A–Z
OF
HORSE
BEHAVIOUR
& TRAINING

Jackie Budd

RINGPRESS

ACKNOWLEDGEMENTS

The publisher would like to thank the following
for their help and co-operation in providing
photographs for this book:
The Horse and Pony Protection Association, Brockweir,
Glos; Hartpury College, Glos; Lesley Dunn, Warrens Hill
Arabians; Lyn Tovey; and CAM Equestrian.

RINGPRESS

Published by Ringpress Books Ltd.,
PO Box 8, Lydney,
Gloucestershire GL15 4YN

Designed By Rob Benson

First Published 2000
© 2000 RINGPRESS BOOKS

ISBN 1 86054 192 5

Printed and bound in Singapore

10 9 8 7 6 5 4 3 2 1

CONTENTS

Section I

UNDERSTANDING YOUR HORSE

TIME TO TALK

The fortunes of the horse have been closely tied to man's for the past several thousand years. Although we no longer ride him into battle, harness him to get us from A to B, or put him to work down the mines, that link shows few signs of weakening.

Horses today are no longer our bread and butter but our friends and playmates. Yet, despite having more time than ever to simply enjoy our horses, how well do we know them? How much time does the average owner spend simply being with their horse: watching him doing what comes naturally? Quietly listening for the replies he is giving to the many and demanding questions we ask of him? Finding out about what kind of animal he really is? Getting to know him as an individual within his species?

A better understanding of a horse's world will lead to an improved relationship.

The raw material we have to work on – born with all the instincts of his wild cousins.

Domestication has given us a false sense of familiarity with our horses. It has also handed us a legacy of training approaches that developed during times when management and handling revolved around maximum convenience and obedience, and minimum consideration for the horse. Many of these techniques are still in use today, and little thought has been given to the appropriateness of such techniques to the natural needs and instincts of the horse. Too often, people pay scant attention to their horse's behaviour until it becomes misbehaviour. Instead of combating a problem by looking for something to blame (this being far too frequently the horse), solutions would be far better if based on examining the problem from the horse's perspective and looking for training solutions based on natural equine behaviour.

It is easy to become complacent about our horses doing what we want, when we want them to. We forget that the new-born foal, struggling to stand for the first time in the straw, is not a dressage horse, a quiet hack, or a three-day eventer in miniature – he is raw material, born with every survival instinct of his wild cousins intact and on stand-by to activate.

A responsive, willing horse is the product of years of careful training which has gradually taught him to accept living alongside, and doing the bidding, of another species he would instinctively fear. This has been made possible by setting up communication between two distinctly separate species. After long and careful negotiations, a pact has been agreed: in return for his co-operation, we agree to be a fair 'leader', with all the responsibility that entails.

However, despite this agreement, training can only ever be a veneer. Whenever it is inadequate, or those communication lines break down, the raw material shows straight through. In these circumstances, the horse will fall back on survival tactics that have served him well for millennia – and who can blame him?

Where problems really begin is if the human involved does not recognise what is happening, does not listen to or understand what the horse is trying to say, or does not know how to go about re-establishing effective communication.

This book is designed to give all owners and riders an introduction to the real nature of the horse and how to be his teacher. As much as an A to Z, it should be viewed as an ABC – a basic alphabet to start building the words and sentences that will get you talking with your horse in a language that makes sense to you both.

RAW MATERIAL

Horses are expensive and demanding animals. As a result, few people want horses who cannot return some degree of the time and money spent on them. Consequently, most horses will only have a secure future with humans if they have been well trained.

Training can take two forms: that based on domination; and that based on willing co-operation. In the past, training relied heavily on domination. The sheer size and strength of the horse meant that men felt they had to dominate the horse to get him to co-operate, and this type of training *did* produce rideable horses, as respect based on fear can.

However, the result of confrontational training is a poor imitation of the level of co-operation achieved through true teamwork. Not only was the former technique unnecessary and unfair on the horse, but the absence of any real trust meant that the horse was not as reliable or skilled as he may have become through training based on understanding and mutual respect.

The benefits of co-operative training are now well recognised. However, this type of training relies on the handler's ability to gain the horse's trust. The handler must have an intimate knowledge of the horse's natural and instinctive behaviour. Co-operation is all about understanding these instincts and getting the horse to use the 'correct' instinctive behaviour in response to a specific aid. It is not about confronting or trying to suppress them.

The first task of any would-be horse owner/trainer, is to learn about these instincts, and to find out what they are and how

The horse is a prey animal, and survival is the name of the game.

they shape the individual character of their own particular horse.

If there is one thing that shapes the behaviour of every horse, above all else, it is this single fact: he is the hunted. The behavioural repertoire of the prey animal has been honed to perfection over the last 56 million years, as a consequence of avoiding being dinner for every passing lion or tiger. While for the domestic horse, carnivores are no longer a threat, the survival code has not diminished as a factor shaping the horse's behaviour. To truly understand the horse is to understand the nature of what it is to be a prey animal.

BORN TO RUN

Today's horse has all the physical adaptations his ancestors needed to stay alive on the open grasslands that are his natural environment. These are:

The Head: The horse has an elongated head, to accommodate the large powerful jaw full of grinding teeth, and to raise the eyes and ears above the level of the grass. Other features are the extremely sensitive nose and lips which help to sift and sort herbage.

The Neck: This is long, strong and flexible to help with ground-level feeding and to give lookout height.

The Body: The horse has a very efficient cardiovascular system, comprising of a large heart and pair of lungs. The efficiency of this system, when working to optimum level, allows the horse to make an extremely quick escape from a predator. The spacious body cavity of the horse houses the intestines, the size of which is due to the need to process a continuous supply of low-grade fibre.

The Limbs and Feet: Over the course of evolution, these have

Large eyes set on the sides of the head produce a near all-round field of vision.

become specialised for running ability. The limbs and feet are designed to produce speed, stability and strength during forward motion. The lightweight lower limb saves energy, which increases stamina.

The Skin: Horses have highly sensitive skin. In addition, their coat hair adapts to changing weather conditions.

EARLY WARNING SYSTEM

The horse's senses co-ordinate to act as a sophisticated early warning system. Although individuals may be more or less reactive depending on their breeding or experience, the basic way this network operates remains the same. Understanding how a horse experiences his world is essential to understanding his behaviour. Many reactions that may seem 'stupid' or deliberately awkward to us are in fact automatic, almost reflex responses, indelibly programmed into his brain.

The horse's world is sometimes the same as our own, but not always and this is the source of many misunderstandings between us. Even where similarities exist, we need to remember that the horse interprets what he sees, hears and feels in terms of his own needs and preoccupations, not ours. To truly understand the horse's behaviour, we have to try to understand how *his* perception differs from what *we* see.

The Horse's Vision: This is the most important sense to the horse, taking up a huge area of the brain. The eyes are large and positioned high on the sides of the head, creating a near all-round field of vision. Narrow blind spots exist only immediately behind the body and in front of and below his nose.

Each eye produces a one-dimensional image. Focusing ability is relatively slow and clumsy due to the comparative inflexibility of the lens. This means the horse relies largely on moving his head to get images sharp. Depth perception is only possible in a narrow zone to the front, covered by both eyes. Instead, vision has evolved to pick up the tiniest details of movement. This is in direct contrast to the predator, whose forward-set eyes allow sharp 3-D vision and so precise evaluation of distance and depth over all his foreground.

A light-intensifying device (the *tapetum lucidum)* increases night vision ability, although equine eyes take longer than ours to adjust to sudden changes from light to dark, for which allowances should be made (e.g. when going from bright sunlight into a dark trailer or stable interior).

The way in which equine vision works has a direct correlation with some of his behavioural characteristics:

- He is particularly alert to threat from behind.
- He is nervous of movements in front of his face.
- He will frequently 'miss' or misjudge the location of something, often when he is almost on top of it.
- The horse is hypersensitive to tiny movements in his peripheral vision.
- He has poor depth perception, except in the few strides directly ahead (with obvious significance when it comes to jumping).
- He feels anxious when his head is over-restricted.
- He needs to be allowed time to investigate and assess strange or unusual sights.

Hearing: The ears are the horse's radar, central to both communication and defence. They are set high, with mobility around 180 degrees. Each ear can act independently, homing in on sounds coming from different directions. The external ear is designed to pick up the slightest sound and precisely locate it. Horses are able to detect a far greater range of sound than we can, of higher and lower frequency. The horse's different pattern of hearing to our own means:

The high-set ears have mobility around 180 degrees.

- A horse who cannot receive auditory signals feels vulnerable (note how unsettled horses are on windy days compared to calm ones).
- Sudden, loud or jarring noises are threatening and put the horse on constant, nerve-jangling alert.
- Odd noises are treated with suspicion and interest, particularly if potentially worrying (e.g. slithery).
- The horse is far more sensitive to the tone of our voices than we may appreciate.

Smell & taste: Smell plays a leading role in the horse's means of identification. It combines with taste to check out the safety of everything from recognising a friend, assessing a stranger, to testing the readiness of a mare to mate, or the suitability of a plant to eat. Extensive elongated nasal passages have a vast capacity for absorbing airborne information. Interesting smells can be forced back into the supersensitive *Jacobsen's organ* for deeper analysis. The importance of smell to the horse means that:

- Familiarity equals security. A horse is happiest in surroundings that have his own odour.
- He is suspicious of strange or strong-smelling substances (e.g. medicines in feeds, or the scrubbed-up odour of the vet!).
- The role smell plays when horses meet and greet each other, and status is established, should be appreciated.

Smell and taste are used to test if a plant is safe to eat.

Be aware of the sensitive areas when grooming.

Touch: Sensory cells throughout the skin are specialised into groups that pick up feelings of pressure, pain or temperature. Tactile stimulation is used extensively in communication. In the herd, horses touch each other constantly, helping to interpret mood and intention, for reassurance or to strengthen bonds.

The muzzle, neck, withers, shoulders, back of the lower legs and belly are particularly touch-sensitive. Pain sensors are concentrated around the mouth, whereas the feet are hyperalert to surface vibration. 'Hot-blooded' horses, e.g. Arabs and Thoroughbreds, tend to have thinner, more sensitive skins and so are generally more reactive in temperament. Touch is important to all horses, and should be to any human trying to establish a dialogue with the horse. Remember:

- Be aware of areas which are particularly sensitive, and be considerate when grooming.
- The mouth is easily damaged and deadened by rough riding or bitting.
- Whiskers are invaluable antennae and should never be removed.
- Being able to touch, as well as see, other horses can make all the difference between happiness and anxiety for a stabled horse.
- Horses clearly enjoy and respond to us using touch in the same way they use it between themselves. Do not limit friendly rubs and scratches to grooming sessions. Make the most of their huge 'getting to know you' potential.

FREEDOM TO RUN

Nothing panics a prey animal faster than the feeling of being trapped. Horses evolved to spend each day, dawn till dusk, wandering miles across open grasslands; finding their own food, selecting their own shelter, and constantly scanning the entire horizon for danger. At the slightest alarm, the wild horse

9

EQUINE COMMUNICATION

BODY OUTLINES

- **Low, droopy, 'tucked in':** relaxed. Smooth curves soothe other horses.
- **Head up, ears pricked, neck arched, and tail raised:** alert or aroused. Any elevation of the tail excites or alarms other horses.
- **Male presenting a proud, 'puffed-up' impression:** stallion displaying.
- **Male with head and neck lowered and'snaked', but high steps:** Stallion herding.
- **Female with fore-feet forwards, ears submissive, and lifted tail:** mare displaying.

EARS

- **Pricked:** if both are strained forward, this indicates intense concentration in that direction. Pricked slightly forwards, indicates a relaxed but focused stance.
- **One forward, one to side or back:** attention is split between sources of interest in different directions.
- **Both to the side:** dozy, dull, submissive, or focusing attention behind.
- **Both pressed back:** extreme effort, anger, or fear:

TAIL

- **Up:** excitement. The angle of the tail depends on the degree of arousal.
- **Down:** dullness, e.g. when dozing, in discomfort, or when being submissive.
- **Pressed down:** afraid, in pain, or about to kick in self-defence.

NOSTRILS & LIPS

- **Mouth tight, nostrils slightly-flared, and muzzle/lips dimpled:** tension, fear, or anxiety. The stiffness increases with the degree of worry.
- **Nose lengthened, lips sagging:** content and dreamy.
- **Skin around muzzle and nostrils wrinkled back:** irritation, disgust, or mild discomfort.
- **Nostrils flared:** excitement or fear.
- **Foal 'mouthing':** submission.

- **Flehmen:** stallion testing mare's receptiveness, or investigating of any strange smell or sensation.
- **Mouth slightly open:** threat. The teeth will be visible if the threat is serious.

HEAD & NECK

- **Nudging:** seeking attention.
- **Jerking backwards:** withdrawal from fear or dislike.
- **Upwards thrust:** aggression.
- **Shaking whole head and neck:** annoyance, irritation or frustration. Also done to remove flies, and frequently seen after rolling.
- **Shaking nose:** showing off.
- **Bobbing:** trying to focus on a source of interest.
- **Neck 'wringing':** anxiety or conflict.

LEGS & QUARTERS

- **Presenting rump:** a mild threat to kick (usually defensive).
- **Hind-leg lift:** Likely to kick (usually defensive).
- **Fore-leg lift or strike:** A quick, high flick of the fore-foot (mild kick) is often used in meetings as a warning (usually aggressive).
- **Pawing:** curiosity, impatience, frustration, or a displacement activity.

CALLS

- **Neigh/whinny, made with mouth open:** an information-seeking call for contacting, locating, and identifying. It is often answered.
- **Snort:** usually indicates alarm, and alerts others to possible danger.
- **Nicker (soft, low-pitched greeting):** From a stallion to a mare, this is usually a deep, pulsating call. A mare greeting her foal uses a gentler, quieter version.
- **Blow (short snort):** curiosity or *joie de vivre*.
- **Squeal:** usually a loud, indignant protest or warning, which is often heard in meetings. It may also be emitted as a sexual sign from a teasing mare.
- **Roar:** anger or fear. May be fierce, raw, low-pitched, or even a high-pitched squeal. It is seldom used in domestication.

knew all he had to do was put his engine into overdrive and in seconds he could be sprinting away from harm in any direction he chose.

Every one of our horses is still programmed to behave in exactly this fashion, yet, for our own convenience, we confine them in small pens with high sides, a roof and, if they are lucky, one window. Here there is no escape from any threat or unpleasantness, perceived or real. For many horses, the only time spent outside those four walls is when their every move is still controlled and dictated by a rider on their back. Stabling need not pose a problem, but only if certain conditions are met:

• Providing the opportunity for every horse to relax loose in the field (or other enclosed area) is essential to both his physical and mental wellbeing. More management and training problems are caused by lack of exercise (often coupled with inappropriate feeding) than any other single issue.

• Horses are likely to become wary and defensive in any situation where their escape option is denied them. This is particularly so in a confined area where their personal space is threatened.

• We must be responsible for replacing the mental stimulation that would occupy the free-roaming horse's mind, or boredom and frustration are inevitable and may become intolerable.

• Physically, the horse must be given the chance to move about as much as possible. He must be able to chew almost constantly, as he would naturally, and to fill his digestive system with low-grade fibre (i.e. hay) for at least two-thirds of the day – a few hours is not enough.

Stabling goes against all the horse's natural instincts.

COMPANY COUNTS

Few prey animals are solitary. Throughout the animal world, society provides safety in numbers for the hunted, and the horse is no exception. In the horse's mind, the herd equals safety and security and survival.

Herd living has many advantages. Included within these is the fact that not only one, but many, pairs of ears and eyes are constantly on the lookout for danger, food and shelter. As a result, more time is available for all members to eat. The herd also provides constant companionship, in the form of friends and potential mates. There is no need to wander in search of others of the same species. There is also less chance that, should a predator strike, one particular individual will be the target.

A horse's whole mental and behavioural make-up is geared to community living. The need for social contact is one of the strongest of all his built-in urges. He wants to be part of a team. Whether inside a stable or outside, an isolated horse not only feels insecure, but also misses out on all the satisfying activities that fill the hours of the field-kept horse in a social group. He may come to *accept* living by himself, but this does not mean the home-alone horse enjoys it, or would not choose companionship if he could. It is up to the owner to minimise the stress to the horse of being separated from his group.

- Social contact with his own kind is essential for the horse's peace of mind and has a positive knock-on effect on his physical wellbeing.
- Groups should be kept as settled as possible and any new horses introduced carefully *(see Herd Behaviour, page 130; Introductions, page 149).*

A horse is geared up to community living.

- Stable design and location should be geared to allowing every horse the opportunity to see, hear and touch friends.
- Training must aim to instil every horse with the confidence to do things by himself, looking to his rider or handler for the security he needs. With less-assertive characters, this may not be easy. Under pressure, gaps in training often show, magnetising the horse back to the 'herd'.

BODY TALK

Like everything else in his world, the language the horse uses to communicate is also tailored to survival. Predators would soon be alerted to the whereabouts of a herd that used vocal signals for every newsflash or snippet of small talk. A system based on body language allows the horse to transmit the subtlest of messages silently (or almost silently) and rapidly throughout the whole group.

The principles of horse-to-horse communication (and likewise, horse-to-human) are simple and based on three straightforward statements that fit almost any situation: "I submit to you", "I want you to submit to me", and "I'm OK with things as they are."

The ability to interpret and use his language is as essential to understanding and training a horse as it would be if we were attempting to teach another person any foreign language *(see table, pages 10-11; Body Language, page 53)*.

FOLLOW MY LEADER

Constant squabbling would put the whole herd at risk. Time taken up with fighting is time that cannot be spent on the lookout for predators. Similarly, horses are programmed to run when threatened, rather than to stay and fight. Turning to face an attacker would mean almost certain wounding, or worse.

Horses understand co-operation, not confrontation. Everything about the way their mind works tells them to stay away from trouble. This policy works well for an individual's own sake and for the good of the herd.

While the range of personalities and roles within any group means there is always a status-structure of sorts, threats are usually sufficient to maintain the status quo. Generally, individuals get on. Everyone knows the rules and sticks to them. Horses are happy to accept direction from a strong, clear leader – as long as that leader has proved worthy of respect.

Be alert to the signs a horse gives that he is trying to reassess his relationship with humans or that all is not well. These are

In a herd situation, horses define their status, and live at peace with each other.

likely to be subtle at first. If he reaches the stage where objections are strong, things are serious. Gear your training programme towards becoming, in your horse's eyes, the leader he craves. Set fair rules, make sure they are clearly understood by everyone, then keep to them. This is what the horse knows, understands and feels safe with.

Utilise the horse's desire for acceptance as part of your 'team', acknowledging with praise every effort he makes to understand and do as you ask. Realise there are some things you cannot teach a horse about, namely, being a horse. Youngsters must grow up in the company of other equines, preferably of mixed ages as in the herd, to become socially well adjusted.

These are the deep-rooted drives and strategies that helped the horse look after himself extremely effectively, without any help from us, for 56 million years. In the blink of an eye (in evolutionary terms), not only have we have taken away that self-sufficiency and replaced it with our own, often inappropriate, 'care', but we have insisted the horse come in to an alien, predator's world full of unnatural and confusing demands. It is a tall order.

THE RIGHT START

An awareness of the 'mustang in your stable' is the cornerstone of a real partnership with any horse. For anyone considering breeding and bringing up their own foal, or taking on the education of a youngster, it has to be the starting point.

Buying a young horse is a popular option which, on the face of it, seems to have numerous attractions. There is the initial saving on the purchase price, of course. A two- or three-year-old can appear substantially cheaper than a ready-made four-year-old if the 'hidden' costs of his education and keep are discounted. Furthermore, who has not been tempted by the idea of starting with a clean sheet, perhaps after years of struggling to put right the results of other people's mistakes? The two questions to ask if you are thinking of a buying a youngster are: just how clean is that sheet?; and, can you keep it that way?

WINDOW OF OPPORTUNITY

The moment the new-born foal opens his eyes he is learning. Young horses are like young children – their minds are like sponges, soaking up learning experiences, good or bad, at a staggering rate. Rapidly, however, the sponge fills. Learning ability and capacity levels off. When the young horse reaches adolescence, at the age of two or three, like any teenager his attitudes to life have largely already been shaped and are beginning to set. By the age of four or five, he is effectively an adult. His mind is fairly well made up about his place in the world, his relationship to those around him and his attitude to their requests. The open window that gives us the chance to shape his behaviour has all but closed.

A young horse who has had a well-structured education during these receptive early years is equipped with all the tools he needs for a lifetime with humans. By the time he is expected to take a rider on his back, he is already familiar with much of the language he will need to understand. He knows he need not fear new experiences. He has become open-minded and flexible in his thinking. He is a practised and skilful learner (and remember, it *does* take practice, for humans and particularly for horses, whose brains are geared to flee, not to solve problems like our own). Having already encountered most of the situations he is likely to come up against, life is going to hold few nasty surprises.

Compare this to the experience of the youngster left in the

Young horses soak up learning experiences.

field for three or four years, barely handled, then suddenly plunged into an alien environment where he is faced with a barrage of complex and alarming (from his viewpoint) scenarios. The worst turn anyone can do a young horse is to mistake training for merely riding, delaying the start of his all-round education for life until he is a big, strong and opinionated adult, when it is really too late.

Think very carefully before taking on the responsibility of a youngster's education. If this literally once-in-a-lifetime opportunity to teach the young horse how to fit into our world is abused, misused, or missed altogether, 'scrubbing' that sheet clean or trying to colour it the way we might like becomes increasingly difficult. Sadly, awkward, unco-operative horses soon become a liability no one wants to know or spend good money caring for.

These precious early years need to be used to make yourself the most important person in your young horse's life, in the same way as a teacher you respected in your childhood imparted to you the motivation and values you still hold today.

BEING PREPARED

Teaching is a demanding job as well as an important one. It is demanding on resources of time, finance and facilities. Most of all, it is demanding on your personal qualities. A young horse will test your skills to the limit, both as a horse-person and a human-person! Even the best-laid plans and most carefully considered training programme are, sooner or later, going to come up against the fact that a horse has a mind of its own – a mind which has not read the textbook.

Dealing with a youngster will throw up constant challenges. Every time he feels threatened, uncomfortable or confused,

Teaching a young horse is a demanding business.

you must expect the young horse (or any horse) to revert to instinctive survival behaviour (to a greater or lesser degree depending on his training level and temperament). This may involve reactions that can be physically quite intimidating – situations which you will need to deal with. Here, a good trainer comes into their own: spotting trouble brewing, knowing how to tell 'normal' youthful naughtiness from an out-and-out challenge to authority, making allowances for personality, and adapting approaches to suit each situation.

Take as an example a youngster which always pulls threatening faces as you tighten the girth. Do you reprimand him sharply? Ignore it? Perhaps he is particularly sensitive about having his girth tightened, so it is better to be more careful about the girth than to discipline him. On the other hand, he may have begun to realise that nipping is a handy tactic to keep humans at a distance, and must be taught that this is not acceptable.

To tackle situations like this effectively a trainer needs to:

- Have the confidence to let the horse make a mistake, then use that mistake to teach him how the correct response can be achieved.
- Look at each lesson from the horse's perspective and make requests clear by expressing them in a way the horse understands.
- Be able to pitch and pace each lesson at a level that gives the horse every chance of achieving the aims.
- Recognise the slightest sign that the horse is struggling and be ready, instantly, to give just enough help to guide him back on track (but not too much so that he never gets the chance to think things out for himself).
- Have the ability and self-assurance to work out strategies to overcome the inevitable training hiccups, and the commitment to see these through, however long that may take.
- As with any teacher, gain and keep the respect and attention of their pupil.
- Have the answers ready for the questions the horse is going to ask – or at least, know where to go to find them out!

Before taking the plunge, consider the qualities of a good trainer and see how you measure up. Do you have:

- Confident horse-handling and riding skills?
- Self-control; patience; a calm, considered approach; the ability to concentrate and listen to the horse's feedback?
- Flexibility of attitude, allowing you to adapt to the

individual's needs and be practical about your approach, being prepared to use what works for you, whether accepted practice or not?

- Physical resources: time, finance and facilities?
- Knowledge of what is important to your horse?
- Knowledge of the way a horse's mind works and how it learns?
- Knowledge of your horse as an individual and what helps him learn best?

EFFECTIVE TRAINING

Plenty of talented trainers have produced many talented horses without ever giving a thought to 'habituation', 'conditioning', 'reinforcement' or any other theories of psychology. However, while 'feel' rather than theory has, in those cases, resulted in a well-trained horse, the reasons why the horse has learned his lessons will have been exactly the same. We may not all be intuitively gifted horsemen and women, but the skills of a good trainer *can* be learned.

- Find out about the circumstances in which a horse learns well (e.g. consistency, security) and those when he does not (e.g. when tense or afraid). Try to ensure everything you do with your young horse encourages him to understand and accept you, not put up barriers between you.
- Help him be a happier, more relaxed animal both mentally and physically, by using horse-friendly management methods.
- Understand your horse as a horse and treat him like one.

Enjoy your horse's training – and make sure he enjoys it too!

- Know your horse as an individual – be adaptable and take his training at his pace, without pressurising him.
- Enjoy your horse's training, and allow him to enjoy it. Do not take training too seriously! Have fun together and avoid getting hung-up on achieving.
- Work at problems calmly and systematically, starting by looking back to where things went wrong and trying to mend the broken communication lines from that point. Keep an open mind, looking at all possibilities and doing so from the horse's point of view. Be prepared to give him the benefit of the doubt, but be aware that horses are adept at training us to do as they want, too!
- Develop your own skills so you become more effective at communication and instilling motivation.
- Never become complacent or take the horse's co-operation for granted.
- Remember, the horse is not by nature a problem-solver. In order for him to develop the mental skills needed to become good at answering the complicated questions he is asked, he requires lots of practice, time, and your help.
- Acknowledge with praise or reward every little effort he makes towards trying to do as he thinks you wish. Horses crave acceptance – if he is making a stand against you, there is a reason why.
- Give your relationship the best chance of success by aiming for compatibility from the start: in build/size, temperament and talents.
- Set up training situations that allow the horse to make his own choices. Your aim is a horse that co-operates because he wants to. The skill of the trainer is in facilitating the 'right' decision.
- Assess difficulties quickly and realistically. Nip potentially significant problems in the bud before trouble escalates. Get help before a worrying situation deteriorates too far. Seek advice only from those whose proven skills and success with young horses you respect.
- Take on a young horse for the right reasons. Be sure you are committed to building a partnership and giving him an education for a secure future.

SECTION II

A-Z OF HORSE BEHAVIOUR AND TRAINING

An alphabetical listing of terms, methods and definitions

AUTHOR'S NOTE
Where the initials q.v. appear in the text after a term, e.g.
"...the horse may develop a tendency to be head-shy
(q.v.)," q.v. refers the reader to the description of the term,
in this case 'head-shy', given elsewhere in the A-Z.

ABOVE THE BIT
An instructor or dressage judge will describe a horse as being 'above the bit' when he evades the rider's rein contact by raising his head. A hollow outline is created, breaking the straight line from the rider's elbow to the bit. *See Hollow, page 138; Outline, page 192.*

This can be caused by a number of schooling problems:
• Loss of balance by the rider or horse.
• Uneven rhythm.
• Inconsistent rein contact.
• Lack of control over speed.
• Poor co-ordination.
• The rider asking too much for the horse's level of training.
• Tension (which may be created by any of the above).

AGAINST THE HAND
See Evasions, page 94.

AGE
While it is true that it is never too late to learn, young horses, like young children, make the most able learners. The excellent equine memory means lessons absorbed at an early age will stick for a lifetime. For this reason it is vitally important that good habits are taught from the onset. Re-education of an adult horse with bad habits can be a long and difficult task.

There are key stages in the natural development of a horse which act as windows of opportunity for successful training and education. Teaching a particular lesson at a point in the horse's life when he is naturally susceptible to it results in much easier training. Correlating training with mental development has the added advantage of avoiding many unnecessary conflicts.

KEY STAGES OF DEVELOPMENT
Within hours of birth: Smell and touch are important to the new-born foal, who is looking for reassurance. This is an ideal time to introduce ourselves in a non-threatening way, establishing the human as an important person in the foal's new world *(see Imprinting, page 141).*
Early weeks: The foal is still susceptible to imprinting, so many procedures can be introduced, e.g. the halter, first leading and loading lessons alongside 'mum' etc. He has a strong urge to follow, and the presence of the mare makes him feel brave.

The foal has a strong urge to follow.

Before weaning: The foal roams further from the dam, enjoying his new-found freedom. Widen the range of his leading lessons, increasing the distance from the mare but giving plenty of time for him to weigh up new objects and experiences.
Weaning: This is a potentially stressful time. Make the most of the foal's appreciation of your company. The reassurance you provide goes a long way towards gaining the foal's trust and respect.
Yearling: The yearling lives to play and explore. Increase his experience of the world beyond home by walking out further afield and travelling to shows. The yearling is beginning to question the boundaries of relationships with humans and

other horses. To avoid the development of any bad habits, be decisive and quick to set the rules of play, bringing into line any behaviour that oversteps the mark *(see Discipline and Respect, page 82).*

The yearling is just starting to develop his personality. Be aware of his individual characteristics. Is he a natural leader who needs his enthusiasm kept in check, or a natural follower who needs his confidence building?

The yearling starts to question the relationships he has made – both human and equine.

Two-year-old: The two-year-old is increasingly less submissive and more likely to test out his status at every opportunity. Fair, consistent discipline is more important than ever. He has a bright, enquiring mind, wants to be independent and absorbs new lessons like a sponge. Introduce long-reining and get out and about. Keep him logging new and enjoyable experiences. Remember, the more chances he has to learn, the more skilled a student he becomes.

Three-year-old: The three-year-old is a typical teenager – full of himself, but coming to realise that things don't always go his way. If early handling has been effective, the three-year-old should drift into the initial stages of ridden training with no unpleasant shocks. He is used to being asked questions and the right reply being insisted on. Lessons still need to be short, frequent and low-key, but he is learning to think and to calmly apply previous experiences to new situations.

Four, five and six-year-old: At this age, the adolescent horse matures into adulthood. Now an expert student, he is ready for increasingly demanding lessons.

By six years of age, a horse is ready for more demanding lessons.

AGGRESSION

Horse society is based on co-operation. Even so, that harmony is still based on an undercurrent of threat, and aggression is a perfectly natural part of equine behaviour.

Aggression may be barely noticeable – such as the lifted leg or flicked-back ear of a more dominant horse telling its subordinate to watch their step. In this way, many a more violent conflict is generally avoided *(see Herd Behaviour, page 130)*. However, horses are big, powerful creatures whose defences are designed to pack a serious punch. 'Normal' aggressive behaviour can still be frightening and potentially dangerous. Abnormal aggression – that which occurs often, too intensely, or is used at inappropriate times – can pose a serious risk to humans and to other horses.

Signs of equine aggression include:
• A tensed body.
• Lowered head with out-thrust neck.
• Bared teeth or biting.
• Widened eyes (often showing the whites).
• Nostrils tensed and flattened.
• Ears pressed back.
• Barging or chasing away.
• Kicking.

ABNORMAL AGGRESSION

There is always a reason behind over-aggressive behaviour, and usually a way to avoid it. Frequently, domestication is at fault – either the unnatural way in which the horse is kept, or inconsiderate handling and riding. Humans often provoke aggression by putting their horses in confrontational or stressful situations.

Sadly, all too often the horse is labelled a 'bad 'un' and treated even more roughly. A little time spent viewing the circumstances from an equine perspective could pinpoint the trigger for the outbursts and suggest a remedial course of action.

Genetics and early experiences of growing up can turn a horse into a naturally more dominant individual. He may become particularly assertive, less willing to 'come into line' with human requests, or more touchy about his personal space. He may also be particularly prone to stress and anxiety *(see Individuality and Temperament, page 144)*. Stress and frustration are usually at the bottom of any aggressive behaviour.

Abnormal aggression is often the result of stress.

HORSE-TO-HORSE AGGRESSION

In a settled group, aggression is usually seen only in competitive situations (e.g. at feeding time), or when a new individual joins the herd and relationships are adjusted. Most of this behaviour is actually defensive rather than attacking. Each horse is protecting its own meal, personal space, status in the group or group territory. Within an established herd, each horse will avoid confrontation, even at feed-times, when lower-ranked horses wait for those above them to take first turn.

Horse-to-horse aggression is usually manifested as one of the following:

Maternal: A mare's natural instinct to protect her foal can lead to her displaying aggressive behaviour to any horse she suspects of wanting to harm her foal. This can often be reduced by carefully introducing the pair to other mares and foals. Reintroduction to the herd may help the mare to relax. However, avoid an overcrowded situation as this is also stressful.

Overenthusiastic play: Normal play-time nipping and barging can sometimes go too far, suddenly turning nasty. Invasion of personal distances *(see Herd Behaviour, page 130)* is usually at fault. Allow much more space so all the horses have plenty of room to get out of the way.

Self-defence: Going on the offensive is actually a form of self-defence for the horse who feels anxious or under threat. Watch the group to see if your horse is being bullied. If so, separate him from the rest but provide an amenable companion from one of the more confident group members. Once these two are established friends, they can be reintroduced to the herd.

Feed-time: This also has its roots in fear – the threat of losing its food supply to a more dominant horse. Whether fed indoors or out, always provide enough space between individuals to allow each to feed in peace without feeling threatened.

Territorial: A group will naturally be wary of a strange horse. Any meeting is a touch-and-go time that cannot be rushed. When insufficient care is taken over introductions, established

Lack of space can lead to aggressive behaviour.

Arguments over status can be prolonged.

horses may defend their territory aggressively *(see Introductions, page 149)*.

Dominance: Arguments over status can be prolonged. These usually resolve with time, but owners must make sure there is plenty of escape room in the field. If disputes continue, separate the horses and reintroduce them slowly and carefully.

Pain: Discomfort or pain will cause irritability and aggression, which may be directed towards other horses or humans. Have the horse checked by a vet. Protect older or convalescing horses from more boisterous or dominant companions.

Redirected: Horses are easily frustrated, either by having a need or desire thwarted, or by facing a conflict of choices. Frustration often leads to aggression being directed at whoever just happens to be nearby! For example, the horse in the next stable may be the victim of a bite by an impatient horse whose feed is being dished up.

AGGRESSION TOWARDS HUMANS

Most aggression towards humans is based on self-defence. The horse's preferred form of defence is flight – instinctively a much less risky option than fight. Most situations involving aggression (both between horses and horse-to-human) are the direct result of the horse being denied the option of getting out of the way (e.g. by being confined to a stable, or tied up). He then feels compelled to go on the offensive.

From the earliest days, handling must aim to reduce this perceived threat from humans. If training is successful, a horse will accept these situations, and any signs of discomfort or worry are confined to fidgeting or restlessness. An untrained, or inadequately trained horse (or one with a tendency towards being extra-sensitive), is more likely to resort to aggression.

Handling or management is usually at the root of

aggression to humans. Always look for, and, as far as possible, deal with the cause before getting tough with the horse. However, far better a solution is to prevent aggressive behaviour ever emerging.

Respect his personal space: This applies to all horses, but particularly those with no escape option (i.e. stabled or tied up), or those with an excuse to be defensive (e.g. a mare with a foal). Give warning of your approach, enter tactfully, and avoid sudden movements. Habituate your horse to accepting your presence at any time.

Allow sufficient freedom: Restriction is the primary cause of frustration, often leading to redirected aggression. Stables must be large enough so the horse does not feel stressed. Avoid boredom and over-confinement, making sure that there is ample provision for lots of mental and physical stimulation. Turn out for free natural exercise daily. Train the horse to stand still when being groomed, tacked up etc., so he need not always be tied up (only use a safe or enclosed area, however).

Socialisation: Put aside lots of time to get the young horse used to human contact. Start socialisation lessons from birth and continue sessions frequently until maturity. Do not breed from nervous or poorly-socialised mares – their foal will imitate their antisocial behaviour. Spend time with your horse, sharing fun experiences.

Expect respect: Over-confident or dominant characters can transfer play aggression from the field to their human companions. Keep the horse occupied and divert him if necessary with a hay-net etc. Deal firmly with over-familiar behaviour and any aggression stemming from lack of respect. Beware of reinforcing bad behaviour by giving up and letting someone else tackle the situation – this is only allowing the aggressor a victory and will encourage a repeat performance. Learn and practise effective handling techniques on easier

Be tactful when entering a stable, which a horse regards as his personal space.

horses, so you are then able to show you are in charge *(see Discipline and Respect, page 82).*

Check for pain: Be aware of your horse's normal behaviour, so you can quickly detect any signs of discomfort and have them checked out.

Avoid overfeeding: A hyped-up horse will be stressed and touchy. Do not overfeed for the amount of work being done.

When faced with aggression, weigh up what the situation requires and make full use of the horse's ability to interpret your body language.

Few horses will attack another animal giving off submissive signals, so, faced with a very angry horse, you are safest adopting a passive, non-threatening posture *(see Body Language, page 53). Quickly* taking up a dominant stance will often avert aggressive or threatening behaviour, especially with a pushy or bullying horse trying his luck. This reminds the horse to show you respect, without you having to resort to physical discipline, which only causes further resentment or fear.

AIDS
The signals used by a rider to communicate with the horse.

Natural aids are given by the seat, legs, hands and voice. Artificial aids, such as the whip and spurs, are for extra reinforcement or precision and must be used with care.

HOW THE AIDS WORK
All the basic aids utilise the horse's finely-tuned balance reflexes. The horse instinctively readjusts his balance when the rider shifts his weight (even very slightly) in the saddle. Emphasis and timing can then refine this into the incredibly subtle, complex language understood by an advanced horse and rider.

It is too simple to say the horse always moves away from pressure given by the rider. He moves whichever way he needs to, to make himself more comfortable and balanced – the direction depends on the precise place the pressure was applied.

The main agent of pressure is the rider's body weight and seat. When used in a particular way, this will cause the horse to move in a certain way.

Downward pressure: If the rider sits down more on the right seat-bone for example, the horse moves to the right to shift the weight to the centre of his back.

Lateral pressure: Applied to one side of the body, pressure causes a sideways movement to return the horse underneath the rider's centre of gravity *(see Lateral Work, page 167).*

The seat aids are used in combination with the leg aids, which make use of another natural reflex to create forward movement.

Inward pressure: A flight animal instinctively moves forwards on feeling constriction around his rib-cage (i.e. the rider's legs used simultaneously). This is backed up by the response of the sensitive intercostal nerve (just beneath the skin by the girth). An inwards nudge here provokes a spontaneous arching of the lumbar vertebrae, causing the horse to bring the leg on that side underneath his body, so stepping forwards.

It is easy to see how the rider must have complete control over their body position to train a horse well. If the rider can remain still (i.e. in 'neutral'), directly over the horse's centre of balance, and use aids correctly when he needs to, the correct response from the horse will come easily.

TEACHING THE AIDS

Most schooling involves stimulating these natural balance reflexes and then conditioning them to our cues, i.e. the aids *(see Conditioning, page 71).*

The position and balance of the rider is an essential aid in training the young horse.

For example, to teach the forward, GO aids, someone leads the horse forwards as the rider applies his legs (or handler sends a quick flick down the long-reins). A click of the tongue can further back up the link between rider's action and the forward movement. Once the connection between the two is made, this help can be dropped and the leg alone used.

POINTS TO NOTE
Training a young horse involves teaching it a whole new language. Time and constant repetition are needed for the horse to link the rider's signal with his action, and so come to understand that the next time that signal is given, the same response is expected:
- Make all instructions clear and consistent.
- Avoid any unnecessary shifts of body weight. Teaching young horses is not a job for novice riders!
- If the horse does not respond, repeat the same aids until he 'clicks', making the signal stronger if necessary.
- It is essential to stop asking as soon as the horse obeys the request, otherwise he has no way of knowing if he has got it right and is allowed to stop that particular reaction. He would also have no reward.
- Use as light an aid as possible, or you will have nothing in reserve if you need to ask again.
- At first, use the voice to help, as the youngster already understands this from earlier work on the lunge and in long-reins.
- Only attempt to teach a response when the horse is in a receptive frame of mind, i.e. relaxed and focused *(see Attention, page 35)*.
- Make lessons short and progressive, building up in small stages and establishing basic skills well before increasing demands.

AMERICAN HORSE SHOWS ASSOCIATION (AHSA)
The national equestrian federation of the USA, which acts as the regulating body for all Olympic and World Championship equestrian sports.

In this capacity, the AHSA oversees the sports of driving, dressage, endurance, show jumping, eventing and vaulting, in addition to 19 other competitive disciplines and breed associations.

ANTHROPOMORPHISM

We are drawn to horses by our love of their combination of strength, sensitivity, and their amazing willingness to please us. Given this, it is all too easy for horse-people to attribute feelings and motivations to their animals which would probably be unrecognisable to the horses themselves.

Horses are not humans. Anyone who treats one as such is doing their horse a great disservice. This is not to say that we should not show the same degree of respect and kindness to horses as we do (hopefully) to our fellow humans. Rather, it is a recognition of the fact that the equine mind works along different lines to the human one.

Even the most dedicated horse-lover will never know what it feels like to be a horse and to see life through a horse's eyes. However, successful training is reliant upon trying to see things from an equine perspective as far as possible. Lessons are better learned by giving the horse suitable motivation to give the correct response. Providing a reward which the horse would appreciate is far kinder than giving him a reward which we, as humans, would consider far better.

ANTICIPATION

Once a horse gets the hang of the learning game, he will often begin to anticipate the rider's aids, acting on them even before they are given.

Although we want the horse to be quick-reacting and sensitive, many a mark has been lost in the dressage arena by over-keen horses taking over the driving seat in this way!

Far from telepathy, anticipation usually stems from repeatedly giving the same cues in the same place or sequence, so the horse comes to think he knows what to do next. Another factor at work is the way many riders will give subtle, involuntary clues with their body as they prepare for an aid – perhaps a tiny shift in balance or slight tensing.

Work on individual movements in a dressage test to avoid anticipation.

Plan schooling sessions to avoid always asking for the same movement in the same place in the arena. When practising for a dressage test, work on individual movements in an open area or in different parts of the arena, before stringing these together into sections of the test. Run through the test as a whole, only a few times before competing. Work on improving your position and technique so you do not give out preparatory cues.

ANXIETY
See Tension, page 254.

ASSISTANCE
However experienced a trainer, the help of a calm and capable assistant is a must. This makes obvious safety sense, but is also a practical requirement. When it comes to needing a leg-up for mounting, or moving around poles during jumping work, a rider clearly needs an extra pair of hands.

A sensible and calm assistant is a bonus.

Choose an assistant you can feel completely confident in, as the horse will soon pick up on any tension or nervousness between the humans around it.

Helpers on the ground need to be level-headed but quick to react if needed. If the trainer is on the ground and working with a rider, the rider must have a very secure seat and good technique, be as unflappable as possible and not put off by the repertoire of antics and evasions the young horse will inevitably come up with.

ASSOCIATION
Creating connections in the horse's mind between a

particular cue and a particular response is the basis of the training of many specific lessons, such as teaching a horse the aids for riding.
See Conditioning, page 71.

ATTACHMENT
See Herd Behaviour, page 130.

ATTENTION
Effective learning depends on each lesson being fully understood before the next is introduced. For this to happen, the horse must have his full attention on what is being asked of him. Due to the nature of horses, this is not as straightforward as it sounds!

Prey animals are acutely aware of their surroundings. Even the tiniest of change in the environment is noticed, and often reacted to. A horse's brain is constantly bombarded with a myriad of stimuli. Subconsciously he is filtering these stimuli and assessing their importance at that minute in time.

The rider's challenge is to make sure his 'conversation' with the horse takes priority over everything else that is 'coming in'. If the horse is preoccupied by other stimuli, lessons will not be learnt well.

Attention may be taken by:
Internal feelings: e.g. discomfort, hunger, fear, anxiety.
External stimuli: e.g. other horses, windy weather, barking dogs, a strange smell, etc.

There is no point trying to persist with teaching a horse whose attention is elsewhere. This can only lead to frustration, resentment and tension all round.

Effective schooling cannot take place when a horse's attention is elsewhere.

ATTENTION-GRABBING TIPS

- Tackle important and accurate lessons, that require focused attention from horse and rider, in a quiet area away from the bustle of the yard.
- Horses, like young children, have a limited attention span. Keep lessons short and interesting.
- As with humans, individual horses learn at different paces. Some have a 'talent for languages' and some do not. Know your horse and make allowances accordingly.
- Young horses are also easily excited, less committed to their trainer and, as yet, weakly conditioned to what is being asked. Keep outside diversions to a minimum.
- Avoid over-stimulating the horse with high-energy feed or keeping him confined too long in the stable. Handling and riding should be calm and confident *(see Tension, page 255)*.
- Get a youngster used to working with lots of activity around him through visits to shows, schooling out on a hack, etc.
- If a horse is very distracted, it is always best to wait until he settles rather than forcing him into a battle of ever-stronger demands and resistance. If you can see the source of the distraction, remove it. If not, and the horse seems to be being deliberately inattentive or awkward, be patient. Try to work out what is drawing that attention, from the horse's viewpoint. Where something in the distance has caught his eye, for example, reassurance and persistence are going to be far more productive than domineering the horse.

RIDER ATTENTION

It goes without saying that, just as the horse needs to be concentrating on the job in hand, so the rider must be totally focused too. Young or difficult horses can be unpredictable, so paying attention is obviously a safety issue. However, concentration is more than that.

A trainer has to be aware of many things at once – his own body, the horse's body, and anticipating and planning every move. Riding is not just about sending out signals. It is a dialogue. The rider must also receive and interpret feedback from the horse. The horse is communicating with us all the time, indicating whether he has understood something, how he feels about it, any anxiety, and so on. His big problem is that riders are often too intent on giving out instructions (or the mechanics of riding – 'sit up', 'shoulders back', 'turn left/right' etc.) to listen to the horse's response.

Obviously, the rider cannot afford to be distracted.

- Make all signals clear and consistent.
- Not assume the horse is being deliberately evasive, if he does not react as you hope to an aid. He may not have heard or understood it.
- Try to develop 'feel' and quietness as a rider.
- Give the horse your full attention. If there are other things on your mind, go for a hack that day rather than schooling.

ATTITUDE
See Motivation, page 184.

AVERSION (AVOIDANCE) BEHAVIOUR
See Reinforcement, page 207.

BACKING
The stage of a young horse's education when he is first introduced to having a rider on his back.

Most youngsters are backed between the autumn of their third year and spring when they are rising four. The exact timing, however, depends on:
- The horse's level of physical maturity.
- His attitude and whether preparatory work has been fully understood.
- Outside factors, such as the time of year (once started you need to be able to carry this stage of training through. If you have no all-weather facilities, take the weather into account).

PREPARATION FOR BACKING

Before backing, the horse must be:

- Fit and healthy – have the teeth and back checked to make sure.
- Sensible and co-operative in all ways.
- Obedient on the lunge and in long-reins.
- Completely familiar with all the equipment, people and setting.
- Used to having a human stand above and over him, e.g. when grooming.
- Establishing join-up (q.v.) prior to backing will have helped with this process and built a foundation of trust. The sacking out procedure (q.v.) is also useful preparation.

If all has gone well in the horse's training so far, backing should be accepted as merely another one of those odd but harmless things that humans want to do! It is only lack of understanding that will cause anxiety. With careful and logical preparation, the horse should have no reason to fear any part of what he is going to experience. Apart from carrying a rider, he will have encountered almost all of it before. Indeed, well-prepared youngsters often accept the experience with little more than a querying flick-back of the ear.

Even so, it is important to remember that the experience of seeing and feeling something on his back is a new sensation that will instinctively alarm him. In a horse's natural environment, this set of circumstances is not just unnerving, it is life-threatening. So, be prepared for fireworks, but do not behave as if you anticipate trouble. A calm, positive approach will transfer to your horse.

If you have any doubts about whether your young horse is ready for backing, he probably is not.

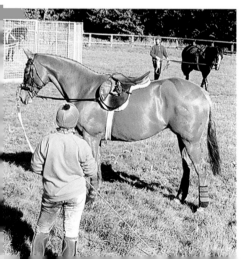

Start off by lungeing or long-reining.

BACKING PROCEDURE

Backing takes two people, both of whom should be familiar to the horse and trusted by him (but especially the handler). It is the handler's job to do all controlling of the horse. At this stage, the rider must simply sit quietly and calmly in the saddle - come what may! Whatever happens, the youngster must not learn he can dislodge the rider whenever he fancies.

- Use a confined area, but make it relatively spacious – your usual schooling area is the best place. Although some people prefer to back in a stable, it is safer, less intrusive, and more instructive to the horse, to give him the space to 'escape' if he so wishes.
- Kit the horse out in his saddle, bridle, breastplate and head-collar (or lungeing cavesson) and lead-rein. Begin by long-reining (or lungeing) for a few minutes. Only carry on if all is going well.
- Check the girth and stirrup length.
- Give the rider a leg-up, so he is lying across the horse's back. Talk calmly to reassure the horse and distract him with friendly rubs. Take care not to hold the lead-rein too tightly.
- Lead the horse slowly around, with the rider patting his side, reaching further and further forwards, back and down. If there is any adverse reaction, halt before calmly moving on again.
- After halting, the rider slips off (this can come as a surprise to the horse, so be prepared). Repeat this process from the other side.
- If all is going well, move on to the next stage. The rider brings his leg quietly over to sit astride, leaning down low with his weight slightly off the back. Inadequate preparatory work usually shows up now!

Remember that any weight on the back will feel strange to begin with, so take things very gradually.

- Remaining hunched in the saddle, the rider puts his feet in the stirrups, sits down a little more and takes up the reins slightly. Keep stroking and reassuring the horse as he is led around.
- At halt, the rider gradually sits up more. The horse is then walked around for a while with the rider sitting up. After a few repetitions, this is enough for a first session.

Repeat this session again over the following few days. Once the horse gets the idea, the rider can start to use subtle leg and rein aids at the same time as the handler's directions. Gradually the handler takes a back seat, so the horse has to rely on the rider's instructions.

When the horse is ready, the lead-rein can be taken off. Keep aids simple – GO, STOP, STAY, TURN etc. Try to be as low-key as possible, but focus on being effective and clear rather than subtle! Rein contact must be light and unrestrictive at all times. If the horse is reluctant to go forwards, give a light flick with whip or soft rope behind the leg, rather than resorting to ever-heavier leg aids. Lungeing with a rider can also be introduced now.

Once walking is going smoothly, try some trotting (the rider will need to take up a little more contact at this stage, but must keep it very light and rise to the trot). This is often where the youngster tries to put his head down and buck, so be prepared to push him on actively if you feel the warning signs. Encourage him up a gear heading towards the gate, using the legs, voice and very little rein contact. A few strides are enough at first.

It is crucial not to rush any part of the backing process. Go at the horse's own pace, and if there is any sign of nervousness, work some more on that stage before moving on. Give the horse time to think about what is happening. What you are aiming for is a confident, willing partner.

AFTER BACKING
The sessions following backing simply confirm what has been taught – being mounted from both sides, walking, and trotting with a rider, on both reins. The youngster needs this time to readjust his balance, get used to the sensation of having a moving weight on his back, and start to develop the muscles he will need.

- Don't ask him to learn anything more at this stage.
- Canter requires much more balance. It is usually best left until later, and should be introduced outside the arena,

where the horse has more natural 'go' and space to move in a straight line.

- Keep ridden sessions short. Build up gradually.
- Make work varied, interesting and enjoyable – mix ridden work with lungeing, long-reining and loose schooling.
- Once he is going happily (if not stylishly!) in an enclosed area, venture out onto quiet roads and tracks *(see Hacking, page 115)*.

A backed horse is not a fully 'broken' horse. Backing is just one step further up what is a long ladder. The next stage, learning more about the aids, should be left until after the horse has been turned away (q.v.). Most horses will need a year from the time when they are first backed, to consolidate this basic work before they are physically and mentally ready for more serious schooling (e.g. to be expected to work in a correct outline).

BALANCE

Balance – the distribution of body weight – plays a crucial role in the horse's world. In nature, the horse's ultra-sensitive balance reflexes keep him on his feet and off the predator's menu. In domestication he must learn to adjust those responses to accommodate the weight of a rider on his back – a weight that is itself constantly moving, to a greater or lesser degree, depending on the rider's ability.

Think of the horse as a see-saw, the fulcrum being his centre of gravity. To stay upright and perform the athletic movements we ask of him, he must stay in balance over that fulcrum. The more difficult the movement, the more balanced he has to be.

As 60 per cent of a horse's body weight lies in his forehand (i.e. in front of the saddle), a young or unschooled horse naturally goes 'downhill', with a relatively forward centre of gravity. This makes it difficult for him to be balanced and agile, particularly with the weight of a rider on his back. For this he must shift his centre of gravity back, so he is carrying more weight on his hindquarters. Rather than using his forehand, he must use his quarters and back to get forwards impulsion by stepping right underneath his body with his hind legs, so they can take more weight and create more activity.

All this is very difficult for the young horse, whose muscles will be stiff and resisting. Balance improves gradually, with correct schooling and general fitness work. This will

Working on a circle will help to improve the horse's balance.

strengthen the muscles and make them more supple. In this way the horse becomes more relaxed, ready and able to listen to the rider, and able to achieve a good outline (q.v.). Now the rider can use his seat and leg aids to ask the horse to round his back, step underneath him and really use his quarters. The centre of gravity of the schooled horse moves backwards, shortening the whole outline. The horse is now like a coiled spring, full of impetus and ready to go easily and smoothly in whichever direction, at whatever pace, the rider asks.

CAUSES & SIGNS OF LOSS OF BALANCE
If the horse loses balance, it may be because:
• The rider cannot keep him straight.
• The rider is unbalanced.
• He has slowed down or speeded up.
• He has lost rhythm.
He is likely to become uncomfortable, resisting and unco-ordinated, perhaps slipping down a gear or rushing to try to regain some equilibrium himself.

An advanced horse will hardly need telling how to adjust himself to maintain a fluid balance: for example, he will intuitively do a flying change to swap canter leads on a change of direction. However, loss of balance is frequent with young and more novice horses, who rely on their riders to help re-establish their equilibrium by using the aids to engage the quarters more.

EXERCISES TO HELP DEVELOP BALANCE
Balance can be improved by encouraging a better acceptance of the bit, improving suppleness, strengthening the quarters, and keeping up a steady rhythm at all times. Useful exercises include:

- Correct transitions.
- Changes of direction.
- Turns and work on circles.
- Ground-poles.
- Use of half-halts.
- Lengthening and shortening the stride.

RIDER BALANCE
At all times, the good rider sits still with his weight upright
over the place where the horse can carry it most easily – i.e.
his centre of gravity. Any deviation from the ideal position
will be reflected in the horse's locomotion or attitude to his
work. In the 'classical' position, the rider is best placed to
influence the horse by using his body weight and other aids to
help the horse stay in balance. Even in the 'forward' jumping
position, this equilibrium can be maintained.

Some riders do seem to have a natural, in-built 'feel' for
balance. Others get a mental block, or seem to lose all of their
own natural physical balance reflexes when they get on the
back of a horse. For these it may take much time and practice
to develop a truly balanced seat, independent of reins or
stirrups.

Rider balance can be helped by:
- Good instruction, to develop awareness of the rider's own
  body and the horse's, and to work on a 'classical' seat.
- Exercises on the lunge.
- Reducing tension in the body.
- Improving general posture.

BARGING
Horses understand the idea of personal space – it is the
basis of the threat behaviour that helps relationships
within the herd stay on an even keel. If these same
principles are applied in horse-human relationships, with
the human established fairly and squarely as the
dominant 'horse' whose space is only to be entered 'by
invitation', then there should never be any pushy, bullying
horses.

Horses that try to squash you against the stable wall, or barge
past in a gateway, lack any respect for their handler's personal
space. This is domineering, threat behaviour from the horse
and is certain to lead to injury sooner or later. Respect needs
to be established, just as it would be for another assertive

individual in the herd, and preferably from square one with the young foal. As always, prevention of misunderstandings and disputes is better and easier than a cure.

As with all kinds of bullying behaviour, the caring owner should consider first whether their horse's attitude has anything to do with poor management or handling. In the case of horses who barge in the stable, factors responsible may be: too much tidbitting; or careless intrusion into the horse's own personal space. Another possibility is that past abuse may have created mistrust and aggression. The solution lies in establishing clear rules, without resorting to bullying tactics yourself.

Make use of aggressive body language to teach the over-confident youngster to watch his step – this way you can ward him off without ever needing to raise a hand to him.

DEALING WITH THE BARGEY HORSE
- Use a well-fitted head-collar at all times, until the pushy character is 'reformed'. A short length of rope (about 10-20cm/4-8ins) can be attached. Take hold of it the moment you enter the stable. Have a long schooling whip in the other hand.
- If the horse moves to barge you, pull his head round towards you, at the same time flicking the whip at his quarters to move them away. Give the verbal command STAND.
- If the horse obeys, reward him with a friendly rub on the neck or between the eyes.
- Repeat this every time the barging behaviour is shown. Lessons may need to be frequent and intensive.

Be firm, but fair, when dealing with the bargey horse.

- If the horse stands in a corner and refuses to face you, tempt him to face you amicably by offering a small feed in a bucket. However, work towards being able to dispense with the food reward before it becomes relied upon.
- For a horse that tries to push you against the wall when being groomed, remember that short, sharp jabs in the side are more effective than trying to lean your (insignificant) weight against his.

BASCULE
A term used to describe the rounded shape made by a horse that is using his body correctly over a fence. When the horse is basculing, his withers are the highest point of the body and the head and neck stretch forward. This is the optimum position for the horse to maintain his balance and to achieve the lift needed to clear the jump.

All jumping training is aimed at encouraging the horse to bascule, or 'make a good shape' over his fences. Flatness or hollowness over the fence can be caused by:
- Poor or rough riding.
- Too fast an approach.
- Uneven rhythm in the approach.
- Taking off too far away.
  It can be corrected by:
- Slowing down, to get a more balanced approach. Try jumping out of trot rather than canter.
- Using placing poles in front of the fences, encouraging the horse to get underneath his fences more. After starting with an 'easy' distance, shorten it a little so the horse must take off closer to the fence.
- Using grids with slightly short distances between the elements.

The withers are the highest point when a horse is basculing.

- Jumping plenty of low, slightly wide parallels. Sometimes a keen but 'green' jumper will jump too big, ballooning over his fences. Again, use grids with short distances to develop a better rhythm and encourage the horse to fold up its fore-legs. A line of small cross-poles using bounce distances in between (3.3-3.7m/11-12ft), is particularly useful for this problem.

BEDDING (EATING)

As horses are fibre-digestors, designed to be processing a constant trickle of low-grade forage through their systems 24 hours a day, it should come as no surprise that the temptation of a clean straw bed is often too much.

A horse or pony will seldom prefer his bed to good-quality hay. Most bed-eating is usually down to the horse either not being provided with enough forage to fill his stomach, or too much time spent in the stable. More time when the horse is turned out and the provision of more hay in the stable will usually make all the difference.

A little clean straw will usually do no harm if it is eaten – it is useful fibre! Greedy ponies inclined to gorge should be bedded on shavings, paper, flax or hemp. Avoid treating the straw with potentially harmful chemicals.

BEHAVIOURAL CHANGES

Far from 'suffering in silence', horses communicate clearly to us when something is amiss – if only we are prepared to listen. The tell-tale signs are there, not only in the constant, subtle conversation of equine body language that every owner should familiarise themselves with, but also in broader, very obvious ways (see Body Language, page 53).

Thinking, caring horse-keepers know the behaviour of their animals inside out. Being aware of what is 'normal' for each individual allows an owner or carer to spot quickly any suggestions that something may be wrong.

Behavioural signs that should ring alarm bells include:

- The horse is looking dull and lethargic, taking little or no interest in his surroundings or companions.
- The horse is agitated, e.g. sweating excessively, looking around at or biting his flanks, rolling frantically.
- The horse suddenly begins behaving aggressively or erratically.

- Development of 'vices' *(see Vices, page 274; Stable Vices, page 241)*.
- Eating dung.
- Any other unusual or out-of-character behaviour.

Any of these should be a cause for concern and investigated immediately.

'BEHIND THE BIT'

A horse that has stopped going forwards actively and brought his nose behind a vertical angle to the ground, so 'dropping' the rein contact, is referred to as being 'behind the bit'. Generally the horse is not 'working from behind' fully – that is, he is not using his hindquarters to create impulsion to propel him forwards. This may be due to lack of training, stiffness, not accepting the bit, or the rider not giving the aids correctly.
See Over-bent, page 194.

'BEHIND THE LEG'

A term used by instructors or dressage judges to imply that the horse is not responding to the rider's leg aids. The rider may have to ask the horse again and again, or the horse's reaction may be slow or even non-existent! The problem usually lies in lack of confidence, misunderstanding or laziness on the horse's part, and poor co-ordination or 'feel' from the rider.

BEND

A term used to describe lateral flexion of the horse's body around a curve, such as a corner or when travelling around a circle. Correct 'bend' means the horse appears to follow the exact line of the curve he is travelling with his whole body, which will be evenly bent from the poll to the tail.

BITING

Biting is a deliberate act of aggression, although it is usually preceded by a series of threatening early-warning signs. Remember that horses are not natural bullies. Look for evidence of discomfort, frustration or insecurity that might be pushing the horse into irritability or going 'on the offensive' *(see Aggression, page 25)*. If you have an entire, then expect to have to get to grips with this typically dominant behaviour early on.

Horses do not try to bite their 'superior' in the herd. Dealing with biting successfully relies on establishing that the human has 'boss' status. Hitting a horse that has bitten is a total waste of effort – it will either be ignored or seen as provocative by the horse. It is also likely to make him head-shy. The many occasions during day-to-day handling that require the handler to raise his hand to the horse's head, mean there is too much to lose to risk the horse coming to regard a raised hand as something to fear and avoid.

Effective retraining of a biter depends on the horse linking his misbehaviour with self-imposed unpleasant consequences, at the same time as asserting the human's personal space as 'non-violable'.

- Firstly, investigate the horse's management and exercise regime, diet, handling, ridden behaviour and relationships with other horses, to try and pinpoint any environmental triggers for his attitude. Rectify any stress factors. Have him checked over physically.

- Begin a programme of regular handling lessons, insisting that the horse allows you to feel, gently but firmly, over every area of his body and pick up his feet. There must be no no-go areas *(see Sacking Out, page 222)*.

- When handling the horse, have the left hand on the head-collar. Watch carefully for the signs of a nip being planned. As the thought crosses the horse's mind, push his head sharply away. Now bring it quickly back towards you and reward him with a rub or pat. The following suggestion is implanted in the horse's mind: aggressive intentions are dealt with roughly, as from another horse; whereas turning his head politely towards the human handler has pleasant results.

- This method can be backed up by using a light whip or short length of rope to send the quarters away at the same time *(see Barging, page 43)*, but this does mean the right hand is not free to be grooming etc.

- Test whether the lesson has been learnt by turning your back – a heaven-sent opportunity for a nip. Once this is ignored, and the horse will even let you feel around and in his mouth, the cure is complete.

- Other options include a tweak to the whiskers, which most horses hate, as the horse makes signs of biting, or, to hold or attach firmly to the sleeve of the handler's jacket, a prickly brush (e.g. a dog-grooming slicker brush) or metal curry comb, which gives the nipper a nasty surprise. The disadvantage of these methods, however, is that they punish the biting but do nothing to reinforce good behaviour.

- Repeat lessons frequently until the biting stops.
- Avoid inconsiderate handling of your horse that can lead to irritability, e.g. rough grooming of 'ticklish' areas, or interrupting his feed times.

BITTING

With 1001 varieties from which to choose, the array of bits available today does little but confuse the ordinary rider. There may well be 'a bit to suit every horse', but it is also true, more often than not, that simple is best. The rider should always look to improving their own technique and their horse's education, before seeing a change of bit as some kind of cure-all for training problems or a short-cut to a better response from the horse. Though a bit with a stronger action may be useful to retain control or curb enthusiasm in exciting situations, e.g. when jumping cross-country, or when used for precision at more advanced stages of training, always aim to achieve as much as possible using the simplest and mildest of bits.

Most commonly used for general purposes is the snaffle bit, the majority of varieties of which are considered to be suitable for all levels of rider. Remember though, that any bit is only as gentle as the hands on the reins.

A loose-ring snaffle bit suits many young horses.

FITTING THE BIT

A horse has every excuse to evade a bit that is causing discomfort due to poor fit or condition. To avoid this:

- Fit all types of bit to just wrinkle the lips at the corners.
- Allow 0.5cm (¼ inch) of mouthpiece between the lips and ring of the bit. Less and the bit is too narrow and will pinch. More and it is too large and could knock on the teeth or damage the lips or roof of the mouth.
- Check regularly for wear and sharp edges, particularly on

The bit must be fitted correctly.

loose-ring types. Avoid soft, easily-breakable metals such as nickel.

Signs that a bit might not suit, or fit the horse, include:

- Resistance.
- Stiffness in the neck, poll and jaw.
- Chewing the bit.
- Crossing the jaw, opening the mouth or grinding the teeth.
- Refusing to go forwards or accept a contact.
- Swishing the tail.

Look to the possible cause of any resistance before clamping the mouth shut with a noseband, restricting head movement with schooling gadgets or opting for a more severe bit.

INTRODUCING THE BIT

Youngsters are usually introduced to the bit (known as 'mouthing') at around 2½ years of age, although it can be done earlier, particularly if needed for showing in-hand. Beforehand, it is important that the horse is perfectly at ease with being handled around the head, including having his ears touched and gums felt. Also have the horse's mouth and teeth checked before starting.

- Common practice has been to accustom youngsters to the bit by leaving them with a bridle on (with noseband and reins removed) in the stable for short periods (no more than 15 minutes). Stay and supervise. Make sure nothing can get caught up on the bridle or bit – a traumatic experience now could create serious future problems.
- Choose the type of bit carefully. Take into account the youngster's mouth and jaw shape, which may better suit a thinner or thicker mouthpiece, an unjointed or double-jointed

A sweet iron bit encourages salivation.

bit. Straight-sided D-rings or cheeked bits can help with steering. Nylon or rubber bits have a softer, warmer feel than stainless steel, but are vulnerable to chewing. Becoming popular are black iron and copper bits, which seem to encourage salivation without making the horse fidgety in his mouth. Traditional 'keyed' mouthing bits may encourage the horse to salivate by playing with the bit in its mouth – but this is not a habit you should encourage. A lightweight, jointed snaffle allows room for the tongue and suits most horses.

- Make sure the bit fits comfortably. A short coupling strap under the jaw will keep it in position. Rubber ring-guards prevent pinching, particularly of loose-ring bits.
- Coating the bit with honey or molasses may make the bit more acceptable for the first few times. Take great care to put the bit and bridle on (and take it off) carefully.
- Allow the horse to get used to the feel of the bit in his mouth over a period of time before he is backed and asked to accept contact on the reins.
- Make allowances for the teething process. Few young horses are settled in their mouths until their baby milk teeth have all been replaced by adult ones, at five to six years of age.

COMMON PROBLEMS WITH THE BIT
Before trying to 'cure' any problem with the mouth or acceptance of the bit, make sure the rider is being sensitive and effective. Also check the condition and fit of the bit and whether the horse's teeth need rasping.

Chewing the bit: This may involve anything from slight grinding of the teeth to significant head-shaking, making a steady contact very hard to maintain. The cause is tension, particularly in the jaw, which then has a knock-on effect making it impossible for the horse to relax through his poll, neck and spine. Chewing is hard to discourage once set as a habit, but may happen mainly when the horse is excited.

- Check the fit of bit and bridle. Too large or loose a bit is often a cause. Examine the horse for any source of discomfort.
- Try a bit with a straight-bar or mullen mouthpiece rather than a jointed one, and with fixed rather than loose rings. It will move less in the mouth.
- Try using a drop, Flash or Grakle noseband. Avoid fastening it so tightly that the horse then fights to resist it!
- Avoid heavy-handed riding, or allowing the horse to constantly fall behind the bit, as this may cause fussiness in the mouth. Plenty of impulsion and a steady, yet soft and giving contact is essential.

Tongue over the bit: Discomfort, unsteady hands or boredom may be behind this habit. To change this:

- Make sure the bit is fitted correctly and is high enough in the mouth.
- Consider a change of bit to one that either gives more play in the mouth (e.g. a linked or rolled mouthpiece), or is ported (e.g. a Kimblewick).
- Make sure the rider maintains impulsion, and keeps a firm, consistent but relaxed contact.
- Make schooling sessions varied and interesting.

Drawing back the tongue: This can lead to a very dry mouth, making the horse even less comfortable and prone to sores.

- Try a bit with different metals in the mouthpiece, such as copper and steel, or experiment with other types of

A Flash noseband (pictured) or a Grakle may help to prevent bit-chewing.

mouthpiece which may be more acceptable or better suit his mouth shape.

- Check fit of the bit. Try adjusting it a little higher in the mouth (taking care not to cause pinching), or consider a cheeked snaffle, which tends to sit higher on the tongue. Try a drop-type noseband.
- Encourage salivation by offering a mint before inserting the bit.

BODY LANGUAGE

Unlike our own vocal system, communication between horses is primarily based on visual cues. Posture, muscular tension and movement combine to create a 'body language' understood by equines the world over. These signals can be as obvious as the pinned-back ears and bared teeth of the aggressor – but many are far more subtle and complex. The 'meanings' of different expressions are shown in the table on page 10-11.

One of the greatest steps forward in recent years, in our long-standing relationship with the horse, has been our growing understanding of the way horses use body language, both between themselves and to express their reactions to their human handlers and riders. Now, instead of relying solely on teaching the horse our language (i.e. the aids) to convey what we expect of him, we can back this up with better attempts to communicate with horses in their way, and be aware of the feedback the horse is constantly giving.

Understanding of equine body language forms the basis of training techniques such as join-up, advance and retreat, and Parelli Natural Horsemanship (q.v.). However, body language is a subject everyone who comes into contact with horses, at any level, should be familiar with. Knowing how to read the signs of a horse's mood and intentions are part of thinking and caring ownership, preventing many problems and misunderstandings from developing.

Body language also gives us another way of communicating our own intentions and wishes. Super-sensitive to the most minute of body cues, horses read every action we take. We need to be constantly aware of the way we act around horses, who will take behavioural cues from our bodies, just as they would from other horses, and react accordingly.

- Always be calm and relaxed – this instils a sense of security in horses. Avoid sudden movements and noises.

- As prey animals, horses are particularly alert to body stiffness and tension, which is instantly translated into a warning signal, creating anxiety in the horse and putting him instantly on the alert – often with unfortunate consequences for novice handlers and riders.
- Riders must be aware of the effect of body tension on the horse's way of going and work to reduce this.
- Study horse communication and how to use your own body language to key into that system and assert your position in your relationship with any horse.

USING BODY LANGUAGE

Passive/submissive: This is a non-threatening posture, used to encourage a horse to accept your presence or approach, in meetings (especially with an unknown horse) or for reassurance of an anxious horse. Your horse will infer a non-threatening attitude from:

- Deep, slow breathing.
- Arms which are held down by the sides.
- Shoulders which are low and rounded.
- Eyes which are averted or to the ground as opposed to direct eye contact with horse.
- The visitor's body being at an angle to the horse's.

A passive body posture is non-threatening.

Note the effect of an assertive posture.

Assertive/aggressive: This should be used only when going on the offensive, e.g. to warn off or reprimand threatening or bullying behaviour, or to send a horse away from your personal space. Horses use assertive body language in the herd to warn off or discipline others. If you learn to use it in the same way, it can be a tool for quiet, effective discipline, preventing you from ever needing to raise a hand or whip against your horse. An assertive posture is characterised by:

- Arms lifted away from the sides, to create a 'bigger' appearance.
- Shoulders held high and squared up to horse.
- Eye-to-eye contact with the horse is kept up.

BOLTING OR RUNNING AWAY

Flight is the horse's first-option survival technique. Whenever he is up against pain or conflict, his natural reaction is 'run first, think later'. This formula has proved successful for millions of years. It is only the veneer of training that provides other options for the domesticated horse.

The flight reaction is never far beneath the surface, however. In a young horse or untrained horse, genuine fright can easily tip over into panic, setting off a stampede. Physical strength, combined with the power of the instinct to run away, mean that a runaway horse that is truly panicking (as opposed to getting a little bit stronger than the rider would like) is very frightening and dangerous. His tension creates a total mental block, so he is no longer listening to his rider but is thinking of nothing but his own fear. Almost any further stimulus or signal will only 'fuel the fire' more.

Fortunately, true bolting is a rare occurrence, and few horses are confirmed bolters. There is usually a reason for the underlying tension and plenty of warning signs for an eruption, which a good rider or handler will act upon.

CAUSES OF RUNNING AWAY

- **Fun:** Some horses simply have far too much energy! This could be the fault of diet or lack of turn-out and play opportunities. It can be solved by a non-heating diet, increasing exercise and giving the excitable horse chance to let off steam before real work (e.g. with a gallop, or if this will rev him up more, time on the lunge or loose schooling).

Avoid further exciting the horse by cantering alongside companions on hacks.

- **Habit:** A horse may have effectively been trained to bolt (as with racehorses), or simply 'got away with it' before and realised his own strength. Careful re-schooling to the aids for slowing down, in a safe, enclosed space, is the only answer. Riders should avoid always cantering in the same place when out on rides.

- **Panic:** A regular bolter is a horse in an almost permanent state of nervous tension. His whole lifestyle and schooling must be completely reassessed to promote relaxation and confidence in his riders and handlers. This should result in his being more thoroughly conditioned to the rider's aids and habituated to all potentially alarming situations he might meet.

- **Tension from inexperience or poor riding:** There are usually plenty of warnings during a build-up to loss of control through sudden fright or over-keenness. If the horse has been well schooled, the horse will respond to the rider's signals to steady him. However, an unschooled or worried horse is likely to be tense and switched off, and can take a rider by surprise.

A nervous or novice rider can find themselves getting carted off simply because they do not start slowing the horse early or effectively enough. Rider anxiety and tension can then transmit to the horse, worsening the situation.

ACTION TO TAKE
Strength has nothing to do with riding a 'strong' horse. Technique, i.e. balance, 'feel' and a secure seat, is everything.

- Riders must be aware of their horse's pace at all times, but particularly when riding out in the open. Use half-halts to help steady the horse before he becomes too tense. Sit up in the saddle so your body weight can be used. Tipping

Use half-halts to steady a horse before he becomes too tense.

forwards, or the legs slipping back, will only urge the horse on more.

- Keep a sensitive, giving contact at all times. If a horse becomes strong, never pull both reins at once. Shorten the reins, then use one to give short, sharp give-and-take tugs, forcing the horse to flex his neck.
- 'Bailing out' when a horse is truly bolting is not an option. If possible, head for an open space and bring the horse around in decreasing circles. Sit quietly and try to ease back gradually, talking in a calm voice. Alternatively, allow the horse to gallop on until he begins to tire. At this point, continue to urge him on when he would rather slow down.
- Where a horse is constantly in a state of tension, look to management changes to relax him. Investigate the possibility of pain or discomfort.
- If a horse panics while being led, let go of the rope – do not try to hang on.

BOOTS & BANDAGES

With four legs to organise and a variety of relatively unnatural athletic exercises expected of them, horses are very prone to lower leg injuries. These are often self-inflicted (i.e. caused by knocking one leg into another) or can be the result of hitting an obstacle when jumping. A few extra minutes spent fitting leg protection makes particular sense with the young, unbalanced horse. Deep or poor going can add to the likelihood of 'interference' (self-inflicted injuries), but protection is advisable for all work in the school.

CHOOSING LEG PROTECTION

Boots have the advantage over exercise bandages in that they are simpler and quicker to fit correctly. Different types are available to suit differing activities or to focus protection on particularly vulnerable parts of the leg.

Commonly-used boots include:
- Brushing boots (these fit around the cannon bones, with padding concentrated on inside of legs).
- Tendon boots (these may be closed or open-fronted. They offer protection for the tendons at the back of the fore-leg cannon bones).
- Combination/sports boots (these are available in a variety of designs to cover extended areas, e.g. the cannon bone and fetlock joint).

Brushing boots.

Tendon boots.

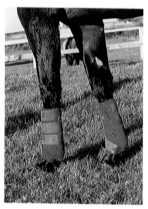

Combination boots.

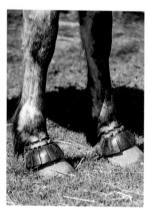

Over-reach boots.

- Over-reach boots (these fit around the pastern, covering the heel area to protect against the hind-leg toes clipping the fore-leg heels).
- Fetlock boots (these fit above the fetlock, protecting the inside of the joint).
  Crepe exercise bandages may offer a degree of additional support, but must be very carefully applied.
- Bandage from below the knee/hock to just above the fetlock joint only. Do not interfere with movement of any joints.
- Always use padding underneath, e.g. gamgee, fybagee, synthetic pads. Tendon shells can be used in addition.
- Bandage firmly but not tightly, with consistent pressure, covering about half of the width of the previous wrap. Aim

to finish half way up the leg. Fasten tapes securely at the sides of the leg only.

• Bandages will shrink if they become wet. When this happens remove them immediately.

INTRODUCING BOOTS AND BANDAGES
See Equipment, page 92.

BREAKING-IN
A traditional term used to describe the early training of a young horse for riding. More recently, this term has been replaced by that of 'starting.'

BRIBERY
See Reinforcement, page 207.

BRITISH HORSE SOCIETY (BHS)
The leading organisation for leisure riding in the UK and the governing body for professionals teaching in the equine industry.

Through its various departments and membership, the BHS works to improve horse welfare, standards of riding and horse care knowledge and access to the countryside for riders.

BRITISH SHOW JUMPING ASSOCIATION (BSJA)
BRITISH HORSE TRIALS ASSOCIATION (BHTA)
BRITISH DRESSAGE
Governing bodies in the UK for the sports of show jumping, horse trials and dressage respectively.

With the exception of special schemes to introduce newcomers to the lower stages of competition, participation in official ('affiliated') shows and events at all levels in each of the disciplines, is restricted to members of the relevant organisation.

BUCKING
All horses buck – it is part of their natural repertoire of behaviour. A buck may range from a playful expression of *joie de vivre* out in the field (or on a ride!), to the gut-wrenching aerobatics of the rodeo bronco, whose twists and dives hark back to the primitive instinct of a prey animal trying to dislodge an attacker from his back.

CAUSES OF BUCKING

Exuberance: 'Small' bucks are often simply a symptom of exuberance, a certain amount of which is no bad thing and to be expected in youngsters in particular. There does come a point at which excessive energy gets in the way of education, however, and can even become unsafe. If bucking is frequent, the owner must look to:

- Management and exercise regime (is turn-out time sufficient?).
- Diet (i.e. is the horse being given too much high-energy food in relation to the work done?).
- Schooling routine (is it varied enough, or is the horse having to make up his own entertainment?).
- Other factors that may be involved (see below).

Most experienced horse-people can distinguish a playful buck from one that seriously intends to eject the rider. Take care before punishing a buck, unless you can be certain it is down to disobedience. Other factors include:

Pain or discomfort: This is the most common reason for persistent bucking, particularly when the problem begins suddenly or is erratic. The problem may stem from relatively minor, easily rectified causes, e.g. crumpled numnah, to the more serious sources of discomfort or pain, such as a poorly-fitted saddle, sores in the back or girth area, or damage to the vertebrae or soft tissues of the back.

The condition and fit of all saddlery should be checked by a professional *(see Saddle-fitting, page 222)*. Arrange a visit

Bucking may be simply an expression of exuberance.

from the vet, who should thoroughly check not only the back but also the horse's teeth, mouth and ears and investigate any possible unsoundness. Pain may be present anywhere in the body, but still cause bucking. The vet may need to refer the horse to a specialist physiotherapist, chiropractor or osteopath.

Poor riding: Rough or unbalanced riding, with a rider bouncing around heavily in the saddle or jerking at the reins, are all enough to cause the sensitive horse to protest with a buck. The rider must work at gaining better 'feel' and a secure, independent seat. Riders too heavy or tall for their horse will sit awkwardly and be difficult to carry comfortably.

COPING WITH A BUCK
- To buck, the horse must get his head down. A rider who feels the horse might buck must sit up, drive him forwards and use one rein to try to lift the head.
- Keep your upper body slightly back and legs more forward than usual. The rider's weight is better pushed down through the stirrups, however, rather than the seat. Hold on to the mane or neck-strap for extra security.
- Use short, sharp, give-and-take tugs on one rein to prevent the horse bearing down on the rein and taking hold of the bit.
- Horses find it near-impossible to buck going uphill. If you anticipate overenthusiasm out on a hack, plan a canter going up a slope, early on in the hack.

BULLYING
See Aggression, page 25.

CANTER
Canter is a three-time pace. It is set in motion by a hind-foot, followed by the other hind and its diagonally-opposite fore landing as a pair. The final leg to hit the ground is the remaining fore-foot. This is known as the 'leading leg', as it stretches slightly further forwards. A moment of suspension completes the stride.

To help the horse stay balanced around a circle or turn, canter is always ridden so that the sequence begins with the outside

Striking off into canter on the correct 'lead'.

hind-foot. The inside fore-leg then completes the sequence. On a right-handed circle, this should be the horse's right fore-leg, and on a left-handed circle, his left fore-leg.

A quick glance downwards will reveal if the horse is on the correct leg, stretching his inside shoulder furthest forward with each stride. Aim to learn to feel this by its effect on your hips and balance.

CANTER TRANSITIONS

- Achieve a balanced trot. Sit up, but think of bringing the inside hip forwards a little and stretching the inside leg down into the stirrup.
- Use gentle squeezes on the inside rein to soften contact and ask for inside flexion. Open the rein slightly to suggest correct lead (but don't draw it back). Keep a light contact on the outside rein.
- Keep your outside leg steady just behind the girth. This helps indicate to the horse which leg to strike off and keeps the quarters in.
- Nudge the inside leg in towards the body, on the girth, to ask for strike off and to keep up energy during canter.
- Keep the outside rein steady, using as needed to control speed.
- The rider's body must stay upright and stable, absorbing movement with open hips but not tipping forwards, sideways or stiffening. Follow the movement with the hands, without giving away the contact.

TEACHING CANTER TO A YOUNG HORSE

Once a youngster is trotting in reasonable balance and moving away from the rider's leg, he can be introduced to canter. Expect it to take a while for him to understand the aids and make a good transition. Keeping balanced and co-ordinated with a rider on board is difficult at first.

A safe place, outside the arena, is ideal for practising canter.

- The first canters are best done in a safe place outside the arena where the youngster will have more natural 'go' and space to continue in a straight line.
- Avoid running or pushing your horse into canter. Get a well-balanced, active trot, with the hind-legs stepping well under the body. Do some exercises to sharpen his response to your leg.
- In the arena, work on canter transitions by bringing the horse on to a 15-metre (14-feet) circle. This will make it easier to strike off correctly.
- Shorten his frame, by squeezing with the knees while keeping the lower leg on. Now release.
- Slide the lower leg back slightly and nudge your inside leg against the girth. Stay as upright as possible, keeping the hands still.
- If the horse does not respond, re-balance the trot and repeat. Be patient – understanding may take some time.
- If the horse strikes off on the wrong leg, quietly return to trot and try again.

COMMON CANTER PROBLEMS & HOW TO OVERCOME THEM

Wrong strike off: This is often due to stiffness on one side. To strike off correctly, the horse must be able to bend around the rider's inside leg, so that his outside leg is free to come forwards. Target schooling at loosening and strengthening muscles on both sides, with exercises in trot, to maintain suppleness.

- Before asking for canter, make sure trot is balanced. Ride a circle to set up correct bend, and use a half-halt to get the horse's attention.
- Asking for the transition over a pole on the ground in the corner of the school can help.
- Ask on a smaller circle.
- Check the correct aids are being given and that the rider is upright.

Rushing: Horses often speed up their canter to try to keep their balance. This is particularly true of youngsters.

- Stay on a large circle. Sit up but sit lightly, squeezing the outside rein gently to steady the horse.

- For a horse that tends to increase pace down the long side of the school, ride a large circle whenever he picks up speed.

Disunited: Where lack of balance makes the horse change legs in front and not behind (or vice-versa), come down to trot, re-balance and try again. Take care to keep contact with outside leg and rein on turns and circles.

Four-time: Instead of coming down together, the diagonal pair of legs splits to create two separate beats. This is usually caused by lack of impulsion. To cure this, try riding forwards into a light, soft contact.

Crooked: The horse should move on two tracks, hind hooves falling in the same track as the fore-feet. Keeping straight is particularly difficult in canter.

- Focus on co-ordinating aids to move shoulders over in line with the quarters.
- Make sure over-strong hand isn't asking for too much bend in the neck.
- Use the inside leg to the outside hand to straighten the horse.

IMPROVING THE CANTER

To increase responsiveness to your leg aids:

- Try decreasing and increasing the size of a circle exercise.
- Place two poles on the ground, a set number of strides apart. Aim to increase or decrease the strides you use between them.

To encourage the horse to engage his quarters and create more 'bounce':

- Use lots of trot-canter transitions.
- Ride forward strongly, to increase impulsion. Ask the horse for shorter steps by using half-halts.
- More advanced horses can work on walk-canter transitions. Ask for canter from an active walk with correct bend, as the horse is about to step onto his outside hind-foot.
- Work on exercises aimed at improving suppleness at all paces, including lateral work.
- Horses able to canter in balance will benefit from occasionally working for a few strides in counter-canter (i.e. on the 'wrong' leg). Introduce this carefully using a shallow loop down the long side of the school. Ideally the horse should not change his bend, even though he is using his outside leg to lead with.
- Work on accurate transitions by placing a pole on the ground at X and riding a figure of eight over it. Ask for

canter over the pole, ride half a circle then return to trot.
Repeat, turning in alternate directions.

CATCHING

**Nothing is more frustrating than a horse or pony that
refuses to be caught. Simply avoiding the issue by not
turning out is not an option. Tackle the problem from
three angles:**

*Make sure your approach to catching a horse is always
positive and convincing.*

Make him want to be caught: No horse is going to rush to greet you if there is little or nothing in it for him! Being caught should be linked in his mind with pleasant experiences, not invariably hard work. Catch your horse regularly to feed, groom, and spend time together, not only to ride. Make it an enjoyable part of his daily routine.

Stack the odds in your favour: A hard-to-catch horse in a 10-acre field is always going to come out the winner.

- Section off a small area of the field and use either as permanent grazing or as a holding area he can be herded into where there is less room for evasion. Electric fencing is useful for this purpose.
- Turn out in a well-fitting head-collar with a short rope attached underneath (no more than 1 ft/30cm). This must be leather or a quick-release type to avoid accidents.
- Be aware of your body language (q.v.). You have a better chance of getting near if you approach calmly and confidently with a non-threatening posture. With the lead rope in your pocket or held discreetly by your side, walk towards his shoulder at an angle, shoulders slightly hunched and eyes averted.

Be convincing: A confirmed escapee will probably continue to sidle off, just out of reach, despite all efforts. In this case, set aside time to persuade him you do not intend to give up so he may as well give in gracefully! This is a lasting cure, achieved by using the 'advance and retreat' principle. Success may take half an hour, or half a day – but, once learned, the lesson is generally remembered.

- If possible, practise this technique in a confined area such as a large stable or menage so the horse 'gets the idea' before using it in the field.
- Go into the field and try to catch the horse. If he moves away, walk calmly after him. Avoid hassling the horse, but quietly keep moving him on every time he tries to settle to graze.
- Eventually he will show signs of looking towards you to gauge your reaction – an ear cocked your way, possibly even a step. This is your cue to turn around and take a few paces away from him. Check his response, and as soon as he hesitates or stops, send him away again.
- The horse will finally come towards you of his own choice. Immediately give praise with a friendly rub and tidbit from your pocket, despite any exasperation you may be feeling – then let him go again.

• Return a while later and repeat the process at least one more time, preferably twice.

CHEWING/CRIB-BITING

Wood-chewing and crib-biting are destructive habits that can do lasting damage not just to stables and fences etc., but also to the horse's teeth and digestive system. Both are so-called stable vices (q.v.); abnormal behaviours originating from stress and frustration. In crib-biting, the horse takes hold of the hard edge of a fence, stable door etc. with the front top incisor teeth. When air is then gulped in, this is known as wind-sucking.

The initial cause is often related to poor feeding management – frequently, insufficient provision of forage to a stabled horse, who is then forced to spend many hours with nothing to chew and with a near-empty digestive tract. Excessive wood-chewing may indicate a vitamin/mineral deficiency.

As with any stable vice, these habits are hard to shift once established. Focus on relieving stress by turning the horse out as much as possible, providing friendly equine company and making sure when the horse is kept in he has plenty of hay and plenty to occupy him.

Devices such as cribbing straps will prevent the horse performing the action, but deal with symptoms rather than causes. Woodwork can be protected from damage by using metal anti-chew strips or treating with a bitter-tasting solution (take care not to use anything toxic).

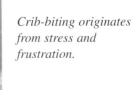

Crib-biting originates from stress and frustration.

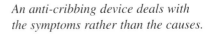

An anti-cribbing device deals with the symptoms rather than the causes.

CLAUSTROPHOBIA

Evolved to survive in the wide open spaces, horses are naturally claustrophobic animals that by instinct would never choose to enter a confined space from which there is no escape. It is a measure of their amazing adaptability and willingness to please that they can become used to living in stables and loading into trailers/horse boxes, etc. Even so, these unnatural procedures need to be introduced carefully and sympathetically, and not taken for granted.

See Travelling, page 262.

Some horses are particularly sensitive to being confined, often as a result of poor handling and training early on. These are best kept out whenever possible or in an open yard system where they can easily see and touch other horses. Travelling will involve patient retraining for very claustrophobic animals.

CLIPPING

Horses which are difficult to clip can leave owners dreading the onset of winter. The noise and vibration of clippers is understandably alarming, yet there is no reason why a young horse should ever develop a phobia about them. Those who panic when the clippers appear usually have unpleasant memories, often from an unsympathetic or impatient handling during their early experiences.

Before clipping any horse, make sure that:
• The machine is safe and in good order.
• Blades are sharp.
• Tension is correct.
• Machine and blades are oiled.
• The horse's coat is clean.
• The horse is standing on a dry, non-slip surface.

INTRODUCING CLIPPING
Avoid future problems by keeping the whole experience as stress-free as possible. Very young horses can be habituated to the sight, feel and sound of the clippers. This can be done during imprinting (q.v.) but is useful at any stage.

   With older horses:
• Allow time beforehand to get the horse used to the sights and sounds of clipping until it is an accepted routine. Clip

With calm handling, most horses learn to accept clipping.

other (experienced) horses nearby. Leave the machine running near the horse's stable while he is groomed.

- In the weeks beforehand, regularly place the switched-off clippers against the coat and move them all over the body.
- On the day, have everything ready. Use a stable or sheltered area, provide a hay-net and a familiar helper to hold and reassure the horse.
- Follow the usual routine. Have the clippers running outside the stable. Once the horse is relaxed, bring them inside. Gradually come nearer to the horse. Now lay your free hand on the shoulder and place the clippers on it, so the horse can feel the vibration through your hand. Once he is relaxed, place them on his skin (without clipping any hair as yet).
- Only begin clipping when the horse is totally accepting and relaxed, however many sessions this requires. Aim to remove only a small amount of hair the first time – leave the hunter clip for the future! Remember to reward good behaviour.

THE CLIPPER-SHY HORSE
Regaining the confidence of a horse that fears clippers takes the same time and patience as introducing clipping to a youngster, and follows much the same pattern. Be prepared for the steps above to take days, weeks or months to achieve.

ADDITIONAL HINTS
- Try blocking out some of the noise using cotton wool in the horse's ears, or playing music (classical, rather than heavy rock!).
- Sensitive horses are often more accepting of the quieter, battery-powered, cordless clippers. These cannot manage a full clip, but are useful for areas like the head, ears and under-belly.
- Never use force. If restraint is needed, a humane twitch can

be used for a short period (up to 20 minutes) by a knowledgeable person. Using a sedative may be the best solution, allowing the process to be completed with least stress to all involved!

To deal with horses that will tolerate the clippers happily on their body, but object to having them around their head and ears: *See Head-shy, page 128.*

CLUBS
Whatever your ability or ambitions, joining an equestrian club is an opportunity to meet like-minded horse-people. Joining allows you to take part in locally-organised training sessions and competitions with your horse – not to mention to socialise! In the UK, membership of riding clubs is generally open to all adults (and sometimes juniors), and many are affiliated to the British Horse Society (q.v.). Others may be based at a particular riding establishment or yard, a system also more commonly used on the continent and in the USA.

COLLECTION
See Gaits, page 101.

COMMUNICATION
See Body Language, page 53.

COMPETITIONS
Once the basics of a youngster's education have been established, it is time to broaden his horizons. The more

Do not be too ambitious when you first start taking your horse to competitions.

new situations a horse encounters in his early years, the calmer and more confident an individual he is likely to become. Each adventure successfully negotiated teaches him not to fear the unknown, and builds trust in his human partner. Getting out and about to small shows and competitions are ideal opportunities. The crucial factor is to keep things as enjoyable and stress-free as possible, introducing all new experiences gradually and in stages.

- Build up by boxing to a different area for a hack, along with a friend on an experienced horse.
- Look for a low-key event, such as a sponsored ride, that will involve being among other horses.
- Keep everything well within your youngster's capabilities and fitness level.
- For a first outing, aim for a small show nearby, where there is not too much going on (e.g. a local riding club show, ideally with horses only).
- Prepare well beforehand and allow plenty of time on the day.
- Don't rush to enter classes. Walk around, allowing your youngster to take in the experience.
- Next time, aim for simple classes such as Best Turned Out, Riding Horse, unaffiliated dressage or Clear Round jumping.
- Be patient and relaxed – you are there to let your horse learn how to behave in a competition environment, not to school or discipline him or show him off. Collecting ribbons comes later if you get these basics right.
- Build up to more demanding classes as confidence and experience grows. Most horses (and riders!) tend to perform less well when under the spotlight. Prepare thoroughly, then enter classes at a level just below the one you are working at back home.

CONDITIONING
Conditioning is part of everyday life for all of us, including horses. It is one of the principal ways we learn and is based on making links between two events. The ability to modify behaviour according to the consequences (good or bad) of specific experiences is a vital part of survival.

For the trainer, whatever lesson is being taught, conditioning involves:
- Deciding on the response you would like.

- Setting up a situation where that response is given.
- Linking that response with a precise signal.
- The horse's mind then links the signal with the response. Whenever the signal is given, the response follows automatically (a 'conditioned reflex').

This 'classical' conditioning is the basis of the way horses are taught the aids and most other signals and commands we use to communicate with them. Incredibly complex patterns of responses can gradually be built up in this way. However, to avoid confusion and misunderstanding, conditioning must be used skilfully.

USING CONDITIONING
- Start with the simplest possible link between cue and response.
- Make only one request at a time.
- Only move on, add or refine a response, when the previous step is thoroughly learnt, e.g. establish HALT before asking for a SQUARE HALT.
- Timing is crucial. Prompts must be immediate and consistent. The cue must come immediately before or at the exact time as the response, e.g. teaching HALT on the lunge, the rider gives the aids for halt as the assistant helps stop the horse.

A correct response needs an instant reward.

- Reward reinforces the link. Correct responses need to be instantly backed up by a reward, so the horse knows he has done well and is encouraged to repeat the response next time. The reward may simply be that the aid/signal stops.
- Repetition fixes the link in the memory. Connections that are not used regularly, no longer rewarded or are not fixed well enough in the mind can become extinct or forgotten, (although horses are amazingly resistant to extinction). Once a link between a stimulus and action is made, it is likely to get stronger, whether good or bad *(see Habit Strength, page 115)*.

TRIAL AND ERROR
'Classical' conditioning can be backed up by, or used

alongside, operant or instrumental conditioning, i.e. trial and error learning. Trial and Error learning takes place when:

- The horse performs an action or behaviour, usually by 'chance'.
- That action has consequences, that may be pleasant or unpleasant, resulting in the horse either repeating the same response next time, or making a different one.
- Pleasant results (e.g. rewards) mean the same behaviour is more likely to be performed again in the future (positive reinforcement).
- Unpleasant results (e.g. no reward, or 'punishment') mean the action is less likely to be repeated (negative reinforcement). It also increases the chance that an avoiding action will be taken instead, to escape the unpleasant stimulus.

An example is the way horses learn to lead and tie up – i.e. yield to pressure applied through a halter. By moving his head in the direction of the pull, the pressure releases, bringing the reward of instant comfort. If the handler's timing is good, he will learn to react to a lighter and lighter contact.

This is all about giving the horse a choice and making the 'right' choice obvious and beneficial. A complex skill (e.g. jumping) can be learnt in this way, by 'chaining' simple actions together or building them up one step at a time towards a final goal (known as 'shaping').

AVOIDANCE CONDITIONING

Much of even the kindest conventional training programme is actually based on avoidance, e.g. the horse learns to react instantly to the slightest pressure, to avoid the harsher aid that might follow if he does not.

This tactic can produce a very obedient horse, but one that may well be tense, stressed and unhappy in its work. Relying on avoidance conditioning will never produce the willing, alert, relaxed partner that has been trained through repetition and reward. When mistakes happen, look for the cause of the communication breakdown. If a foreigner doesn't understand your English, does it help to shout louder?
See also Reinforcement, page 207.

CONFIDENCE
Self-confidence does not come automatically to horses. Millennia spent at very real risk of finishing up as another animal's dinner has put the horse at the top

of the insecurity league. This instinctive nervousness is constantly challenged by the unnatural things we ask horses to do on a daily basis.

Even so, most horses are happy to oblige and enjoy new experiences, showing that experience and training can override insecurity, and replace it by confidence and independence *(see Conditioning, page 71; Habituation, page 113)*. A look at any racecourse or three-day event shows that when training and trust is complete, horses are capable of remarkable courage.

Numerous problem behaviours are rooted in lack of confidence. Put under stress, any gaps in training or lack of trust in handler or rider will surface. Stubbornness, evasions, nipping and other apparently 'bully-boy' tactics often have their roots in anxiety, mistrust and the drive to get back, anyhow and any way, to the security of the yard and other horses.

Confidence is crucial for a happy horse – and precious. It takes many years to build and can be lost in seconds. Building and keeping the horse's willingness to face the world independently and enjoy new experiences is a vital ingredient of good training. Of course, it also requires a trainer who is confident themselves, and able to instil that 'feel-good' factor in a young or nervous horse. Confidence comes from:

Character: Some horses are more confident characters to begin with. Inherited temperament can be helped (or hindered) by the mare.

Experience: From earliest days, exposure to new experiences and help to negotiate them successfully add to the youngster's knowledge and self-belief, making him less reliant on others.

Training: Good training makes learning easy and fun, building trust through consistency and judgement of when to 'push' and when to reassure.

CONFORMATION

Conformation is the way a horse is put together. Far from being simply a case of 'good looks', correct conformation is all about soundness. Details of 'ideal' conformation will vary between breeds and types, and according to the purpose for which the horse is to be used. Common to all is a balanced, symmetrical framework that gives a horse the best possible chance of standing up to the strains and stresses of his chosen discipline.

Learning what makes a sound horse is a fascinating subject

A balanced, symmetrical framework is a key to good conformation.

which owners and riders should study, particularly before looking for a youngster to buy, or when choosing parents for breeding. Always keep in mind that a horse whose conformation and way of moving are well suited to a particular activity will find progress comes easily, will enjoy his work, and will be more likely to show talent, and ultimately to succeed. On the other hand, working with a horse that is simply not 'built right' for the job is going to be an uphill struggle.

CONSISTENCY
Predictability is critical to all learning, but never more so than with horses. Keep anxiety and stress levels down and create a positive environment for learning by always being consistent and fair with what you ask and the way in which you ask it.

This applies not just to the way the rider gives aids etc., but to everything we do. If we let a horse get away with something one day and next day discipline him for exactly the same thing, his understandable confusion is going to lead to him resisting or switching off. Give your horse the reference points he needs to learn by keeping the goalposts securely fixed in the ground!

CONTACT
Taking up the reins, the rider is able to feel the horse's mouth at the other end as a weight. This feel is called the 'contact'. Ideally, it should be the same in each hand – at all times and all paces.

Training is aimed at teaching the rider to keep this contact constant, and the horse to accept it happily, without resistance. As the head and neck are constantly moving, this consistency can only be achieved if the hands can 'follow' that movement. The rider must be supple and mobile enough in his shoulders, elbows and wrists to allow the hands to move totally independently of their body (i.e. have an independent seat).

A good contact should:

- Be soft, elastic and 'giving' – so a consistent, equal weight can be kept in both reins whatever the horse is doing.
- Not be too light, too heavy or fixed – just enough to give security and confidence.
- Stay constant as the height of the hands is adjusted to keep up the line from the elbow through the wrists to the bit.

With the hands too low and 'fixed', the rider loses all softness and elasticity in the rein contact.

CROSS COUNTRY
See X-Country, page 283.

CURVES & CIRCLES
Turns and circles – or variations of them – are a staple ingredient of schooling sessions and are used to improve suppleness, co-ordination and obedience. As the horse moves around the curve, the muscles along the outside of his body are stretched. Working on a bend also encourages the horse to use his quarters more, lightening the forehand and coming into a better outline as he puts more weight onto his inside leg.

Riding the circle correctly is crucial to achieving these aims – and not as simple as it seems!

RIDING A CIRCLE

- The amount of bend asked for depends on the horse's training level. As a guide, expect to be able to just see the horse's inside eyelashes.
- Aim for uniform bend along the whole spine, from poll to tail, so the hind-legs follow the same track as the fore-legs.
- The rider uses the inside leg to support the horse, keeping up impulsion and encouraging the correct bend through the rib-cage. Think of nudging it inwards, not backwards. The outside leg is quiet but ready to use behind the girth if needed to stop the quarters drifting out.
- The rider must take care not to collapse their body either in or out but to sit centrally. Turn the shoulders and body slightly towards the inside of the circle.
- Never demand bend. Ask, using your legs. Invite bend by flexing the fingers on the inside rein and 'giving' a little with the outside rein. Keep the hands level and even.
- Think of steering the shoulders around the circle rather than the head – the quarters will then follow.
- Plan turns and changes of direction well in advance, using half-halts as needed to steady and re-balance. Thinking 'leg yield' around turns and corners will help prevent falling in.
- From time to time, use counter-flexion for a few strides, i.e. bend to the outside of the circle/turn. Besides helping create suppleness on both sides, this keeps the horse thinking about what he is doing.
- Do not overdo circle work – it is physically and mentally tiring. One well-ridden circle is worth 20 poor ones!

The rider must sit centrally when riding a circle.

COMMON FAULTS

Falling in: The horse leans in, putting too much weight on the inside shoulder/fore-leg. Work on increasing responsiveness to rider's inside leg. If the shoulder is falling in, use leg-yield aids to move it out. Raise the inside hand slightly (without moving it backwards). Check that the rider is upright and that his inside shoulder and hip are not creeping forwards. If the quarters are falling in, think of shoulder-in aids to help guide the shoulders back level with the quarters. Move both hands as a pair slightly towards the inside.

Falling out: The quarters drift out from the line of the circle. Decide if you need more outside leg, or less inside leg. Check the rider is upright. Work on increasing the horse's respect of outside leg and rein.

Too much bend: The horse is bending through the neck but not the body, often falling out at the shoulder and/or quarters, or tilting his head to the inside. This is usually caused by over-strong inside rein, or not enough contact on the outside rein.

Rider becoming unbalanced: This happens easily on smaller circles, with the rider's seat slipping to the outside, making the inside leg slip forwards and outside leg back, losing contact with the horse's sides. Stretch the inside leg down to increase weight on the inside seat-bone.

EXERCISES

Use a combination of these in schooling sessions, aiming to keep up a continuous 'flow' and including regular transitions.

- Circles of varying sizes. Keep circles large (no less than 15-metre diameter) for young or novice horses – even bend on small circles needs a very supple, balanced horse.
- Figures of eight, loops (5m/10m) and serpentines. All excellent for creating bend and working on changes of bend.

Spiralling inwards and outwards from a 20-metre circle will improve bend and flexibility.

- Leg yielding. Moving from the centre line to the outside track, then from a 20-metre half-circle back to the track teaches the horse to move away from the rider's inside leg and helps prevent falling-in. Moving from the outside track in towards the ¾ line helps teach obedience to the outside leg and rein, preventing falling-out.
- Spiralling inwards from a 20-metre circle then outwards again builds on the leg yielding exercises above.

DECISION-MAKING & CONFLICT

Horses are not good decision-makers. Their survival has been best served by running first and thinking later. Problem-solving and weighing up options are not skills evolution has given the horse much need for.

Most horses crave a quiet life. When the horse is relaxed and able to make a considered decision, it is usually still based upon securing his own safety: what action is most likely to increase his survival chances?

Loose in a field, the horse can usually perform whichever option he chooses and so feels comparatively in control. Unfortunately, the way we keep and use horses denies this choice to many, constantly facing the horse with stressful and frustrating situations. Most of these can be avoided with a little thought:

- Plan training exercises carefully. Make any choices clear and easy, setting up learning situations so that the horse can hardly help but make the 'right' decision.
- Always be consistent and fair.
- Make sure a lesson is understood before asking a more difficult question.
- Avoid 'grey areas' and creating unnecessary conflicts.
- Help keep your horse happy and relaxed by managing him in an environment that meets his natural needs for freedom, company, security and constant access to forage.

SIGNS OF CONFLICT

Conflict can be shown in many ways. Some of these, such as stable vices, are obvious, others are harder to interpret.

Any horse in conflict is stressed. Stress, whether it be from

Pawing the ground is a sign of frustration.

confusion, frustration or fear, is often displayed as displacement activity. This is commonly seen when the horse's instincts are driving him in two opposing directions, and he is unable to make up his mind. Often, restriction is behind the frustration – because he is confined or tied up, he is prevented from acting as his instincts are urging. With no instant escape from this dilemma, he gets increasingly agitated and is forced to take some form of action – because any is better than none.

Pawing the ground or pacing in circles are clear signs of frustration. But often the action the horse takes to relieve his conflict is a seemingly irrelevant behaviour: a normal action now being performed 'out of place'. This occurs particularly when the horse is torn between wanting yet not wanting something (e.g. wanting to get to the other horse on the far side of the stream, yet not wanting to cross the water).

Displacement activities are usually hurried, nervous versions of behaviours that an animal spends a lot of time doing. They can include:
- Yawning.
- Pawing the ground or raising a fore-leg.
- Banging at the stable door before feeding.
- Snatching at grass/hay-net or drinking.
- Chewing (e.g. the lead-rope or reins, or catching hold of the bit).
- Head-tossing.
- Nipping himself or another horse.

Where displacement activity becomes a real problem, try to identify the cause and relieve the horse's frustration or fear. Avoid punishing the behaviour, but use reassurance and positive reinforcement (q.v.). Look for harmless ways in which he can fulfil his instincts (e.g. for a horse that chews the lead-rope when being groomed, provide a hay-net) and try to remove anxieties using habituation.

Chronic conflict, where frustration is long-term and unresolved, can lead to neuroses such as stable vices (q.v.).

DIAGONALS
In trot the horse moves in two-time, using one pair of diagonally-opposite legs then the other. A rider doing rising (posting) trot sits to one pair, then rises to the next. Correctly, he should sit as the horse's outside leg comes back, and rise as it goes forwards – known as using the outside diagonal. On a right-handed circle this would be the horse's left diagonal. On a left circle, it would be the right diagonal.

- Sitting to the correct diagonal helps the horse balance and stops the muscles developing unevenly.
- Change diagonals whenever you change the rein, and regularly when riding in a straight line (e.g. hacking out), by sitting down in the saddle for an extra beat (e.g. up-down, down-up).
- Practise being able to tell which diagonal you are using by 'feel' rather than looking down.

DIET
Correct feeding is fundamental to keeping horses of all ages happy and healthy.

Knowledge about equine nutrition has advanced far in recent years, and with so much information available, there is now little excuse for horses being fed inappropriately. A major advance has been the realisation that the closer we can get to the horse's natural way of feeding, the more content and healthy he will be. Modern management systems have not lent themselves to this, but fortunately things are changing.

Provide plenty of roughage in the diet.

There is now a feed product to fit every possible equine need, but for the young horse, focus on providing:

• Plenty of roughage, in the form of hay or haylage, and preferably, daily turn-out. Roughage should make up at least 75 per cent of the diet of a horse in light-to-medium work and never less than 50 per cent, even for a hard-working competition horse.

• A concentrated ration in the form of a balanced low-energy, high-fibre feed.

Feed each horse as an individual. The major feed manufacturers all operate telephone help-lines to give advice on diet planning and any feed-related queries. It is a free service, so make use of it!

DISCIPLINE & RESPECT

In the wild, discipline is part of herd life. It is dished up liberally from day one not only by the mare to her foal, but by other more 'senior' herd members to their subordinates of whatever age. It is quick, clear, consistent and meaningful. With each individual aware of the unwritten rules of social living, the group co-exists happily and the survival chances of all are increased.

In our relationship with horses, domestic harmony is also best served by clear rules and effective discipline. Horses are big, immensely strong animals – too big, and too strong to be treated like house-pets. If a horse is going to adapt to life alongside humans and have a secure future, he must be trusted not to use his size and bulk against his human handler or rider. We must take over the role of teacher and disciplinarian most frequently seen in the wild from the dominant mares and stallion.

Teaching this respect must begin from day one, but, as in the herd, that respect must be earned by using fairness and consistency – never force. In any battle of strength between horse and human, the horse will always win. The only leverage we have, both to stay safe and to teach the responses we would like, is to establish ourselves as a worthy leader in a way that is meaningful to the horse.

If discipline is given in a form the horse instinctively understands, it is usually accepted readily. It should be seen as an extremely positive and fundamental part of training. Some rebellion should be expected, particularly during the adolescent years when the horse would naturally be challenging the authority of others, including his 'leader'. However, by working through this using the same consistent principles, you can strengthen your relationship and reassert your authority.

Unfortunately, all too often, force is used inappropriately or excessively in an attempt to discipline. This may have the effect of quashing the resistance – temporarily or permanently – but the end result is a resentful, evasive horse, rather than a willing partner with a healthy respect for the human half of the team.

Making consistent, clear rules about behaviour and sticking to them is important at all times, but particularly with youngsters, who like all children and teenagers, are keen to test the limits of what is allowed, and quick to make capital out of any perceived areas of weakness!
See also Reinforcement, page 207.

DISCRIMINATION
Among the horse's varied repertoire of survival techniques is a remarkable ability for visual discrimination. This eye for detail is a skill common in social animals. It enables the wild horse to recall the most minute of details in his environment, logging even the slightest differences, and to communicate with others using the subtlest of body cues.

Our domesticated horses are no less clever. Many times your horse will have noticed, and reacted to, the smallest of differences in his routine or surroundings. A jump of a different colour; a new road sign on a familiar route; granules of wormer mixed in a feed etc. are all enough to grab his interest. Likewise, any change in your emotional state and the way you are using your body *(see Body Language, page 53)* will arouse his suspicion.

Horses are *not* good at generalisation – i.e. making assumptions, or applying a lesson learnt in one situation to another set of circumstances (even if very similar to the first). Generalising is a risky survival tactic. The sensible horse takes every situation as it comes!

For this reason we must be careful to:
• Introduce any change, however small, gradually and sympathetically.
• Familiarise the horse with every possible variation on each lesson, making experiences as wide and varied as possible.

Horses have a great eye for detail – but they are not good generalisers.

For example, familiarise your horse with all different types and colours of fences, and school in different locations (on hacks, at other yards, at shows).

- Never assume because a lesson seems to have been learned, its principles will be applied in a different situation, especially where there is added stress. For example, he may box like an angel at home, but panic and refuse to go near the lorry for the return journey.

Better generalisation skills can be taught. Habituation plays a large part in getting horses used to the fact that change need not necessarily be for the worse! Trust and confidence come through thorough training. An experienced event horse, for example, has learnt that, whatever obstacle he is faced with, it is generally safe to take off. Competition horses must come to accept a new home almost every night during the busy show season. Even so, it's worth remembering that though generalisation may be something we take for granted, it does not come naturally to the horse.

DISPLACEMENT ACTIVITY
See Decision-making and Conflict, page 79.

DISTANCES
Accurately measured distances between trotting poles, elements of a grid, or combinations of fences are vital when the young horse is learning to jump, to encourage a good rhythm and correct take-off point. As training progresses, distances can be gradually increased or decreased to increase athleticism, practise skills such as lengthening/shortening the stride, or improve the shape over the jump (bascule). Standard distances are generally used in competition, although at more advanced levels the course builder may choose to use a more challenging distance between some fences.

Measuring the correct distances between poles or jumps is vital when teaching a horse to jump.

FACTORS AFFECTING DISTANCE

- **Length of stride:** Each horse is an individual, and average distances may need to be adjusted for long or short-striding horses. Ponies will usually require a shorter distance, and unco-ordinated or big horses a larger one.
- **Speed of approach:** An approach in canter will make the horse land further out, so the distance to the next element must allow for this.
- **Type of fences used:** A horse lands further out over a spread than an upright, so the distance from a spread to the next element will be further than if it were an upright.

If a distance is set to fit six or less strides between two fences, this is said to be a 'related' distance.

The average canter stride measures 3.7m (12ft). Where the fences are small (no more than 1m/3ft, most horses suit distances between fences in multiples of 2.7m-3.7m (9-12ft).

AVERAGE 'CORRECT' DISTANCES

Trotting poles:	In walk:	1 metre (3 feet).
	In trot:	1.3-1.4m (4' 3"-4' 6").
	To fence:	2.6-2.9m (8' 6"-9'6").
Placing pole:	No stride:	2.6-3m (8' 6"-10ft).
	One stride:	5-6m (16' 6"-20ft).
Bounce (no stride):	From trot:	2.7-3.3m (9-11ft).
	From canter:	3.3-4.2m (11-14ft).
One stride:	From trot:	5.4m (18ft).
	From canter:	6.6-8.7m (22-27ft).
Two strides:	From trot:	8.7-10m (27-33ft).
	From canter:	10-10.8m (33-36ft).

Remember that half a stride must be allowed for taking off and half a stride for landing. Check at the first attempt whether the horse gets too close to the second element, or has to bend his fore-legs backwards (distance too short), or flattens and has to reach for the second element (distance too long).

DITCHES

Horses are understandably wary of holes in the ground, but, with careful training, can usually be persuaded to overcome their fears. The ability to tackle a ditch is crucial for those planning to tackle cross-country competitions and horse trials, where obstacles including ditches are a regular feature. It makes sense for *all* riding horses to be happy about negotiating a ditch – it could get you out of many a sticky situation!

- Introduce ditches gradually. Start in the earliest stages of training by leading (and later riding) the youngster in and out of hollows and dips in the ground.
- Use an experienced, forward-going horse to lead and boost the confidence of the novice horse.
- Ride positively, using forward-driving aids and looking ahead, not down.
- Make the pace active but not too fast. The horse must be allowed to see the ditch and choose his own take-off point. Hesitation is likely, so the rider must be ready to sit up, keep him straight and encourage take-off.
- Be prepared for an awkward jump at first. Be ready to go 'with' the horse and possibly let the reins slip on landing to avoid interfering with his mouth or stopping him in his tracks.
- Always approach any ditch at a right angle – even if there is an angled pole placed over it, e.g. in a trakehner fence.
- Only introduce a pole over a ditch once the horse is taking the ditch confidently by itself.
- Ditches in the show-jumping arena can be practised by introducing a shallow version at home, or working over a (well-secured) sheet of plastic. Once the horse accepts this, try adding a small fence over the top.

DOMINANCE
See Aggression, page 25; and Hierarchy, page 133.

DRESSAGE

The word dressage means training or schooling. The 'rules' of dressage are based on principles of classical equitation that were first explored by ancient Greeks and later developed into the art of 'haute école' by the riding academies of Renaissance and Baroque Europe.

The FEI (Fédération Èquestre Internationale), defines dressage as "the harmonious development of the physique and ability of the horse. As a result, it makes the horse calm, supple, loose and flexible, but also confident, attentive and keen, thus achieving perfect understanding with his rider."

Training to achieve these standards begins from the horse's earliest days, but when he moves on to ridden work it becomes a long-term, structured process. The aim is to make the horse's movement, when carrying a rider, as balanced and light as it would be without. The horse must also be totally responsive to the rider's commands. This can take many years to achieve using a systematic programme of gymnastic exercises to build the horse's physical and mental agility.

Today, dressage is frequently referred to as a discipline of equestrian sport where riders perform a set test, involving a sequence of movements within an arena. As a result, many riders look on dressage as somehow separate to other forms of riding. In fact, dressage is as much a means to an end as an end in itself. The training of a horse to make him a pleasure to ride – balanced, supple, athletic and obedient – should form the basis of all forms of horsemanship, not be just for those who 'do dressage'.

Dressage is now a highly competitive international sport.

THE SPORT OF DRESSAGE

Riders in the UK are usually introduced to competitive dressage through Pony Club or Riding Club classes. Although these are not affiliated to the sport's UK governing body, British Dressage, they are usually run under the same rules.

Serious competitors may then register with British Dressage and take part in affiliated shows. Levels of competition range from those aimed at the young or inexperienced horse to international-standard horses and riders.

Tests are set at Preliminary, Novice, Medium and Advanced levels. Progress up the ladder is through the accumulation of points, awarded for the achievement of a certain percentage of marks.

ENDURANCE

One of the friendliest and most accessible of all equestrian sports, endurance riding is rapidly increasing in popularity. At the lower levels of the sport any horse and rider can take part. There is little to beat the boost in confidence that hours spent in the saddle getting into shape, enjoying the countryside and getting to know each other can give to any horse and rider, including a youngster.

Rides are organised over various distances, covering all standards. In the UK, riders must complete a 20-mile qualifier and 30-mile final at Bronze Buckle level before progressing to complete two Silver Stirrup qualifiers (40 miles each) and a final (50 miles) before reaching Gold level. Gold standard rides may be up to 100 miles, usually over two days.

Horse welfare is paramount at all levels. To have completed the course successfully, the horse must pass a strict vet's examination both before starting and after the finish. Presenting the horse in top condition is not the only skill the endurance rider must develop. To finish sound and well in a good time, the ability to judge pace, keep the horse balanced so that he uses himself efficiently, know your horse's temperament and capabilities, are all as important as map-reading and an efficient back-up crew.

In the UK, three organisations are currently involved in the administration of endurance riding and all run their own rides.

To succeed in Endurance you must be able to judge your horse's pace, and be aware of his capabilities.

These are the British Endurance Riding Association (BERA), the Endurance Horse & Pony Society (EHPS) and the Scottish Endurance Riding Club (SERC).

ENERGY

It is easy to underestimate the energy at the disposal of our horses, kept in comfort and confinement on high-calorie concentrated rations. After all, wild horses on the poorest of diets and riddled with worms, think nothing of covering many miles a day.

The energy overload we create through modern feeding regimes needs an outlet. If there is not one (in the form of freedom or exercise), it will find its own release – usually through mischief, explosive high spirits, resentment or abnormal behaviour. The amount of energy a horse has depends on various factors, some easily within our control and others less so:

Good health: Persistent lack of energy should be looked into.

Fitness level: This must suit the work expected of the horse.

Diet: Check the amount of digestible energy provided by the ration you are giving. Most horses do best on a diet high in fibre and containing slow-release energy sources. Keep sugars and starch levels low unless the horse is in very hard work. If a restricted diet is needed, top up energy levels and ensure sufficient vitamins and minerals are being provided by using a feed balancer or broad-spectrum supplement. Too much energy, either from overfeeding or underwork, is at the root of more behavioural problems than any other management issue.

Age: Youngsters, like children, tend to be dynamos that have to tick until their energy levels are manageable and it is reasonable to ask them to settle down to some 'school work'.

Temperament: As with humans, some horses have more natural 'fizz' than others, and some are more sensitive to energising feeds or other factors, such as the state of the weather. Highly-bred horses like Thoroughbreds are commonly naturally hyped-up in comparison with cold-blooded breeds.

EXCESS ENERGY

Energy to spare is not helpful for listening and learning *(see Attention, page 35)*. Over-exuberance usually leads to a tense, frustrated rider and the horse being punished simply for feeling good. If you have a hyperactive horse:

• Check his diet and exercise regime.
• Allow him to let off steam before expecting any serious work. This can be achieved in the field, on the lunge, by going for a short hack, or loose schooling.

However, be aware of the difference between high spirits and evasion.

Incorrect diet may be a reason for excess energy.

SCHOOLING THE RUSHING OR 'HYPER' HORSE

Excess energy is not the only cause of rushing. A horse may feel the need to rush because he is unbalanced, tense, being insensitively ridden or is in pain. To try to stop these symptoms in your horse:

• Be calm but positive. Stay relaxed, so as not to increase tension. Keep a soft contact, avoiding hanging on the reins.
• Use half-halts, so the horse learns to wait and listen for the forward aids, and to accept the rider's legs.
• Sit upright to help keep the horse off his forehand.

- Don't be afraid to use your legs, but be subtle with them.
- Highly-charged horses usually settle and unwind gradually if the rider concentrates on rhythm and balance. Improving suppleness from poll to tail will also help the rider acquire more control over the energy being produced.

These exercises should stop the horse rushing in most situations. However, other ways to manage rushing include:

- Working in circles, serpentines and other school figures, for easier control. If the horse will not walk calmly, let him trot slowly (not run on) on a large circle until he steadies and can be balanced using half-halts. Slowing down the rider's rising will also help. When the horse feels like slowing down, then use the legs and seat to ride him forwards.
- Spiralling in on a circle also helps to slow the pace.
- Introduce lots of successive transitions to get the horse thinking and listening. Make them accurate!
- Rushing horses usually have a short, choppy stride and often over-bend (q.v.). Increase the stride length by encouraging the horse to stretch his neck, take the contact forward and work into it. Use the legs quietly, yielding the inside rein slightly. Once the horse is accepting the contact and connected from poll to tail, create more impulsion without speed by working on lengthened strides.
- Teach the horse to relax on a long-rein (see Loose Rein, page 177).
- Do not move on to canter work until the horse is listening in walk and trot. Be patient – rushing takes time and frequent repetition to correct. If the horse hollows or over-bends, return to the earlier exercises.
- For rushing when jumping, see Jumping Problems, page 162.

LACK OF ENERGY/TIREDNESS

Loss of interest or too little energy is as much of a barrier to learning as too much. Although the horse should be calm, he should never become apathetic or 'switched off at the mains'.

Unresponsiveness can be largely down to temperament (big, young horses are often lazy, as are more 'common'-bred types) but management and schooling issues also often play a part:

- Check that the horse's diet is giving sufficient energy, and there is no vitamin/mineral deficiency.
- Make sure the horse is fit enough.
- Learn to recognise signs of tiredness. Serious problems can be created in the future by working young horses so long

their joints and muscles become fatigued. Signs include the horse slowing and trailing its head, tripping or stumbling, becoming more unbalanced, dragging feet or 'brushing' uncharacteristically.

- Work youngsters for two shorter sessions a day (e.g. 15 minutes) rather than one longer one.
- Work and ride out on good, level terrain.
- Allow youngsters a few weeks rest after an intensive period of work.

SCHOOLING THE LAZY OR UNRESPONSIVE HORSE
See Responsiveness, page 211.

EQUIPMENT
There is no reason to wait until the horse is about to be backed before suddenly expecting him to accept a whole stack of restrictive straps and strange objects fastened to his body, in addition to his first experience of a rider.

By introducing a youngster to all the items of equipment he will have to wear well in advance, when ridden work begins he will already be familiar with virtually every part of the process, short of the actual rider.

Begin at any time from around 18 months to 2½ years old – but only once a basis of trust and respect has been set up (*see Join-up, page 153*).

Allow exploration: Whatever the item, give the horse opportunity to find out about it in his own way, discovering for himself that it poses no threat. Sniffing, biting, even stamping on gear (saddles excluded!) is part of this process, so use old gear.

Allow a young horse to get used to the smell and feel of the equipment he is going to wear.

Work in an enclosed space: Conventionally this would be a loose-box, with an assistant holding the horse. Youngsters familiar with work in a round-pen (or similar larger space) are better having all their lessons in that particular 'classroom', one-to-one with the handler. This allows the horse total freedom to act naturally and come to terms with the feel of each new piece of equipment at his own pace. This freedom of choice is consistent with the principles of the join-up process (q.v.).

Be positive: Act calmly and confidently and this will transfer to the horse, who then knows where you are. Slipping on a piece of gear when he isn't looking, or stretching out to ease it on at arm's length gives all the wrong messages. Once you have begun to put on a piece of equipment, finish the job – backing off only teaches him he can control what you ask him to do.

Start simple: Begin with simple items and work up to those that demand more tolerance from the horse.

Work on both sides: The youngster must get used to being tacked up from either side.

TYPES OF EQUIPMENT

Boots and bandages: These can be introduced as soon as the youngster is totally accepting of having his legs handled. Begin with boots, which are easier to put on. Work up to using bandages, which must be well fitted and secure.

Surcingle: A surcingle gets the youngster used to the feel of a restriction around his girth. A breast-plate will stop it slipping backwards and accustom him to the pressure around the chest felt later when wearing a rug. Start by flopping a soft, short length of rope over the back during grooming/handling sessions. Progress to an actual surcingle and finally do it up (firmly but not too tightly). Repeat this often, leaving it on for longer periods.

Saddle: Check the back is comfortable. Properly prepared, the youngster should accept the saddle and girth as simply a heavier version of the surcingle. Use an old saddle to allow the horse to investigate it first. Then put it on carefully but confidently and do up the girth firmly. Expect an instinctive flight/fight reaction to this unnatural, threatening feel – but he will soon work out it is staying put – and he's still alive! Stirrups should be removed or fastened up until a later session. Put on and take off the saddle every day from now on. *See also Saddle-fitting, page 222.*

Bridle and bit: *See Bitting, page 49.*

Rugs: The all-over restriction and feel of a rug flapping against the sides makes many youngsters apprehensive and some even react violently. Allow plenty of time for sniffing etc. Leaving the rug overnight in the stable may help. Prepare by draping a small sheet or cloth over the horse during grooming. Progress to putting on a light sheet fastened with a surcingle (see above), then a stable rug. Leave the turn-out rug until he is relaxed with other types less stiff and heavy.

EVASIONS
Any method the horse uses to avoid a request from the rider is called an evasion.

Evasions range from opening the mouth or chewing the bit, to more extreme tactics such as bucking or napping. Most evasions are down to:
- The rider giving unclear aids.
- The rider asking the horse to do something which is physically too demanding (possibly due to stiffness or even pain).
- The exercise is too difficult for the level of education.
- The horse simply does not want to go forwards into the contact.

Tension quickly causes evasions to escalate and become habits. Avoid giving the horse an excuse to evade by keeping work within his physical and mental capabilities. The rider needs to understand what he is asking for and why, and to be able to explain this clearly to the horse. Be alert to any sources of physical discomfort that may be giving a genuine excuse for the lack of co-operation.

Rather than repeating a mistake that is perpetuating an evasion, abandon that lesson for now and focus on the root cause of the problem. Punishment only creates more anxiety and resistance. Try to find circumstances where the desired movement or action happens more naturally, and use that to condition the horse with plenty of positive reinforcement (q.v.).

EXTENSION
See Gaits, page 101.

FALLING IN / FALLING OUT
See Curves and Circles, page 76.

FARRIERY
See Feet and the Farrier, page 96.

FEAR
Evolution has programmed the horse to fear in order to live. Suspicion is an evolved survival device the horse has brought with him to domestication; he instinctively leaps sideways at a bird fluttering from a hedge, even though it is millennia since his ancestors were at risk from ambush by a tiger.

Signs of fear *(see table, page 10-11)* are highly infectious. Other horses rapidly interpret and respond to these cues. Alarm can spread like wildfire from horse to horse, or human to horse. In order of priority, the horse's response to any situation where he feels threatened are:

Flight: Escape by running away is always preferred. This is why confinement is such a source of potential stress, denying the horse his first-choice survival option. In ridden work, flight would translate to behaviour such as rushing or shying.

Fight: Fighting is a risky business. Always keep this in mind, particularly when tempted to blame a horse for apparent bad temper. Aggression is rarely used offensively by horses – it is almost always an act of self-defence, often when the horse is 'cornered' in a situation from which he cannot escape. Evasions and resistance in ridden work such as bucking and napping, can all be fight responses.

Freeze: Extreme fear, particularly in a situation where the flight/fight choices are denied, can cause an 'emotional overload' in the horse which literally paralyses him. The 'freeze' reaction is often the prelude to panic – a very dangerous scenario.

Most training is targeted at damping down the horse's natural fearfulness. Fear of strangeness is overcome through habituation (q.v.). Learning can only be effective if tension levels are kept as low as possible and any situations are avoided where the horse may feel threatened or anxious.

A farrier must be both skilled and sympathetic.

FEET AND THE FARRIER

"No foot, no horse" is an old adage that cannot be repeated often enough. Our horses are totally reliant on us to keep their feet comfortable and usable. Neglected feet can lead to severe problems and is a major welfare issue.

To ensure your horse's feet remain in good condition:
- Clean out your horse's feet daily (twice-daily for stabled horses).
- Learn to recognise the signs of when a foot needs trimming or re-shoeing, as well as the features of a well-shod foot.
- Use a farrier who is skilled and sympathetic.
- Call your farrier regularly (the average length between visits should be around six weeks for most horses).

FOOT NOTES

Horses themselves know the importance of their feet to their survival. Youngsters are understandably reluctant to 'surrender' their precious get-away equipment to a human handler, but do not ignore this basic lesson in life. It will be far more difficult to gain the co-operation of a big, strong four-year-old determined to fix his feet safely to the floor!

Unfamiliarity makes even the simplest process an ordeal. Once any horse links lifting his feet with a problem, the farrier's job becomes increasingly hard. This applies equally to older horses whose owners are too busy to pick out feet regularly, or who do not insist on good manners. Any horse that is difficult to shoe will be vulnerable to abuse and have a shaky future.

TEACHING THE YOUNGSTER TO HAVE HIS FEET PICKED UP

- Where possible, use imprinting *(see Imprinting, page 141)*. If the new-born foal learns to accept his legs and feet being handled from the very start, it is unlikely that problems will be encountered later on.
- Allow the foal to see the mare having her feet handled and become familiar with the farrier.
- Gradually progress to picking up the horse's feet yourself. Only ask for a slight lift at first, for a few seconds. Give praise and put the foot down carefully.
- Picking up a foot involves redistribution of the horse's balance – a potential source of stress. Ask for the fore-leg which is furthest forward. This has the least weight on it. Move next to the hind-leg on the same side, then the other hind-leg and finally the remaining fore-leg.
- Ask while the horse is distracted with something pleasant, e.g. feeding.
- Ask properly. Stand alongside and run your hand down the back of the leg. At the fetlock, give the command UP and give a little squeeze. At first, you may need to nudge his side a little to indicate more clearly what you want.
- Once lifting the feet for cleaning is accepted as routine, gently tap the hoof-pick on the hoof wall and sole, in preparation for the farrier.

With regular routine attention in the early years, the first shoeing should not cause any alarm. When buying a youngster, make sure he is happy with this process before arranging for the first shoeing. Choose a particularly patient farrier for young horses.

Always give yourself plenty of time when handling a youngster, and make sure you succeed in what you set out to do.

Be firm with the awkward customer.

RESISTING LIFTING THE FEET

With any horse not wanting to pick up his feet, check first he has no reasonable excuse. For example, pain in the opposite foot would explain the reluctance, as would stiffness from arthritis, often found in older horses.

Some horses have never been properly taught to pick up their feet. Others are simply plain awkward; this is a respect issue – there must be no 'no-go' areas which your horse dictates to you. To avoid this problem:

- Insist on handling the feet regularly.
- Before asking for a particular foot, get him to move the weight off it to make it easier. Walk him forwards a step if necessary.
- If the horse plants his feet, use a short, sharp nudge behind the elbow. Do not lean into his side; he will respond by leaning back against you – and win!
- Squeezing the chestnut slightly, or running a hoof-pick or mane comb gently along the sensitive area at the back of the pastern and heels, usually convinces the horse it is more comfortable to lift the foot.
- Once the foot is lifted, unless you feel in danger, do not let go! The stubborn customer must understand that whatever he does, you intend to hold on. After a short time, place the foot back on the ground (avoid simply letting go, which is asking for a kick).
- Immediately repeat the lesson several times. Make sure the lesson is repeated regularly from now on.
- Avoid holding the foot up for too long or too high.

FEAR OF THE FARRIER

Once a horse has had a bad experience connected with being shod, the whole process (or even sight of the farrier) can make him panic. This situation takes tremendous patience to resolve, but is worth the effort. Even if a home can be found for a horse where he can manage without shoes, regular trimming would still be essential.

- Work patiently on the habituation process described above.
- Find a sympathetic farrier and discuss the problem with him. Expect to pay extra to allow him to spend additional time with your horse.
- Consider a calming feed supplement, a therapy such as Bach Flower Rescue Remedy, or working with TTEAM techniques (q.v.).
- It is better to use a sedative if necessary, to ensure the horse stands quietly, than to allow another battle to be linked with the farrier's visit.

FLATWORK
A general term referring to ridden work that does not involve jumping.

Even though flatwork does not involve jumping, it is as essential to jumpers as dressage horses. Whatever kind of horse you want – whether it is a well-mannered riding horse or a winner in any competitive sphere – it is exercises on the flat that produce the essential balance, suppleness, and control needed for the horse to perform at his best.

FLEXION
See Suppleness, page 24; Curves and Circles, page 76.

FOREHAND / 'ON THE FOREHAND'
'The forehand' describes the front half of the horse, forward from the centre of gravity. It includes the forelegs, shoulders, neck and head, and carries 60 per cent of the horse's bodyweight.

Ridden training aims to encourage the horse to take weight off his front end and transfer the centre of gravity backwards. By flexing along the neck and back and bringing the hindquarters further underneath, the forehand is lightened, making the horse much more balanced and manoeuvrable.

Young and novice horses find this difficult. Their natural way of going is with their weight too much 'on the forehand' – an expression many novice riders will have heard from their instructor or dressage test judge!

FORWARD / 'GOING FORWARD'

'Going forward' is a term describing a horse that is truly working forwards into the rein contact, flexing through his spine so that he is carrying himself, rather than leaning on the rein, and stepping right underneath his body with his hind-legs (i.e. engaging the quarters). To have the horse truly going forward is a cornerstone of training.

Going forward is not the same as going fast. It involves the horse tracking-up (q.v.), to create the impulsion that allows him to lighten in front.

Some horses have plenty of energy. For these types, forward impulsion is easy to find (often too easy!), but can often translate into tension, leading to hollowness (q.v.) or over-bending (q.v.). Others are naturally lazy and their schooling needs to concentrate on creating impulsion *(see Energy, page 89)*.

Forward training is the cornerstone of all ridden training.

TEACHING THE FORWARD AIDS

Teaching the horse to go forward from the leg is the first step in ridden training. From the start, forward movement should come from the hindquarters pushing the horse along, not the forehand pulling him along.

- Walk on a long-rein.
- Keeping the lower leg on, squeeze the knees into the saddle and tighten your back muscles slightly. This should shorten the stride a little.

- After a few strides, relax the back and knees, pushing the horse forward with the lower leg. His hind feet will then step further under the body. Practise this exercise until only a light aid is needed for a response.
  See also Backing, page 37.

THINKING FORWARDS

Horse and rider must think forwards at all times. Right from the beginning, ride your youngster positively in all situations. Reassure him and encourage him to work away from the security of friends and the yard.

Whenever correction is needed, give the aids carefully to avoid confusion and the backward thinking that can be the start of evasions such as napping. For example, when teaching the forward aids, if the horse shoots forwards too abruptly, avoid being too heavy-handed when steadying him or he will only be confused as to what you meant in the first place. Give aids for upward transitions clearly and firmly, always ensuring they are not being contradicted by any restraining aids.

FRIENDSHIPS & BONDING
See Herd Behaviour, page 130.

GAITS
A gait (also referred to as a pace) is a method of using the legs to create forwards movement. Horses commonly use four gaits: walk, trot, canter and gallop (q.v.).

The gaits developed as ways of moving that saved energy, kept the horse upright, and enabled him to travel at speed (and without his legs knocking into each other). Each gait has an optimum speed where energy efficiency is greatest. This is the speed at which the horse is most relaxed and comfortable. Pushed beyond this, he either needs to make more of an effort, or, he needs to change gear to regain this optimum.

VARIATIONS IN THE GAITS
Within each gait, the horse can be asked to change the length of his strides and his outline. The extent of that change will depend on the stage of his training and athleticism.

Working trot: the basic movement.

Begin to ask for variations once training has produced gaits which are balanced, regular and energetic when carrying a rider. Work on suppleness and impulsion first – this will take time, but without these, lengthening and shortening the stride will be very difficult.

Within all the variations the aims are:
- To keep the rhythm of strides regular.
- To make each stride of even length.
- For the horse to go forwards freely without tension.

Once your horse has reached this stage, he is ready to learn how to extend the stretch of each gait.

Working: The regular version of each gait (especially trot and canter), used for most of the young horse's training until he has the suppleness and impulsion to vary the gait. Variations are developed from the basis of the 'working' paces. The exception is medium walk, used from the start with the young horse.

Medium: The horse is asked to take longer, freer strides with more impulsion.

Extended: The horse lengthens his stride as much as possible, producing much more activity from the quarters but staying light in front. The neck and head extend and lower. Rushed steps will be stiff – strides must be long and low, with the whole frame stretched.

- Ask for only a few lengthened strides at first – lots of strides require lots of balance.
- Ride plenty of transitions beforehand to activate the quarters and get the horse listening to your leg.

- Prepare with a half-halt to gather impulsion. Squeeze with the legs, then 'yield' the hands, allowing the energy forwards.
- Rhythm is important. Count in your head to stop yourself speeding up, using half-halt if needed.
- Ask in rising trot first. Rise slightly higher to encourage forwards movement, but sit up!
- If the horse does not understand the aids to lengthen, push him up a gear around the whole arena several times, then ask him to come back to you. Gradually reduce to just lengthening down the long sides, then to using a few strides of lengthening only (e.g. across the diagonal or between two markers).
- Asking for lengthening on a large circle helps prevent rushing. Use half-halts for steadying.

Collected: The horse steps right underneath himself, moving weight off his forehand backwards, on to his quarters. Impulsion from the quarters is contained and channelled upwards and forwards, making the steps shorter and higher (but not slower). The shoulders are freed as the centre of gravity moves back. The neck is raised and arched so that the whole frame is shortened, not only the steps.

- Use the legs to create impulsion.
- Keep a softness in the contact, squeezing the reins slightly to contain the impulsion.
- Think of pushing into the contact, not pulling the head back.
- Prepare for collection with half-halts.
- Decrease from a 20-metre to a 15-metre circle.
- Start asking in trot or canter. Walk is more difficult, as natural impulsion is easily lost. In walk, try quarter pirouettes (turn on the haunches) at each corner of a large square.

Collected trot: impulsion from the quarters is channelled upwards.

Extended gait: the horse lengthens his stride.

Free: The horse is given freedom to stretch and lower his neck as he likes. Free paces should be relaxed but still active.

Lengthening and shortening the strides is hard work for the horse. Tired muscles become tense, so alternate these exercises with others to improve general suppleness. After work, encourage him to stretch 'long and low' in free walk.

ADVANTAGES OF VARYING THE GAIT
Teaching your horse to vary his gaits has many benefits:
- He will be more free in his movement, mobile and controllable.
- It increases the horse's suppleness from front to back, so he can relax and use his back more.
- It helps to develop the correct muscles.
- Increases his attentiveness and responsiveness.
- Improves co-ordination and balance.
- Shortening strides improves transitions and allows the rider to get bouncier, more athletic paces (e.g. for doing lateral work, or jumping).
- Develops the rider's 'feel'.
- It is a good way of tackling difficulties faced by uneven terrain or obstacles, e.g. when jumping or going cross-country.

GALLOP
The fastest and most extended gait. The change up a gear from canter is often hardly noticeable. As the horse gathers speed and impulsion, the diagonal sequence of the canter is broken. In gallop, four foot-falls are heard,

followed by a moment when all the feet are off the ground (known as the 'moment of suspension').

In gallop, the centre of gravity moves forward, so to remain balanced the rider must take up a forward position with their seat slightly out of the saddle. Shortening the stirrups helps with this.

Like canter, gallop has a leading leg. When the right fore-leg is the lead, the sequence begins with the left hind, followed by the right hind, then the left fore, and ending with the right fore.

A 'GOOD' GALLOP

In a 'good' gallop the strides should be even in length and rhythmic – the steps producing a regular four-time beat. Throughout the gallop the horse should be in perfect balance and form the correct outline, with the hind-legs following directly behind the fore-legs.

Unfortunately, all too often, gallop is simply left to happen. It then frequently becomes an uncontrolled fling, linked in the horse's mind with an opportunity to stop listening to his rider and let off steam. Taking the time to make sure that young horses are taught to gallop in a balanced, controlled way has many benefits:

- You can enjoy picking up speed when the opportunity arises out on hacks without fear of being run off with.
- It reinforces the lesson that the horse must listen to the rider whatever pace he is in.
- It allows the horse to go across country in an energy-efficient, controlled and balanced way, avoiding injuries and approaching each obstacle in a better position to jump.
- It enables you to show your horse's capability to truly extend himself in the individual show required in many showing classes (particularly important in hunter classes).

In gallop, it is essential that the horse still listens to the rider.

Opening and closing gates

1. Line up your horse's head with the latch.

2. Undo the latch.

3. Open the gate wide, using the aids for turn on the forehand so the horse moves his quarters around.

4. Turn on the forehand again so that you can come back alongside the gate and fasten it.

GATES

Many a horse that has taken to barging through gateways does so because he is in a rush to get through. Either no one has taken the time to teach him to lead quietly through a narrow space, or careless handling (often through too narrow a doorway) has resulted in knocks and worried the horse.

To prevent gateway barging:
- All doors and gateways should be at least four foot wide.
- Lead your horse carefully through any narrow space.
- Introduce gates of different widths (but never narrow) to young horses from their very first outings.
- Use the proper procedure:
1. Bring the horse alongside the gate, head in line with the latch;
2. Reach out and undo the latch;
3. Use the aids for turn on the forehand to ask the horse to move his quarters around;
4. Open the gate plenty wide enough to pass through without it swinging back on the horse;
5. Turn on the forehand again to come back alongside the gate to fasten.
- Stay calm and take your time. Praise the horse when he stands quietly.
- Horses that have become nervous of narrow spaces need their confidence rebuilt. Be patient and avoid battles. Set up 'passages' to negotiate in the field or arena (e.g. with bales of straw), starting wide and gradually reducing the width.

GENERALISATION
See Discrimination, page 83.

GESTALT
A term used in psychology to describe the way that animals (horses, and ourselves included) tend to respond to situations as a whole rather than simply to a specific prompt. For example, whether the horse reacts to an aid depends not only on whether he felt it being given, but also whether he was distracted by an activity outside the arena (e.g. by a gust of wind, or an itch on his knee).

Gestalt is the combination of stimuli that come together to make up any situation at any moment in time. It affects learning in several ways:
- It emphasises the need to create a good training environment and keep it consistent.
- New lessons are best learnt in familiar surroundings.
- A lesson can be learnt in one situation, then apparently 'forgotten' in a different one.
- Altering the gestalt, especially without warning, can completely confuse and unnerve some horses, undoing even well-learnt lessons. Most owners are familiar with the

experience that a horse arriving at a new home can behave quite uncharacteristically in his unfamiliar environment.

- Horses can sometimes be broken of unwanted habits by changing the gestalt, e.g. a horse that pulls hard at the bit may suddenly become softer in the mouth if a severe bit is swapped for a mild one. Even the tiniest of changes in a situation can break a set pattern and make the horse's mind receptive to a new perspective (*see Discrimination, page 83*).

GRIDS

A schooling exercise where a combination of poles on the ground, along with small fences, are set out in a line with set distances in between. It is also referred to as 'gymnastic jumping.'

WHY USE GRIDS?

A well-laid-out grid places the horse on exactly the right stride throughout the exercise, making it easy for him to stay in balance and keep up forward momentum.

Grid-work benefits horses and riders at all levels. It is as invaluable to experienced combinations as it is in teaching a youngster confidence and good jumping technique. Some of the benefits to be drawn from grids include:

- Greater horse and rider confidence.
- A more developed sense of good rhythm.
- Improved co-ordination and balance.
- Increased suppleness and agility.
- Quicker reactions.
- A steady, systematic rate of progress.
- Fun!

Grids are used to develop balance, rhythm and co-ordination.

At a more advanced stage, grids can be designed to polish skills and work on specific problem areas, e.g.:
• Improving the horse's shape over a fence.
• Encouraging the horse to get closer to his fences.
• Slowing down a rushing horse.
• Creating impulsion to sharpen up a lazy horse or make him more careful.

GETTING GRIDS RIGHT
Following certain ground-rules will help you get the most from grid-work.
Riding the grid: Approach steadily and straight, coming off a wide arc. With novices use an active trot, allowing the horse to canter on once over the first element.
• Speed is not important – aim for balance and bounce.
• Avoid interfering with the horse. Look up, keep an even rein contact and the legs on.
• Practise approaches from both directions if space allows (and if all the obstacles are suitable to be jumped either way).
• Grids are tiring – keep sessions short.
Building the grid: Start small and simple, e.g. poles on the ground. Build up the length and difficulty gradually. Increase the demands of the grid only once the previous stage is being tackled successfully.
• If a problem arises, go back one or more stages as necessary. Simplify or lower the grid until the horse is coping confidently again.
• Keep the first element inviting, e.g. cross-pole or small upright/narrow oxer.
• Give every element a ground-line (q.v.).
• Remove any unused cups from jump-stands.
• Always use correct distances for the horse *(see Distances, page 84)*. Awkward distances soon knock confidence. Be ready to adapt distances slightly so your horse can jump comfortably. At a later stage they can be shortened or lengthened little by little to encourage the horse to alter his stride.
• Bounce distances are more demanding, but useful for more experienced combinations. Use low cross-poles and uprights only for bounces, with no more than five in a row.
• Spreads ask for more effort. For novices, include a spread at the start or end of the line only.
• Learn to measure the length of one of your own paces, so

setting out a grid with the correct distances for your horse is straightforward.

See also Pole-work, page 199.

GROOMING

Grooming is about more than keeping a horse smart with a clean and healthy coat. Touch is important to horses and plays an important role in their social life. Horses enjoy being groomed by their friends in the field, and most appreciate when human friends make them 'feel good' in the same way. Regular grooming sessions provide an opportunity for getting close to our horses that few of us make the most of.

GROOMING NOTES
- If possible, 'imprint' the foal to the sensation of being felt all over *(see Imprinting, page 141)*.
- Familiarise the foal to the feel of a soft brush and the sight of his mother being groomed soon after birth.
- Brush for a few minutes only at first, building up little by little.
- Make grooming sessions 'quality time'. Stay calm. Avoid the softly-softly approach – take firm, confident strokes.
- Use the right tool. Avoid scrubbing with hard brushes – where mud is dried on, use the fingers to pick it away carefully.
- Speak reassuringly, so the horse always knows where you are.
- Give the anxious horse an enjoyable distraction, e.g. a hay-net.

Good friends will indulge in mutual grooming.

- Work over every area – all horses must accept being touched all over their bodies. However, be sensitive to ticklish areas and places where most horses feel vulnerable, e.g. belly, between the hind-legs, ears etc. Take particular care with thin-skinned individuals.

DISLIKE OF BEING GROOMED

A horse that is touchy or difficult to groom usually has good reason. He may have especially thin or sensitive skin, or have been roughly handled in the past. Dislike may be shown through fidgeting or pulling back. Being good at persuading us to stop doing things they do not like, many horses soon realise that a lifted leg or head swung round to nip is enough to stop a sensitive spot from being touched.

Dislike of grooming needs to be worked on until trust is regained. A deal must be struck – the handler agrees to be fair and sensitive, but the horse must understand there will be no 'no-go' areas. Achieve this by following the points above and using the sacking out procedure *(see Shying, page 236).*

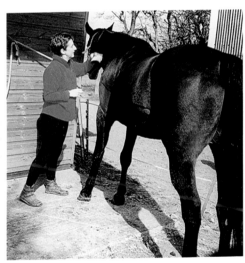

Make sure grooming sessions are quality as time spent with your horse.

GROUND-LINE

Any part of a fence that touches the ground (e.g. a pole or plank at the base, a pole resting on the ground at an angle, or a filler) provides a ground-line. This is a way of helping the horse assess the height of a fence and his distance away from it as he approaches, so the take-off point can be judged accurately.

Although more advanced horses can be expected to jump fences built without, a ground-line must always be used for novice horses and riders. Never use a fence with a 'false' (i.e. misleading) ground-line. The pole or filler used must always be slightly in front or directly beneath the fence. If set back, it can cause the horse to completely misjudge the obstacle.

GROUP RIDING
While important new lessons are best taught in a quiet environment one-to-one, a young horse needs to be given regular opportunities to work in slightly larger groups with other horses.
See also Hacking, page 115.

- Avoid large groups.
- Choose riding companions carefully at first. Do not insist for example, that your horse goes alongside one he is known to dislike. Reliable, easy-going friends are best.
- Alternate between riding behind, alongside and in front of others.
- When working with others in an arena, stick to the accepted rules to avoid confusion and mishaps:
1. Pass riders coming from the other direction left-hand to left-hand.
2. Give warning when entering or leaving the arena.
3. Move to the inside track when in walk and to halt.
4. Be particularly aware of other riders when cantering.

Observing riding school etiquette avoids accidents.

GYMNASTIC JUMPING
See Grids, page 108.

HABITUATION

Almost all of the training that allows us to ride and handle horses is based on the principle of habituation. This simple form of learning is an on-going, lifelong process. Habituation requires horses to become accustomed to living alongside humans and going along with the unnatural things that we ask them to do.

The horse is repeatedly exposed to experiences that would normally provoke instinctive survival responses, but is instead shown that it poses no threat to him. Gradually he learns to suppress his innate reactions, using his memory of previous experience. This ability is what makes horses so much more easily trained than other large prey animals such as deer, or even members of their own genus such as zebra.

USES OF HABITUATION

Habituation can be used in all aspects and levels of training. Examples include teaching the horse to become accustomed to:
- Being approached from all angles.
- Being touched and handled all over his body, including in his most vulnerable areas, such as under the belly.
- Accepting experiences loaded with perceived risk, such as the farrier, clipping, grooming, traffic, or entering a lorry or trailer.

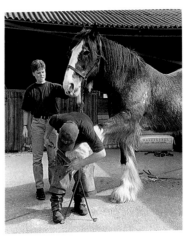

Habituation involves suppressing natural survival instincts and accepting that a situation, such as a visit from the farrier, involves no risk.

- Accepting a saddle and bridle.
- Accepting a rider on his back.
- Tolerating a busy, highly-stimulating environment such as a show ground.

MAKING IT WORK

Whatever its application, successful habituation depends on the lesson being:

Progressive: Introduce an experience gradually, in easy stages. Do not expect too much too quickly. Start with a reasonable request and increase expectations in small, graduated steps, moving on only when the horse is completely happy and confident with the previous stage. Expecting too much too soon will frighten the horse and make progress from that point doubly difficult.

Gradual: Take your time. The longer allowed for the learning process, the more thorough it will be. Rushing inevitably leads to a relapse, usually at the worst possible moment (i.e. when you are both under stress, such as at a show). Let the horse dictate the pace of learning.

Consistent: Horses are easily confused by change. Anxiety about what to expect is a significant barrier to learning. Be clear and consistent in all requests.

Repeated: Regular exposure to an experience, with frequent repetition of short lessons linked to a positive reward, all help habituation sink in quickly and thoroughly *(see Reinforcement, page 207)*. Even when a lesson has been fully understood it must be repeated often, otherwise original, innate reactions can quickly return. For example, a horse may have loaded first time every journey when he was competing regularly, but should not be expected to walk straight up the ramp after a long break from travelling.

Context-specific: Horses are poor at generalising experiences *(see Discrimination, page 83)*. Trainers must work through any lesson in as many different ways, and apply it to as many different situations, as possible, before it can safely be considered learned.

PROBLEMS WITH HABITUATION

Habituation merely dampens instinctive responses – it does not switch them off. Consequently, it is a notoriously temporary kind of learning, that can be rapidly undone, even by one single high-stress experience, such as a traffic accident or attack by an aggressive dog. A strong unpleasant memory can completely block the horse's ability to even start the process.

Occasionally a horse can become sensitised to an experience and begin to over-react to a stimulus rather than learning to ignore it. This is usually due to habituation being rushed or the horse becoming confused and stressed. Care and time must then be taken to go back to the very basics and regain confidence before starting the process once again slowly.

HABIT STRENGTH

Once learned, a lesson becomes more and more firmly fixed in the memory the more often it is repeated. This works to our advantage in training horses. By using a particular command repeatedly, the horse's reaction to it becomes almost automatic, so it can be used in all situations. For example, once trained to the command WHOA, this can be used not only when halting, but also to help steady a horse that is going forwards too strongly.

The effects of habit strength are not always so positive. Horses are particularly prone to forming persistent habits that then 'stick' so firmly they can be all but impossible to replace or eradicate. An evasion that develops due to an unsuitable bit or rough hands is carried on long after the original cause is removed. Getting training right from the start is far easier than trying to retrain a horse that has established an unwanted behaviour.

HACKING

Both horses and riders generally find huge enjoyment in hacking, or riding outdoors away from the confines of an arena.

For the horse, this is an activity that follows his natural instincts and provides variety, relaxation and interest. Hacks over varied terrain and ground conditions and in all weathers broaden a horse's horizons. Hacking also fosters independence and teaches him to face whatever comes his way calmly and with confidence. It builds agility, balance, surefootedness and the horse's ability to look after himself, and also develops his pace and natural impulsion – the basis of good schooling. Riding out is an opportunity to teach manners and obedience in many different circumstances. For the horse, clocking up

Hacking is one of the most enjoyable parts of riding – for both horse and rider.

mileage under saddle is also foundation of fitness and muscle development.

There is nothing like riding in the open countryside for enjoying the companionship of a horse and really getting to know him. Hacking also helps riders to develop a practical ability and feel for their horse's movements and reactions, and to improve their control skills and judgement. Here is your chance to practise lessons away from pressures of the school or competition.

A horse that is not safe and sensible to ride out both alone and in company, in particular on the roads, is going to have an uncertain future. Make the most of time spent outside the arena to teach any horse some important lessons in life.

USING HACKING TIME EFFECTIVELY

Riding out should be relaxing, but viewing it as a complete 'holiday' is a wasted opportunity – and can be unsafe. A horse that is slopping along, falling over its feet, distracted by every sight and sound, is a positive danger. At all times your horse must pay attention to his rider.

Hacking time can be used to improve many aspects of your own riding and your horse's way of going, though take care not to be distracted from what is going on around you. Choose your place and moment sensibly, taking advantage of level ground or a quiet stretch of road to work on areas such as:
• Improving rider position.
• Working 'on the bridle'.

116

- Making accurate, balanced turns and corners.
- Halting correctly, e.g. at road junctions.
- Practising straightness, e.g. using the verge as a guide.
- Practising accurate, obedient transitions.
- Lateral exercises (e.g. to go around a stationary object such as a parked car, approaching shoulder-in, straighten as you go past, then leg yield back to the side of the road).
- Increasing and decreasing the length of stride.
- Turn on the forehand (opening and shutting gates is perfect practice!).

HACKING POINTS
- Follow the Countryside Code when riding in the countryside, and the Highway Code when on the road.
- Use only routes that are official rights of way, or where you have specific permission to ride.
- Be aware of the steps to take in any emergency.
- Expect any horse to be far more switched on when hacking than he may be generally working in an arena.
- Stay alert. Anticipate potential problems, but ride positively.
- Take care riding at speed over unfamiliar ground or in woodland. Do not tackle obstacles without first checking the landing side. Never jump livestock fencing or gates without permission.
- Keep rides interesting by avoiding repeating the same ride too often. Make routes circular wherever possible – rides that involve about-turns, returning home the same way, encourage anticipation and overexcitement on the home stretch.
- Tailor the length and type of ride (i.e. fast, uphill, etc.) to the horse's fitness.
- Start and finish in walk, allowing the horse to settle, loosen up, and later, to cool down.

INTRODUCING HACKING
Before venturing out, any horse should be under control in an enclosed area and fully understand the basic aids. However, remember that, to the inexperienced youngster, everything he encounters in the world outside the yard may be new. Riders should ride confidently, but must also expect the unexpected and not take for granted that a youngster will accept experiences that an older horse takes in his stride. Riders must be competent and strong enough to deal with any difficult situation that might arise.

Make sure your youngster is working confidently in the arena before going out on a hack.

Consider arranging a reliable older companion for the youngster's first few hacks. Choose a sensible escort that is prepared to ignore any antics. He can give a lead past more unusual sights or objects. Bear in mind though that your ultimate aim is an independent horse who looks to his rider for security and direction. There is much to be said for venturing out solo from the start (provided preparation has been sound) and introducing company as a second, rather than first, step.

Keep outings short at first, avoiding any known potential frighteners. Encourage the youngster to go forwards in a straight line, keeping the quarters in. Ride forwards positively, using the voice to encourage and reassure. If riding with a companion, position the older horse between the youngster and the traffic at first.

Introduce early on the idea that the youngster must take whatever place in a group that he is asked to. Vary his position regularly. Start by following, but later ask him to go alongside the other horse and, at times, in front.

Take advantage of natural obstacles. Encourage forward movement through puddles and over dips and hollows. Ask the horse to stand quietly alongside a gate, even if he is not yet ready to learn to let you open it.

As the youngster gains confidence, include short trots and canters, in suitable locations. Canter is best introduced on a slight incline and not when heading towards home. Give thought to your place among other horses in the ride: lazier horses are best behind another, whereas keen, stronger ones would be safest at the front. Once a steady canter is

118

established, however, practise varying the position. The horse must learn to stay calm and do as he is asked, wherever he is.

If you have used a companion horse from the beginning, over a period of time and several outings, increase the distance between yourself and the escort until they are completely out of sight and hearing. Once this is accepted, your youngster is ready to start hacking out regularly on his own. This next stage is best not delayed too long, or a reliance on the other horse can soon develop.

COMMON PROBLEMS
- Refusing to go forwards or to leave the yard, or rearing *(see Napping, page 188)*.
- Becoming excitable or refusing to walk calmly *(see Energy, page 89)*.
- Running away, becoming over-strong or bolting *(see Bolting, page 55)*.
- Nervousness *(see Shying, page 236)*.
- The horse repeatedly puts his head down to eat. Greedy ponies soon spoil a child's riding fun but can be thwarted by fitting a set of home-made 'grass reins'. Take a good length of twine or strong string. Tie one end to one of the front D-rings of the saddle. Pass the twine through the bit ring, up behind the ears, through the bit ring on the other side and attach it to the other D-ring. The 'reins' must be tight enough to stop the pony reaching down to eat, but not so taut that his neck cannot relax.
- The horse constantly pulls at the reins. A horse inclined to 'yaw' or yank at the reins must be ridden forwards actively into a firm but elastic contact. Gloves should always be worn and rubber-covered reins also allow for better grip. *(see Bitting, page 49)*
- Rushing through gateways *(see Gates, page 106)*.
- Reluctance to go through water *(see Water, page 277)*.

HALT
Learning to stand still at halt is among the very first and most important lessons for the young or novice horse. Neglect this fundamental 'house-rule' and you are forever likely to have a fidgety horse or one that is unable to achieve a correct and balanced halt.

AIDS FOR HALT
The aids for halt are the same as for any decrease in pace *(see*

Transitions, page 259), but are kept up until forward movement stops. The horse is pushed into a non-yielding rein, moving forwards into halt with plenty of impulsion and no resistance. The rider's legs stay wrapped around the horse's sides and a soft contact is maintained throughout, so that the horse stays attentive and energy is not lost, even at a standstill. The horse is then 'in gear', ready to move away in balance at whatever pace the rider asks for.

Points to remember:

- The strength of the aids needed will depend on the horse's obedience and training level.
- The rider must soften the rein as soon as horse responds, but maintain contact.
- Never pull back on the reins.
- Ensure you have equal weight in both reins and are sitting upright and central.
- Keep breathing and try not to stiffen during the transition and the halt or the horse will tense. Arms and hands must stay relaxed while still maintaining contact.

INTRODUCING HALT

- Introduce the idea of halting and standing still from an early age with in-hand work and later, in long-reins and on the lunge.
- Do not ask for too much in the initial stages – three seconds is plenty for a novice or youngster before walking forwards again. Avoid hassling the horse if, at first, he does not understand.
- At first, rely mainly on the voice and a very light contact on the head-collar, lungeing cavesson or, after backing, the bit.

As training progresses, you can work on a perfect halt, with the horse standing four-square.

- Do not confuse the issue by being over-fussy about the need to halt square (i.e. with a 'leg at each corner', weight evenly distributed). At this point it is far better to instil the need to be immobile, than to be constantly correcting a halt that is technically less-than-perfect and so suggesting it is acceptable to fidget. As the horse becomes more balanced and supple, he is less likely to leave a leg trailing and more likely to halt with his hind-legs underneath him and weight evenly spread.
- Praise the horse when he does what is asked. If the halt is to be lengthy, allow him to relax on a longer rein.

FURTHER WORK

As training progresses, the rider can work towards a more ideal halt. Here the horse is carefully prepared with the rider using the seat and legs to transfer more weight to the hindquarters and drive him into an increasingly holding, but giving, contact (see Half-halt, see below). The aim is for the horse to react almost instantly to the rider's request, without making the halt too sudden or abrupt.

The horse should stand straight and square with his legs underneath him, carrying himself with the neck and poll as the highest point and the nose slightly in front of a vertical angle to the ground. He should accept the bit, staying still, yet attentive to his rider.

PROBLEMS

Not standing still: Be consistent, insisting on no fidgeting whenever you want your horse to stand still, whether on the ground (e.g. when grooming, doing up the girth etc.) or in ridden work. Be definite with the aids and maintain concentration by keeping the leg and rein contact positive, yet soft. Avoid moving on too quickly from halt – practise counting to a specific number (e.g. 20) before asking for forwards movement.

A few steps back are often taken when the rein contact is too strong or unyielding, or the horse drifts into halt unbalanced or without impulsion. Use more leg to maintain impulsion while keeping the hand soft, yet still. Horses too much on the forehand will often take a few steps forward.

Fore-legs or hind-legs are too far underneath: The horse has come into halt on the forehand, or the rider has used too much leg but forgotten to 'give' contact slightly as the horse halts. Practise plenty of transitions to improve his general way of going.

Fidgeting is a common fault when attempting to sustain the halt position.

Halt is crooked: Any crookedness in the paces will be emphasised as the horse moves into halt. Work on increasing suppleness and straightness generally and improving your riding position, so your body weight is kept central and upright, your legs are used equally throughout downward transitions and there is equal weight in both reins. If the horse is not travelling straight, he will not halt straight or square.

Leaving one or more legs trailing: This is due to lack of suppleness and balance, and loss of impulsion. The horse will find it hard to move off well out of a halt where his quarters are not engaged, so work on improving his impulsion into halt. Riders can practise feeling when the horse does not have his weight evenly spread and identifying which leg is left behind. Sit relaxed and central in the saddle with your seat-bones square. If a hind-leg is trailing or rested, the horse's pelvis will lower on that side, causing your seat-bone to drop slightly. Glance at the horse's shoulders to see if the fore-legs are square and learn how this feels.

During early training, it is better to ask the horse to walk on and then make another attempt at a better halt than to try and make minor adjustments. More advanced horses will become sensitive to small shifts of the rider's body weight or a slight nudge with the leg on the corresponding side to the one on which the horse's leg needs to move forwards. This can then be enough to signal to the horse to adjust his balance. Always ask for adjustment forwards, never backwards, and avoid over-compensating or the horse may take a full step.

Horse resisting or slow to react: The rider needs to work on increasing the horse's sensitivity to the aids by making frequent downward transitions and halts, e.g. every set number of paces. Be positive when asking for halt, but avoid fixing the hand or pulling. Use a series of shorter rein aids that can get progressively stronger if necessary. Sit up and push forwards into halt with the legs. Remember to 'give' a little, when halt is achieved, to reward the horse.

Horse raises his head: Usually a result of the rider lowering the hands during the transition, putting pressure on the bars of the mouth, or fixing the hands stiffly during the halt.

Horse leans on bit: The rider must keep a contact but soften the rein during halt, so the horse learns to balance and carry himself.

THE HALF-HALT

The half-halt is one of the most useful and important of all riding techniques. A crucial stepping stone in a horse and rider's education, half-halt makes it easier for the horse to tackle more demanding exercises on the flat and over fences.

The half-halt is used to:

- Re-balance.
- Increase impulsion.
- Raise the head.
- Maintain a regular rhythm and speed.
- Remind the horse to pay attention and listen for a new instruction.
- Prepare for a smooth change of gait, direction or shortening of stride.

As the term suggests, the half-halt is a check by the rider which slows the horse momentarily, but then lets him go on forwards. This allows the horse to re-balance and reorganise himself, shortening and slowing his steps as his hindquarters come further underneath his body and 'catch up' with his forehand. The centre of gravity shifts downwards and

The half-halt is used before turns and transitions to re-balance the horse and to get his attention.

backwards and the back is lifted, lightening and freeing the forehand. Almost instantly, you have a horse that is better balanced and able to take more active and elastic steps. As the energy created by the legs is contained by the hand, impulsion is increased.

Western-trained horses are masters of the half-halt. With next-to-no contact on the reins, the rider brings the horse's hindquarters right underneath him to prepare for a turn 'on a dime'. The horse's back is lifted and the head acts as a balancing pole.

AIDS FOR THE HALF-HALT

Riders are taught the half-halt in differing ways. Essentially, the rider sits deep and sends the horse forwards from the leg, then tightens the back muscles slightly and blocks the forward movement for a moment by closing the fingers around the reins. Instantly the horse reacts, the fingers are opened slightly to allow him forwards again. It is like approaching a closed door that suddenly opens at the last second. When practising the half-halt, remember:

- A half-halt should last no longer than a stride. Repeat as needed using short, squeeze-and-release rein aids, not a constant or backwards pull.
- A half-halt should not affect the horse's head carriage or interrupt his stride.
- Rather than stiffening the back, think of tightening the stomach and back muscles while keeping the hips and seat supple.
- Keep your weight over the horse's centre of gravity as it moves back.
- Think of pushing the hips forwards slightly towards the hands.
- A half-halt can be used to remedy many a riding mistake. If anything goes wrong, try a half-halt!

INTRODUCING THE HALF-HALT

Teaching a young horse to half-halt will help prevent him leaning on the hand and develop suppleness and self-carriage. Half-halts create instant impulsion and re-balance before turns and transitions, on the approach to a jump or when going downhill.

Introduce the idea of half-halt in walk at first. Take care to come to use both full and half-halts regularly, however, so the horse learns to listen to which is required.

A good half-halt is hardly visible, but tailor your aids to your horse's training level. A novice will need stronger, less subtle aids, but avoid being too heavy-handed and upsetting and unbalancing the horse.

HALTER-BREAKING
Accepting restraint does not come naturally to horses, yet it is fundamental to almost everything we wish to do with them. If respect for the halter is introduced kindly and carefully at a very early age, handling basics such as leading, tying up and loading need never become an issue for argument.

INTRODUCING THE HALTER
Even though new-borns will be happy to follow their dam closely for several months, a foal-slip (a small, soft head-collar) should be put on within a few days of birth. Foals are instinctively wary of being restrained by their head however, so the idea of being led directly is best introduced either on a long, loose lead rope or using a soft towel or stable rubber around the neck rather than rope attached directly to the foal-slip. The handler holds the towel with one hand and uses the other cupped around the top of the tail to push the quarters gently forwards. Take care never to rush or panic the foal.

Make the most of the new-born imprinting period (q.v.) and the young foal's strong following instinct to get him used to being led around with his dam well before he gets too big and strong to want to be directed by someone else. However, do not delay introducing the idea that he must be led by himself too, gradually putting more distance between the two.

BREAKING TO THE HALTER
A youngster may tolerate wearing a foal-slip but, until he has been taught to submit to pressure on his head, he is not considered to be halter-broken.

The traditional method of breaking to the halter has been based on the principle of kindly but firmly showing the youngster that his human handler is more powerful than himself, so resistance is pointless and unnecessary. This approach has recently been joined by techniques using the concept of self-responsibility, where the horse makes a conscious decision to want follow his handler.

All such early lessons should be short (five minutes is plenty), as low-key as possible and take place in a safe enclosed area with the mare nearby. If the foal is already weaned, make use of this period of insecurity as he will be eager to transfer his follow-instinct to another likely candidate at this time.

The conventional method of breaking to the halter requires the handler to place a towel around the foal's neck, and with one hand firmly around the quarters, push the foal firmly forwards from behind (never pull). The mare is led in front to encourage the foal forwards and an assistant encourages him from the rear. Gradually, over several lessons, there is less need for pushing and the towel is used increasingly to direct the foal. Eventually, once the foal becomes accustomed to the idea, the towel can be discarded and a light pull can be used on a lead rope fastened to the foal-slip.

Once the foal has become used to wearing a halter, he needs to be taught how to yield to pressure applied by that halter, and respond to it. The handler passes a long lead rope around the foal's neck, fastens it in a non-slip knot and passes it through the ring underneath the foal-slip. For most effective leading with older animals, a pressure halter is recommended (*see Pressure Halter, page 201*). The handler then needs to create a situation where the foal moves into the pressure. This can be done by using a long stick with a piece of soft material, such as a handkerchief, to tickle the foal's quarters so that he moves away from the source of annoyance, or simply by waving the hand at the quarters. The foal's movement brings him into pressure from the halter, which is uncomfortable.

Expect some protest, but maintain tension until the foal stops resisting. He must now learn how to relieve that feeling,

Applying a slight pressure on the hindquarters encourages the youngster to move forward.

by finding that a step away from the pressure towards the handler brings relief. The crucial element of the lesson is to reward any move, however small, in the direction of the handler. Rewards can be as simple as the release of pressure on the halter, or some kind encouragement and a friendly rub between the eyes or scratch on the neck.

The lesson should be repeated until the youngster's immediate reaction on sensing pressure on the halter is to move towards the handler. The conscious decision to walk away from pressure and to choose closeness to the handler as a 'comfort zone' forms a sound basis for future work. This method can be used to teach, or remind, horses of any age to respect the halter.

Handlers must stay calm and aware of the youngster's body language indicating when he is ready to submit *(see Body Language, page 53; Join-up, page 153)*. Resist the temptation to grab at the foal's head or to hold the lead rope too close to the head when leading: allowing the impression of freedom is important to avoid resistance or inducing panic.

Once the lesson has been learned, the youngster will soon be watching the handler's body language and anticipating the pressure. Now take every opportunity to practise leading in a variety of situations to reinforce the learning:
• From both sides.
• Away from the yard.
• In more open spaces.
• At shows.
• In company and alone.
• From a ridden horse.
Also see Leading, page 172; Tying up, page 270.

HANDEDNESS

As with humans, horses seem to be naturally right- or left-handed. This is one reason why achieving true straightness is one of the rider's most difficult challenges. Most horses will favour a particular side (usually the left), finding it easiest to work on that rein, to strike off into canter on that leading leg, and even tending to paw with the fore-leg on that side. Riders and handlers must take care not to allow any preference to become too pronounced, particularly if combined with a subconscious bias against the rider's own 'weak' side, as this will lead to stiffness and unbalanced muscle development.

As horses have poor ability to transfer learning from one side of the brain to the other, exercises should always be repeated on both reins. It also makes sense to perform tasks such as leading and mounting from either side. This not only means muscles and suppleness build up on both sides, but mentally, the lesson is learnt bilaterally too.

WORK POINTS
- Repeat exercises from both sides or, in ridden work, on both reins.
- Be conscious of the horse's weak side and include a little extra work on this side to compensate.
- Use stretch exercises to keep the muscles on the horse's stiff, or contracted, side supple.
- Work to correct any crookedness or imbalance caused by your own side preference, both when riding and handling.

See also Suppleness, page 250; Straightness, page 248.

HANDS
See Aids, page 30.

HEAD-SHY
A head-shy horse can make life very difficult for an owner. Everyday procedures such as grooming, tying up, tacking up and clipping can all become potential confrontations.

Even if there is no fear or anxiety involved, once a horse realises how easy it is to avoid human touch by raising his head, the lesson he learns is that he can keep control over where and how he is handled. This has unfortunate implications for the trust, co-operation and respect you are trying to achieve. Try to develop your 'feel' for when a horse is simply being evasive and when he has a genuine reason for his behaviour.

CAUSES
Head-shyness is an entirely man-made and avoidable problem. Causes include:

Poor habituation: The horse has never been taught to accept being handled and touched all over his body.

Fear/lack of trust: The horse has been abused in the past by rough or inept handling, e.g. careless tacking up or being hit around the head. Or he has been unnerved by banging his head at some time.

Physical problems: If being handled around the head hurts the horse, he has a genuine excuse for his objection to handling or pressure in this area. Reasons might include neglected teeth, sore mouth, ear problems, neck or back injury, poorly fitting tack (particularly bridles that pinch the ears), or memory of these discomforts.

THE HEAD-SHY HORSE
Thorough imprinting of a foal should avoid him ever wanting to object to being handled anywhere on his body. In older horses, investigate any possible causes of discomfort before taking action. It is possible to get around a bridling difficulty for example, by taking the bridle apart and putting it on literally piece by piece. However, this is avoiding an issue whose implications reach much further.

Nervous head-shyness is best dealt with by making the horse confront his fears and surviving to learn from the experience. The following technique is helpful with nervous and spooky horses, as well as those which are head-shy:

- Securely attach lots of lightweight objects on strings to the roof of the stable, e.g. empty feed bags, empty plastic drinks bottles etc. The more brightly coloured and rustly the better! Though it may take some time for the horse to relax, he will finally have to pluck up courage to move around the stable to his hay, feed or water. Frequent brushing-up against the hanging objects eventually desensitises him to their touch.
- Work in an enclosed space (e.g. stable). Handle the head sympathetically but firmly. Move the flat of your hand

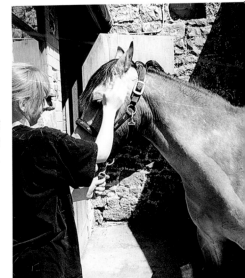

Handle the head sympathetically but firmly.

confidently all around the head area, including the ears. Do not be shaken off by ANY objections.
- When the horse quietens and accepts your touch, then take the hand away and praise him.
- With horses who mean business but have no fear, persuade these to reconsider and gain control of the head with the help of a pressure halter (q.v.).

HERD BEHAVIOUR
Herd living makes good survival sense for prey species. Despite domestication, the instinct to band together for security remains extremely strong in the horse and has many implications for us as effective handlers, riders and carers.

Wherever horses are kept together, they will instinctively form into a group. Within any group, just as within a wild herd, a complex network of relationships will develop *(see Hierarchy, below)*. Whether at a livery yard or in the field, a string of racehorses or line of trekking ponies, as a group, will tend to react as a 'herd' – a process called social facilitation.

From his earliest days, the young horse has copied the actions of older members of his band. This instinct to imitate and join in remains powerful and means the behaviour of other horses, good or bad, can be extremely infectious.

A horse by itself feels naturally vulnerable and under stress. Only thorough training and habituation (q.v.) teaches our horses self-confidence and to look to their human handlers and riders for the security and leadership that would otherwise come from the herd. When this training is incomplete or inadequate, the effects can be seen in horses that nap, refuse to leave the yard or constantly fret for absent companions.

Awareness of this inbuilt desire for company allows us to work with it rather than against it, so reducing stress in our horses' lives, avoiding unnecessary confrontation and utilising it as a training aid.

IMPLICATIONS
Stress from lack of company: Many domesticated horses spend a large percentage of their time in enforced solitude (in the stable or field) or with only humans for company. Denial of natural social interaction, and the feeling of security it

The company of other livestock is preferable to isolation.

brings, creates a constant undercurrent of stress that is exacerbated by sheer boredom. Adaptable and amenable as ever, many horses seem to accept their 'lot'. Sensitive horses however, become prone to health and psychological problems *(see Stable Vices, page 241)*. To ensure that your horse does not develop loneliness and consequent behavioural problems:

- Make the provision of company an essential, not a preference. Ideally this should be in the form of other equines, but even a sheep, goat or cow is better than nothing.
- Spend as much time as possible with your horse.
- Arrange stabling so that all the horses can still see and/or hear each other.
- Fit grilles or talk-holes between stables, allowing neighbouring horses to see and sniff each other.

Attachment to companions: Stress has to be minimised by providing company, but it is equally important to prevent over-reliance on equine friends. Horses are particularly susceptible to forming very strong bonds and this can prove problematic.

Confidence and trust in going it alone takes time to develop and needs to be fostered from day one. Even the educated horse will instinctively hang towards other horses for moral support whenever he is worried, unsure, or having a difference of opinion with his handler or rider. Depending on the degree of this urge, it can either be a nuisance which requires positive action to reassure the horse or convince him of what you expect, or, if allowed to develop unchecked, can become very dangerous or disruptive behaviour that is difficult to cure *(see Napping, page 188)*. From the earliest days, target training at teaching the horse to regard their human handler/rider, rather than the herd, as their ultimate 'safety zone'.

- Make the most of all opportunities to broaden a youngster's outlook and foster his confidence in himself and his handler/rider. Provide as many varied experiences as possible, taking care to introduce them carefully and in a non-pressurised way.
- Use other horses to boost confidence initially, but expect the horse to learn to cope on his own as well.
- Consistency and a step-by-step approach to all learning experiences will build self-confidence.
- Be considerate to the need to pair-bond, but do not allow over-strong attachments to interfere with your own bond with your horse. All horses must become used to being left alone for short periods on a regular basis. A youngster must not come to rely on always having a companion, whether in the field, yard or when ridden. If two friends are becoming over-dependent, add a third individual, or separate them for increased periods. Protests may be dramatic at first, but must be seen through.
- Plan hacks so that no one horse is always in front, or behind, the others.
- In all handling and riding situations, be flexible and sensible about when to insist your horse goes it alone and when to allow him the extra reassurance of company. For example, most horses left by themselves in a field will become unsettled and agitated. If you do not want your horse upset on a particular day, or the field to be churned up, avoid the

Fit internal grilles in the stable so that your horse can see, and smell, other horses.

situation by bringing in another horse at the same time or arranging for other company. When trying to load a reluctant traveller, decide whether putting another horse in first is going to be a help, a distraction, or an obstruction. Take each situation as it comes, but always be aware of the strength of this instinct (even after training).

USING THE GROUPING INSTINCT POSITIVELY

The natural magnetism of one horse to another, and horses' general readiness to accept leadership can be turned to our advantage. Benefits include:

Giving confidence to a youngster/novice: When introducing traffic and road-work to a young or novice horse, a sensible, well-behaved companion will provide reassurance as well as a good example. Anxiety or lack of confidence can be overcome in many situations by providing a lead from an experienced horse, e.g. over a jump, across a ditch or through water.

Easing potentially difficult handling situations: The settling effect of a companion can be put to good use in many an awkward or anxious situation, e.g. when clipping, giving an injection or loading. If his field-mates are brought in first, a horse that is difficult to catch can often be persuaded to come in rather than face the prospect of being left out alone. For best effect in either case, use the horse's pair-bond.

HERD HIERARCHY

The herd system works so well because it is built on 'getting along'. A group of prey animals cannot waste energy, risk injury or be distracted by constant squabbling. Horses understand about co-operation and rarely go looking for a fight. This is easy to forget in the heat of the moment when handling or riding situations do not go according to plan. Indeed, the very reason horses are so amiable and amenable to our requests lies in the way they are naturally 'programmed' not to confront but to please, and to follow positive leadership.

A traditional hierarchy or 'pecking order' is based on rank. A tough guy at the top gets the best deal and gives the orders, whereas beneath him others jostle for the lower steps, with the weakest and most timid at the bottom. This is far from the reality of equine society. Status relationships do exist within horse groups, but are only one of many forces, including family bonds and personality, that combine to create a complicated web of affiliations and preferences.

FACTORS AFFECTING HIERARCHY

Status: Squabbling over status makes no sense in the wild, where food and space is plentiful. However, within domesticated groups a type of status order can develop, leading to arguments and jealousies straining relationships. This is usually the result of competition for a scarce resource, such as food, attention or living space.

Family bonds and age groups: Family bonds between horses are strong, particularly between dams and their fillies, sisters and brothers. Few families are allowed to remain in natural groupings in domestication, but any mixed-age group of horses will still act to some extent in the same way as a wild community *(see table, page 138)*. Expect to find a 'boss' (usually an older mare) and to see the mature horses disciplining boisterous youngsters.

Personality, friendships and pair-bonding: Although rank is not a big issue and co-operation is the general theme, individuals in a group do not all get along equally well. Friendships develop readily between horses who feel comfortable with each other and these will stand or graze close together and even indulge in mutual grooming. A horse who dislikes another or feels intimidated will avoid that other horse.

These affiliations and aversions will link some members and disperse others. They are never static for long, so that group dynamics are forever shifting, even between one context and another. In a danger situation for example, the herd always acts as one.

Special friendships often develop within a herd.

What makes particular individuals get on, or otherwise, is probably (as with humans) largely down to personality. We cannot choose friends for our horses! Shy characters will feel vulnerable and tend to stick with other easy-going, non-threatening types. Bullying or intolerant characters are often loners, but are rarely the 'boss' *(see Aggression, page 25)*. The true 'top dogs' are generally those confident personalities happy to make decisions.

Pair-bonding: Friendships work to help keep the group functioning as a co-operative unit. Although most individuals are on friendly terms with most of their companions, there is generally one special friend that becomes his pair-bond. Between these two, a particularly strong attachment develops.

Pair-bonding occurs whenever a regular group grazes together. The two will graze and even drink closely together, perhaps at a distance from other pairs. Mutual grooming is a favourite pastime. Imitation of behaviour is also more frequent between a pair-bond than among other horses.

Having a pair-bond enhances all the plus-factors of group living. The close presence of a trusted friend increases feelings of security, lowering stress levels and allowing more opportunities for play and relaxation.

The bond may take some time to develop, but can become a lifelong attachment. Even short-term separation can cause distress in an insecure horse. Permanent loss, as when one horse is sold or dies, is potentially traumatic and needs sensitive handling.

- Every horse should be given the chance to pair-bond.
- Be sensitive to the effect of separating pair-bonds. Avoid creating too much dependency. When selling, take steps to reduce the impact of the change as far as possible, e.g. familiarise the new owner to your routine, and take time introducing the horse to new companions *(see Introductions, page 149)*.
- Target training at giving a young horse confidence, independence and flexibility in his attitudes.

Threat behaviour and personal space: Harmony is the keynote of the herd and any settled group. Serious arguments are usually avoided or solved long before coming to actual blows by the use of subtle threat language *(see Body Language, page 53)*.

Crucial to this is each individual's personal space. Like most animals, humans included, horses feel threatened when another individual comes too close without being invited. All horses seem to have an oval-shaped area extending 2-4 metres around them that is considered their personal space. Only intimate friends are tolerated here and others can expect to be driven away. This area is defined by threat-distance. Beyond is a larger bubble defined by flight-distance. Any intrusion into this wider space prompts the horse to move away (an escape reaction). Distances will vary between horses and personalities. Dominant horses, for example, are more touchy about their personal territories, which seem more extensive.

Beyond this lies the 'herd distance', a larger area within which the horse still feels safely linked to the group but out of which he would not choose to stray. Again, the size of this varies for each individual and also group. A settled, relaxed group will spread further than an anxious, uptight one.

Overcrowding: Overcrowding is as stressful for a sensitive horse as being alone. When personal space is constantly being encroached, anxiety ripples through the group, nerves are frayed and all are on edge. In the stable yard, a sensitive horse finds it impossible to relax as his 'safe area' is forever being violated without consent. Stabled horses, who have no flight option, are commonly driven to aggression by our insensitivity to this situation.

MANAGEMENT POINTERS
- Be sensitive to preferences and dislikes when planning stabling or choosing field and even riding companions. Sworn enemies in adjoining stables will never relax. Likewise, friends will thrive if they are neighbours. If space allows they can even be stabled together.

Horses feel threatened when their personal space is invaded.

A settled group is one in which every member is confident of their own status.

- Be aware of personal space and the body language that says "not welcome". Get into the habit of pausing at the stable door to gauge the occupant's reaction. Meetings and greetings are important to horses, so take your time and adopt a non-aggressive stance *(see Body Language, page 53)*. It is only good manners!

- Always take care in a field of loose horses, particularly in situations involving food. Out in the field, herd rules apply. Even a relaxed group may act unpredictably and it is easy to become 'piggy in the middle' in a jealous squabble, or in danger from a panic reaction from the group as a whole.

- A settled group is a happy group, where each member is confident of their place and rank. Avoid upsetting this equilibrium by changing the make-up of the group too frequently. This is a major source of stress to horses in busy yards with ever-changing occupants.

- Tie horses up with a minimum of 3 metres space between them. Increase this by another metre for feeding.

- Introduce newcomers carefully *(see Introductions, page 149)*.

- Occasionally, individuals at pasture seem simply unable to get on peaceably. Most commonly, one dominant horse continues to pick on another despite its signals of submission. Here the most practical solution is to divide the group, separating the horses involved. Electric fencing is the best way to do this, as it protects the intimidated horse but allows group members to continue grazing in sight of each other. Do not isolate any one horse, however; make sure each has an acceptable companion.

SOCIAL STRUCTURE IN THE WILD

The same basic social rules apply in any group of horses but can be seen at their purest in a wild or feral community. Free-living herds usually consist of 4-8 individuals (though any number between 2 and 20 is found) and would be organised along these lines:

STATUS	ROLE
Stallion	Acts as the group 'chairman'. He is the chief organiser of the herd. He is protective of other herd members, but is otherwise aggressive only when challenged.
'Boss' mare	She is the herd matriarch. She is often the main decision-maker, and frequently the one to initiate movement and direction. She is also the chief law-enforcer and disciplinarian.
Other mares	Mares with young foals at foot tend to stick in family groups. Barren mares often act as 'aunts' and help with herding.
Young fillies	Young fillies usually stay with the herd until they reach 2-3 years of age. After this age they sometimes wander off to join bachelor groups, or may be claimed by another stallion from a different herd.
Young males	At around 18 months of age, young males are driven away by the chief stallion. Those driven away in such a fashion tend to form bachelor bands. Particularly strong individuals may challenge the older male for his harem, or claim any drifting fillies as his own.

HOLLOW

A horse working correctly will create a rounded outline, arched from poll to tail (see Outline, page 192). If the horse stiffens and resists, raising his head and neck out of this shape, he is said to be 'hollow'. A hollow outline makes it difficult for the horse to relax through his back and engage his hindquarters properly.

REASONS FOR THE HORSE GOING 'HOLLOW'
Conformation: Good neck and shoulder conformation and correct muscle development helps a horse to achieve, and to keep, an outline that is soft and rounded. Poor conformation, such as ewe-neck, bull-neck or lack of room at the throat, will

create a natural tendency to hollow and make it difficult for the horse to work correctly. The horse compensates for these conditions by altering his posture. He gets into the habit of going 'hollow'. Once muscles under the neck have built up, the problem is exaggerated.

Discomfort: Pain is a common reason for hollowing. Discomfort may be caused by sharp teeth, a severe bit, badly-fitting tack, rough riding or back injury. Have all these possible causes checked by experts before trying to improve the horse's way of going.

IMPROVING THE HOLLOW HORSE

- Use the whole range of schooling exercises to improve suppleness and reduce tension *(see Schooling Exercises, page 230)*.
- Focus at first on getting more activity from the quarters, working on large circles.
- Ride from the inside leg to the outside hand. Keep the hands as still as possible. Ask for softening by squeezing the outside rein. Every now and again, give a little with the inside rein to encourage the horse to lower his head and take the contact.
- Encourage lateral suppleness and activity from the inside hind-leg by spiralling in and then outwards again from a 20-metre circle. Take care to keep the correct bend.
- If the horse hollows in canter, re-establish the outline in trot and then ask again. Keep legs on and hands soft. Bringing the seat slightly out of the saddle can help the horse relax and round his back.
- Try some work over trotting poles.
- Allow regular chances for the horse to walk on a loose rein to stretch his neck.
- Insist on a better outline even when hacking, to avoid bulky muscles building up in the wrong place.
- Encourage correct muscle development and stretching

A hollow outline could be related to pain.

by careful use of a schooling aid such as a chambon (*see Schooling Aids, page 225*).

HOMING INSTINCT
The many reported cases of horses finding their way home, even over great distances in unfamiliar territory are often held as evidence of super-sensory equine powers.

It is hard to investigate these claims scientifically while we still know so little about the scope of the conventional equine senses. The likely explanation of the homing phenomenon is that, in addition to excellent visual memory, the horse's acute sense of smell is used to detect the faintest of airborne clues.

HUNTING
Aside from the political issues surrounding hunting, there is no doubt that following hounds provides an ideal learning and confidence-building opportunity for any horse, but in particular youngsters aimed at an eventing career. Besides the benefits that go along with getting you both in shape for a demanding day 'in the field', horses which hunt regularly become used to being part of a bustling crowd at the meet, standing quietly alone or with others at covert (when hounds are 'drawing', or finding the quarry), galloping alongside others when hounds are running, and taking all types of terrain and obstacle in their stride.

The United Kingdom and Ireland have over 230 packs of fox hounds. Mounted followers can also join harrier packs, bloodhounds and drag hounds (following a human, or artificially-laid scent). In the USA, hunting takes place in both the East and West, over vastly different 'country' with either grey or red fox (in eastern states), hare or coyote (in the West) as quarry.

Hunt membership allows a subscriber to go out one or more times a week through the season, which, in the UK, lasts from November to March. Autumn hunting, arranged to introduce young hounds, takes place earlier. Most hunts welcome visitors, who pay a 'cap' or daily fee, although permission should be sought from the Hunt Secretary beforehand.

I

IMITATION

Much natural horse behaviour is imitative. The new-born foal watches his mother and other herd members and copies what they do. In this way, essential survival skills (and many other routine behaviours) rapidly become part of the youngster's way of life.

There is some debate as to whether specific, abnormal behaviours, such as stable vices, can be imitated. Evidence suggests this happens only when the environmental circumstances add up to encourage the response. Copycat behaviour seems more likely to occur where:

- The bond between the horse performing the action and the one watching it is strong.
- Environmental factors are conducive to invoking that behaviour anyway, e.g. there is a high stress level, for example from unnatural management.
- Both horses have similarly sensitive temperaments and low stress tolerance.

IMPRINTING

Imprinting is a special kind of permanent, subconscious learning that only takes place very early on in an animal's life. Rather than making associations (as in conditioning), imprinting is based on a perceptual experience which makes a deep impression and lasts a lifetime.

The clearest examples of imprinting in the animal world are in the offspring of vulnerable prey species who must key into their species identity and learn rapidly in order to stay alive. It is increasingly thought to play a role in determining the youngster's behaviour in later life.

Imprinting has recently been latched on to as a powerful training tool. It works on the premise that, if foundations are laid during this highly-receptive time, the youngster will have a head start in his relationship with humans. All subsequent training will then be easier and less traumatic.

IMPRINTING THE NEW-BORN FOAL

- Desensitise the foal to all the potentially-alarming sights and sounds he will subsequently encounter.

The process of imprinting must start from birth.

- Sets up a bond of trust between the human (recognised by the new-born as a 'predator') and the foal (effectively born a 'wild' animal).

  This careful and thorough introduction will programme the foal's brain to realise that humans mean him no harm but are going to play a central role in his life – and that the human will be 'in control'. To imprint humans on your foal successfully, and without causing any unwanted side-effects, you will need to:

- Begin within an hour of birth or as soon as possible after this.
- Never move between the mare and her foal. This risks interfering with their bonding, or upsetting the mare and so putting across the wrong message to the foal.
- Start once the foal has been rubbed down after birth and is resting. Kneel beside the foal and start gently but firmly rubbing his head and face in small, circular motions. Move to include the mouth, ears and nostrils, then gradually along the body. Include all the limbs, under the belly and even beneath the tail.
- Make the touch gentle but firm and systematic, imitating the licking pressure of the mare. Rub around each area at least 30 times, continuing well after the foal has relaxed to your touch.
- Work on both sides of the body equally.
- Once the foal is standing, get a helper to help restrain him if necessary without alarming him. He must not realise he can escape if he really tries. Use one hand around the chest and the other ready to cup the quarters. Manoeuvre him around a little forward, sideways and backwards.
- After the whole body has been rubbed and stroked, introduce other sensations the foal will encounter later on. Stimulate all the senses by scrunching plastic bags over the body, running the clippers against the coat, lifting and tapping the feet, wrapping your arms carefully around the barrel and squeezing gently.
- Take a break after about 15 minutes so the foal can suckle. During the first day, work for no more than an hour in total.

- Repeat the process several times the first day and daily over the following few weeks, even if just for a few minutes.
  New experiences that can also be introduced within the first few days include:
- Loading and travelling.
- Accepting water on his legs.
- Sight and sound of a car, other animals etc.
- Following the mare over dips in the ground, through puddles etc.

Once halter-broken *(see Halter-breaking, page 125)* the foal can encounter many new situations further afield, led with his mother if she can be ridden.

Imprinting can still have an effect even if the optimum time after birth is missed. Make sure you can stay in control, however. It would be best to halter-break the foal beforehand.

IMPULSION

The more impulsion a horse has, the more easily he will be able to come into a good outline (q.v.). Impulsion is not speed and is not simply energy – it is *contained* energy. That energy must be being produced by the hindquarters, causing the horse to round his back and bring his hind-legs right underneath the body. It is then being contained by the hand aids, to stop it disappearing out of the front end or pushing the horse on to his forehand.

A horse working with impulsion will go forwards (q.v.) but not in a rushed, hurried way. All the energy he has created is contained, yet he is not yet heavy in the front. This means his shoulders are free to move, and he is extremely mobile and manoeuvrable.

IMPROVING IMPULSION

Some horses move with more natural impulsion than others. However, impulsion may also be created by using schooling movements. These encourage the horse to engage his hindquarters, keeping his back supple in the process. These exercises include:

- Riding long and low, encouraging the horse to 'seek' the rein contact.
- Transitions.
- Lengthened strides.
- Lateral work.
- Rein-back.

See also Outline, page 192.

WORKING INDOORS

In tune with your overall objective, (to include as many new experiences as possible in your youngster's education), take your horse regularly to indoor facilities as well as using outdoor ones.

A trip to an indoor arena should become a routine outing throughout the early years, well before ridden work begins. Include familiarisation with all the sights and sounds of an indoor school, e.g. the doors, lights, mirrors, equipment and audience seating.

INDIVIDUALITY & TEMPERAMENT

Horses would not be half the fun and challenge they are if they were all the same. Personality is just as much a part of horse society as it is human, having a significant effect on behaviour, and so on training.

All riders know that each horse is very much an individual, both physically and mentally. Every aspect of management and training is affected by these differences, so to get the best out of every horse we need to be observant and flexible in our approach.

Physical differences: Build is determined by breeding. It affects the lifestyle the horse or pony is best suited to, what he should be fed etc. Conformation is also important in deciding what activities he is best suited for. There are horses for courses – get it wrong and the result is often much frustration, stress and disappointment all round. A draught horse is never going to be good at endurance riding. A dressage horse will not succeed without free-moving paces and presence. A show jumper whose conformation does not allow him to make a good shape over a fence will never find the job easy and enjoyable, and so is unlikely to be any good at it.

The calmer, slower-reacting Cob is better-suited to a novice rider.

The high-spirited Arab demands more experienced handling.

Mental differences: Breeding is about more than looks. Certain types tend to have particular temperament characteristics too, which all have training implications.

Calmer, horses, often very solid in conformation, are:

- Better suited to less athletically-demanding activities.
- Often easier to train than more sensitive, excitable types.
- Easily bored and dull if not stretched.
- More forgiving, but likely to react by shutting off if angered.

Horses with more reactive and emotional temperaments:

- Suit more athletic activities where they can burn off energy.
- Require very measured, sensitive training with plenty of reassurance.
- Are less forgiving. They can react to misunderstandings with anger or resentment.

Within these simplified broad groups there are invariably the fast learners and the slower learners. Some horses will lift their legs higher after touching one pole, whereas others will carry on knocking up cricket scores for a lifetime!

Personality differences are the result of a combination of genetic make-up and learning experiences. Within each breed type there are shy, nervous characters, the go-getting, assertive ones and every shade of temperament in between. All these characteristics can be influenced and altered by experience. For example, a submissive horse can be encouraged, through learning, to be more confident. A character too full of his own importance needs to be firmly but fairly taught the universe does not revolve around him!

Few horses are born 'mean'. Certainly the mare's influence is strong, so a youngster born to a temperamental and unco-operative mother is going to take his cue from the way she behaves. On the other hand, a horse labelled as having a 'bad' temperament has often been made irritable, resentful or aggressive by humans. His past treatment or present situation, may have taught him to mistrust his handler/rider, feel insecure and threatened, or feel under stress in some way.

Never simply accept a 'bad' temperament without looking into its possible causes and trying to improve the horse's attitude to life.

TEMPERAMENT AND TRAINING
The most important things to bear in mind about personality and training are:
- Appreciate each horse's individuality, value it and work with it.
- Work to alter only areas that will make the horse's life with humans safer, pleasanter and more secure.
- Find a job for which the horse is physically and mentally suited. Choose one he can enjoy, rather than one he will have to persevere fruitlessly with.
- Teach only at a pace dictated by the horse.
- Look at ways of increasing motivation (q.v.).
- If you hit difficulties, investigate the reasons behind the horse's attitude rather than simply blaming character.

IN-HAND WORK
Horses that are hard to handle from the ground are usually difficult under saddle. Working a horse of any age in-hand has many advantages.

In-hand work:
- Builds muscle, suppleness, balance and co-ordination.
- Increases the horse's awareness of his own body.
- Allows the horse the freedom of working without a rider.
- Means you can see how he is moving.
- Is a good way of introducing lateral work and other new movements.
- Encourages the horse to use his quarters and round his back.
- Saves schooling time.
- Encourages the horse to think for himself.
- Improves focus, self-control, obedience and confidence.

USING IN-HAND WORK
Giving the horse 10-15 minutes on the lunge before working in-hand will help him loosen up and let off steam. There are

several ways of using in-hand work:

Classical: Using lungeing equipment *(see Lungeing, page 179)* and either a long light whip or lunge whip with the lash taped up, the trainer stands slightly in front of and to the side of the horse. The STOP command is taught (gentle laying of the whip on the quarters and blocking of forward movement by the hand). After this, by using the whip and controlling the head via the cavesson, the trainer indicates to the horse the way he wishes him to move.

Turn on the forehand, shoulder-in, travers, half-pass and walk-pirouette are among the movements that can be taught in this way. Once the horse understands and trainer is experienced, these aids can be gradually transferred to a rider.

TTEAM work: Ground exercises are also part of the TTEAM approach *(see TTEAM, page 268).*

INSTINCTS

Instincts are behaviours and 'knowledge' which are present in the foal at birth. Instincts are:
- **Innate.**
- **A characteristic of the species.**
- **Controlled by the genes.**
- **The product of interaction with the environment over many millennia, which has been developed through evolution.**

However, not all equine behaviour is instinctive. The horse's ability to learn is precisely what enables horses and humans to form a symbiotic relationship and for horses to be able to adapt to a modern lifestyle under human control. Learned behaviour, of which the modern horse is a prime exhibitor, is most simply described as the product of the individual's own experiences. Habituation relies on this principle.

It is difficult to determine which, horse behaviour are instinctive, and which are learned. A true 'instinct' is behaviour that is inherent at birth and pre-set in the mind, i.e. not affected by experience. However, even behaviour which would be assumed to be instinctive (e.g. the foal struggling to find the mare's teat) has some elements of learning contained within it. Suckling for example, requires quite a lot of trial and error learning. Other so-called instincts only manifest themselves a long time after birth, such as sexual urges.

Many reactions appear to be inherent, but might be a case of 'doing what the others do' as it seems like a sensible idea!

Very little behaviour is really free of environmental influences. For this reason the term 'innate' is now used to describe a consistent reaction that seems to be triggered by a cue the animal can recognise at birth. A better term to describe other shared responses, e.g. in horses, the flight/fight response, is 'strategies'.

INSTRUCTION & TRAINING
Before you can start to improve a horse's way of going, you have to be sure that *you* are not creating any barriers to progress, and that you are seeing the whole picture from all possible angles. This takes experience and knowledge that may go beyond your own.

Even when a rider's personal 'feel' and ability is well developed, an experienced eye on the ground is invaluable. This is the reason why the very best professionals still use trainers.

Do not leave training until you have a real problem you are desperate for help with. Take your horse regularly to an instructor you respect and can relate to. He or she will be able to monitor your progress and that of your horse, help spot any difficulties early on, suggest schooling plans and advise on specific queries. You will then have confidence that you are working along the correct lines at home.

For help finding a trainer in the UK, contact the British Horse Society, Association of British Riding Schools or the governing body of the particular discipline you are interested in. An instructor need not be qualified in order to be worth going to, although qualifications do indicate a certain level of

An instructor will monitor your progress and suggest schooling plans.

competence. Generally it is best to go by recommendation and to someone who has had success in a relevant field, e.g. with young horses, with problem horses, or in your chosen sport.

Expect to feel at ease and motivated by a good instructor – do not persist with one you find isn't helping you or your horse simply because he or she is popular or close by.

INTELLIGENCE

Human beings often arrogantly dismiss many animals, including the horse, as unintelligent. This judgement is usually based on what *we* are good at (i.e. problem-solving, using our hands) and so the comparison is hardly fair.

In fact, the horse's adaptability and trainability point to him being extremely smart. Intelligence is not only judged by insight learning, a human strength which the horse has never had any particular need to develop, but also involves many other mental processes, at which some horses are very clever (e.g. discrimination, which is largely based on acute sensory perception).

Comparing intelligence between species is ultimately pointless, as it is impossible to compare like with like. It is better to acknowledge that each species has developed its own intelligence, supremely adapted to its environment. Horses are simply brilliant at being horses.

There is still huge variation between individual intelligence. Like humans, some horses are quicker on the uptake than others and each have their own strengths and weaknesses *(see Individuality, page 144).*

INTRODUCTIONS

Horses are very particular about who their friends are. Initial meetings between strangers are always touch-and-go. Usually the pair approach each other with interest but caution, extending noses carefully from a safe distance towards the newcomer. With a sniff and snort, breath is exchanged, sending a personal ID message into the nasal passages where it is analysed and memorised. A decision is then taken – friend or foe?

Great stress can be caused by rushing or even ignoring this important ritual. With a little thought and time set aside to allow things to happen at a more natural pace, this is easily avoided. All too often we are quick to punish a horse for a snort or squeal when first encountering a different riding companion. This is most unfair. As long as we are aware of the issues of personal space, it is not unreasonable for the horses to feel they need to meet and greet each other in their own way. Just as with humans, a confident, relaxed horse will soon become more sociable and laid-back about encountering strangers.

INTRODUCING A NEW HORSE TO A GROUP

- Never simply 'dump' a new horse in with an established group.
- Allow opportunities for the newcomer to meet and introduce himself to all the other group members, either in-hand or ridden out with them.
- Turn the newcomer out first with one easy-going, friendly group member in a separate paddock (preferably close to or alongside the main field, with secure fencing between). Let these two become familiar and settled. If the main group is quite small, they can then be allowed into the newcomer's 'territory'. If the main group is larger (i.e. over four horses), firstly add one or two more non-aggressive types and allow to settle before moving the rest of the group in.
- Keep a close eye on proceedings at all stages. Expect sparks to fly, either for minutes or even days depending on the personalities involved.
- If bullying or excessive aggression is still shown to the new horse, try to discover the cause of this and take the appropriate step to remedy the situation (*see Aggression, page 25*).

Give thought to introducing unfamiliar horses.

IRRITATION

All behavioural signs that show a horse is irritated are reflexes – i.e. reactions that are not the result of conscious thought. The twitch of the skin or swish of the tail may have evolved as behaviour patterns to remove annoying flies, but these same responses are also used by the horse to express annoyance with any stimulus – including humans!

Constant or repeated sources of irritation cause anxiety and tension. So, if your youngster does swish his tail during schooling sessions, for example, think whether your aids need to be as strong, or what other underlying causes there may be for his attitude.

JEALOUSY

The structure of the horse's brain suggests he is capable of feeling as strong and as wide a range of emotions as we do. Pleasure, anger, frustration – these emotions can be seen daily in every paddock. The only difference lies in the triggers for each feeling. A horse will be upset by any threat to something that means a lot to him.

Horses are quite capable of jealousy. As with humans, the trigger usually lies in a scarce resource, which in the case of horses is often food. However, the attention of another horse (or human) may be the source of the envy. To the horse, such closeness is crucial to his security and sense of belonging. Jealousy is sign of insecurity.

If a horse is consistently aggressive due to jealousy, look closely at the relationships within his group. Try to establish and maintain a pair-bond *(see Herd Behaviour, page 130)*. When jealousy is shown because the horse's 'human' gives attention to another animal, focus on increasing the individual's self-confidence and sense of security.
See also Aggression, page 25.

JIBBING

A horse is said to be jibbing when he refuses to go forwards and gives little half-rears. Take any signs of jibbing seriously, as it is often the prelude to more serious rearing.
See Rearing, page 204.

JOGGING

An uptight horse that goes everywhere at a jog, unable to relax enough to walk out properly, makes for an extremely exasperating and exhausting ride.

Tense horses are rarely contented, so putting in the effort to pinpoint the cause behind the jogging habit and teach the horse-in-a-hurry to take his time is well worthwhile.
See also Energy, page 89.

CAUSES AND CURES

Joggers are frequently anxious or excitable characters. While it is difficult to change a horse's personality, many other factors that can add to the problem are under your control:

Environmental:

- Make sure the horse's management routine is low-stress, i.e. plenty of turn-out with amenable companions and a high-fibre, low-starch diet. A calming herbal supplement may help.
- Be certain there is no discomfort from badly-fitting tack, neglected teeth or pain in the neck, back or elsewhere.
- Only school in quiet surroundings.

Anticipation:

- Make ridden work varied, encouraging the horse to think for himself.
- Use combinations of movements, rather than repeating the same one again and again. Schooling sessions are best as a continuous flow of different changes of rein, pace and exercise.
- Lessen the anticipation factor by including exciting but uncommon variations, e.g. a canter out on a hack or a jumping session, interspersed with regular work in a less predictable way.

Tension:

- Poor, rough or careless riding can make matters worse. Check the rider is not at fault.
- Choose suitable hacking companions. A pony or small horse may have learnt to jog to keep up with a longer-striding companion. Horses with fast or long-striding trots may jog if made to trot too slowly. Ride out a tense horse with quiet, steady companions.
- Remember that lack of balance can often unsettle a youngster and make him jog.

Riding a jogging horse requires considerable patience – and the ability to relax.

RIDING THE HORSE THAT JOGS

A jogger needs sensitive, patient riding.

- Relax and remember to breathe! Be patient – taking frustration out on the horse will only create more tension.
- Hang the legs by sides, ready to use but not gripping.
- Rather than trying to contain the energy with the hands, keep them still and soft. Use the legs to push the horse forwards into the contact and take longer, more rhythmic strides. Do not have a loose rein.
- Avoid being heavy-handed or abrupt when taking up the reins before increasing the pace.
- Speak reassuringly and praise better steps.
- Focus on improving the walk, helping the horse to relax and stride out *(see Walk, page 275)*.
- Lungeing and long-reining will help and will improve the obedience to your voice.
- 'Think' the forward aids to avoid them being stronger than you need.
- Quietly insist the horse either walks properly or trots properly. Regularly push him forwards into an active trot so he does not feel constantly restricted. Be consistent.
- Only ride out when you have plenty of time. Any urgency will transmit directly to the horse.

JOIN-UP (or 'ADVANCE & RETREAT')

Join-up is a technique used to establish trust and respect between the trainer and horse. First developed by American horseman Monty Roberts, it has become widely acknowledged and practised in the UK, largely through regular demonstrations by Roberts himself, his students, Richard Maxwell, and Kelly Marks.

PRINCIPLES OF JOIN-UP

Join-up aims to set up an understanding between the horse and the human via use of the horse's own communication system (i.e. body language). Arrived at in this way, the lesson is understood so completely it provides a sound basis for all the dealings the horse will have with humans in its long-term future.

In a natural, non-stressful and meaningful way, the horse is helped to realise that a friendly relationship with this 'predator' in his life is not only possible, but positively good news. However, it must be on the man's terms. The man places himself fairly and squarely in the role of the dominant horse. As the horse appreciates strong leadership and clear rules, this is totally a positive experience for the horse. Once he is sure of the terms of the agreement, the horse is almost relieved to 'join the team' and accept the security this partnership offers.

THE JOIN-UP PROCESS

Join-up is not a complicated process, although it does require several important skills in the handler:
- Total confidence around horses.
- The ability to completely relax.
- Knowledge of equine body language.
- Concentration and observation.

Other necessities are:

An enclosed area: Any will do, from a loose-box to a field, although the smaller the easier. It is best to introduce a horse to the idea in a large loose-box, using a head-collar and long, light stick *(see Halter-breaking, page 125)*. For moving on to true join-up, a round pen is safest and most effective.

A soft rope or lunge-rein: Join-up makes use of three of the horse's strongest natural instincts. These include escaping a perceived predator; craving company; and desiring and respecting strong leadership. The steps are:

1. Turned loose, the horse (prey) instinctively moves away from the human (predator). The handler then sends the horse away – not aggressively, but insistently – using assertive body language and gentle flicks towards the quarters using the rope or line (the horse must *never* be hit). Turning the horse and sending it in the opposite direction reinforces the message that control lies with the handler, whichever way he tries to 'escape'.

2. This continues until the horse indicates he has chosen to

reassess his options. The handler must watch very carefully for signs of this, which will include:

- Slowing down and dropping the head.
- Turning the inside ear towards the handler.
- Softening the muzzle, then mouthing (licking and chewing).

Once these signs are seen, the handler must be quick to acknowledge them. If ignored, the horse's offer is being given a most unfair and confusing snub. The handler switches instantly to passive body language – effectively inviting the horse to be friends.

3. If the horse is ready to accept the invitation, he will come in to the handler. There his reward is praise, in the form of a friendly rub between the eyes and reassuring words (i.e. company, *not* food). He must come right up, however. Immobility, or any hesitation, and he must be immediately sent away again.

4. Eventually all horses will make the connection: away from the handler equals hard work and isolation (the natural punishment in the herd); towards and with the handler equals comfort and security. The horse is always free to choose, but the handler creates an environment where making the 'right' decision is easy and worthwhile. Allowing the opportunity to make mistakes gives the handler the opportunity to show the 'right' way.

Although a skilful practitioner can establish join-up with most horses within a matter of minutes, the process may take much longer and should not be rushed. Each individual will react differently. Over-confident, bolshy or mistrustful animals often put up a prolonged resistance to surrendering their 'right to flee'.

Once true join-up is achieved, the horse will follow the handler around the pen as if on an invisible lead-rein. He has accepted that, imagined predator or not, the handler now represents his comfort zone – the best place to be. Join-up creates a partnership, but not a wholly equal one. The handler is still a predator and retains 51 per cent of the shares. The man must always take the initiative (when leading, for example, stay slightly ahead of the horse).

5. After this stage, the handler then moves on to feeling firmly but gently all over the horse's body. This acceptance of being touched everywhere, including the areas where he feels most vulnerable (i.e. feet, under the belly, between the hind-legs) is crucial to reinforcing the relationship.

6. Young or unbroken horses can then be introduced to

equipment such as the bridle, saddle and girth. In this receptive frame of mind, even the feel of a weight on their back and tightening of the girth (both instinctively alarming to a prey animal) is accepted without great alarm, because a pact of trust has been agreed upon that is meaningful to the horse. Any signs of resistance indicate that the pact is not yet strong enough. The process is then taken back a stage and the advance and retreat technique repeated until the bond is stronger. Once the horse is familiar with the rules, suddenly taking up an assertive stance can bring back his attention and serve as a reminder.

MOVING ON FROM JOIN-UP

As Monty Roberts has demonstrated, it is possible for a previously untouched horse to reach the stage of accepting a rider within 30 minutes or so. However, in everyday practice, this is usually for demonstration purposes only. Trainers are advised to:

- Take time, achieving join-up repeatedly with a young horse and progressing each time towards introducing new ideas such as equipment.
- Prepare the horse more gradually for a rider and the use of the aids (a totally new language) by the use of long-reins before backing.

The youngster's education then continues in a conventional way and should progress smoothly from this sound foundation, with the horse being keen to please the 'boss'.

Join-up is not only an effective basis for training youngsters. It is also useful in restoring a relationship with difficult horses or youngsters out to test your authority. It can be used as a natural discipline, where the only pressure is mental, never physical. Always remember, however, that the majority of behaviour problems stem from discomfort or other environmental factors. These must be addressed before expecting miracles from any training technique.

JUMPING

Even if you do not foresee leaving the ground with your horse, jumping should be part of every youngster's education. Jumping not only gives the horse a versatile future, but provides welcome variety and has more than a few follow-on benefits on the flat, including improved collection and impulsion.

A horse will never jump willingly unless he enjoys it. As in every other aspect of training, making the learning experience fun and easy smoothes the path to success:

- Careful forward planning avoids unnecessary, confidence-denting mistakes.
- Learning to jump is mentally and physically demanding. Go at a pace dictated by the individual horse and keep sessions short.
- If mistakes occur, go back one or more stages and get things right before asking for more. Start each lesson by recapping previous work.

WHEN TO BEGIN

Introduce the idea of tackling obstacles as early after halter-breaking as you wish. The initial step is walking over, around and through simple poles on the ground, increasing the number of poles as confidence grows.

At first the youngster can be led in-hand and later long-reined. Poles can be positioned singly around the school; used in a line; on a wide arc, or set in a square with a narrow gap at each corner (*see Pole-work, page 199*).

LOOSE JUMPING

Loose jumping is as the name suggests. The horse is set loose in an enclosed space and asked to negotiate obstacles with no interference from the trainer or a rider. Done well, this can give the horse a useful and fun introduction to the 'feel' of jumping before ridden work has begun.

The crucial rule of thumb is the horse must jump of his own free will, calmly and confidently. If chased into the fence, all he will learn is to career around the arena, avoiding the fence at will or jumping wildly. Set up the exercise properly. If problems arise, you are doing too much too soon and need to go back a stage.

Watch and practise with an experienced horse before trying with a youngster. It is best if the horse has already been taught to respond to voice aids and has been lunged (*see Voice, page 274; Lungeing, page 179*).

Remember that all jumping puts strain on the limbs. Leave loose jumping until the horse is at least three years old and use it no more than twice a week. Five minutes from each direction is plenty.

- Fit a head-collar or saddle and bridle (with reins and stirrups removed) and boots.

- Use a long schooling or lunge whip.
- Use a safely-fenced area with good footing, familiar to the horse. It should be at least 65 feet (20 metres) long but not so large that control becomes difficult.
- Set up pairs of fence stands (at least 10ft/3.5m wide) and work the horse through these first.
- Add a ground-pole between the fence stands and walk, then trot, the horse through. Add another 9ft (3m) beyond. Adjust distance as necessary.
- Encourage the horse to go over in the middle. An assistant about 8ft (2.5m) in front of the pole/fence can help guide him in.
- Move on to a single low cross-pole. Once this is being tackled well, if there is space on a long side or oval arena, add another 18ft (5.5m) beyond, again working up from a pole on the ground.
- Two fences are enough for a young horse. Make the fences solid and vary their appearance once the horse is confident. Raise the fences a little higher as he progresses, but not over 2ft (0.5m).

JUMPING ON THE LUNGE

Again, practise on an older horse before attempting lungeing a youngster over fences. Never use side-reins. Once work on the lunge is familiar (see Lungeing, page 179), the three-year-old can be lunged over poles on the ground.

- Set up the stands first, making sure the inside one is low so the lunge-line will slip easily over it. Work up from one to three ground-poles laid out in a fan with 4 to 4'6" (1.2 to

Jumping on the lunge.

1.4m) between each at the middle point. This distance is correct for walking over the narrow end and trotting further out.

- Once the horse is going happily both ways, picking his feet up and is in a good rhythm, raise the middle pole a few inches at the outside. Progress to also raising the first and last poles.

- Now replace the poles with a single low cross-pole. Allow the horse to approach in a wide circle so he can see it in good time and straighten beforehand. Use verbal encouragement and a slight flick from the lunge whip, but do not hurry him. Once over the fence, move forward a little so the horse has total freedom of movement.

- Progress from a cross-pole to a small parallel. Vary the fillers, but keep the fence solid and low (not over 2ft/0.5m). The horse must be able to jump easily from a standstill if necessary. Discourage rushing if necessary by adding a ground-pole 9ft before the fence. If the horse runs out, increase the length of the wings by adding an angled pole filled in with cones. The horse may canter away from the jump. Let him settle back to trot and re-balance before the next approach.

- Work equally on both reins. A 20-minute session twice a week is enough.

JUMPING WITH A RIDER

Ridden jumping can be started as soon as the youngster is going with a reasonable degree of balance and responsiveness in his work under saddle on the flat. Choice of rider is important as there will be plenty of mistakes at first. A jab in the mouth or heavy thump on the back will soon put off a young horse, so the rider must be able to help the horse, not hinder him – i.e. be 'on the ball', confident and very well balanced. Riding must be positive and encouraging at all times, but without hassling the horse or inviting confrontation. Young horses often lack confidence coming into a fence but this must not be confused with naughtiness. When hesitation occurs, the rider must sit still, keep the legs on and a steady contact.

Begin all jumping sessions with some work on the flat. Focus on achieving the impulsion, control and balance the horse is going to need. Concentrate on achieving an active, bouncy trot and canter.

Build up the complexity of fences stage by stage.

EARLY STAGES

Poles and grids: Begin with poles on the ground, working up progressively to a single low cross-pole. Once this is being tackled well, add a horizontal pole to make the cross into a small upright. The next step is to add a ground-pole about 15cm (6 inches) in front, then create a small spread by using the low cross-pole on the first set of stands and a horizontal pole at the back. You are now ready to introduce simple grids. Remember, always use ground-lines and the correct distances for the individual horse.

See Pole-work, page 199; Grids, page 108.

Single fences: A horse that is at ease with small grids can progress to single fences. At first, use placing poles to help him judge an accurate take-off.

Steps for jumping successfully: Keep questions straightforward.

- Never move on to a more demanding exercise until the horse is tackling the previous stage calmly and confidently.
- If problems or mistakes occur, go back a step (or several if necessary) and correct the basics before moving on again.
- Work from trot at first. If the horse canters the last few strides, allow him on and set up again with a balanced trot before the next approach.
- The horse can only take off and jump well from an active but balanced approach. Coming in off a wide circle helps the rider establish this and gives time to plan a straight, central approach to each fence. Use large circles to re-balance if you feel you are not properly prepared – do not just have a go anyway! Work off both reins (the fence should be suitable to be jumped from both directions).

- Height is not the issue in teaching a horse to jump. Avoid all temptation to raise the fences beyond 2ft (0.6m), even if the horse seems a fast learner. Many promising youngsters are put off jumping for life because they show a little talent or enthusiasm and are then over-faced or pushed on too quickly. Let your aim be to master the basics and to achieve a good style over low fences (*see Bascule, page 45*).

MOVING ON
The next challenge is to widen the young horse's experience so he understands that jumping means taking on whatever obstacle he is presented with. Once the horse has the idea and is going happily, do not leave it too long to present the youngster with fillers and whatever strange and different-looking fences you can come up with (as long as they are safe!). Solid fences, e.g. walls, or fillers, are best introduced by positioning them with a large gap in the middle of the fence that is gradually closed in.

Once the horse is familiar with a variety of single fences, a selection of these can be positioned to be approached from various angles. Now tackle these two or three at a time, aiming for a continuous flow from one fence to the next. Include a change of direction when the horse is ready. Approach in trot at first, bringing the horse steadily back again after each fence. At this point, the focus should be on keeping up an even rhythm. Even three or four low fences are enough to create useful exercises and mini-courses.

Introducing combinations should be straightforward for the horse already familiar with grid-work. Simply remember to build up gradually, keeping distances accurate and the fences low and inviting. Doubles must be being taken on confidently before a third element is added. Bear in mind that a spread out of a combination is more difficult than an upright.

Begin to use more demanding grids to help improve the horse's technique over the fence. For example, bounce distances develop greater suppleness and quicker reactions, helping the horse to really 'round' and pick up his feet.

Try some small courses. Courses are best introduced by working first over groups of two or three fences before putting these together to make up a short six-to-eight-fence track. Keep the fences low and the track straightforward and flowing (e.g. include one change of rein across the diagonal and one one-stride double).

Watch your speed. Give yourself and the horse time to

Once the young horse is more experienced, he can move on to solid jumps.

prepare and see each fence by tackling it from trot. Move up a gear only when the horse is confidently taking on grids and single fences from a canter. Then use circles whenever necessary to re-balance and re-establish rhythm and return to trot and strike off again to get the correct leading leg if the horse lands on the wrong lead. Trying to 'place' the youngster or interfering with his stride before the fence is no help to him and is only guaranteed to put him off.

Once the youngster is enjoying his jumping at home, start to introduce natural obstacles. This is can be done out on familiar hacks if the ground and obstacle are suitable, but much more can be achieved by hiring a purpose-built novice course and knowledgeable instructor. Again, avoid all temptation to over-jump your youngster. Jumping once or twice a week for half an hour is plenty.

COMMON JUMPING PROBLEMS

Youngsters will make many mistakes. Even with the best of riders, there are times when the novice horse will come in on a tricky stride or hesitate at the last moment, jumping awkwardly, or even knocking the entire obstacle flying. However, with good planning and sound basics most horses make steady progress. Any faults are picked up quickly and worked through, not allowed to become 'set' into bad jumping habits that then prove a problem once the fences get higher and the courses more demanding.

Persistent problems tend to be the result of one, or a combination, of:

Inadequate training: The horse does not sufficiently understand what he is being asked to do, or is not physically capable of it.

Poor riding: The horse has not been set up well enough by

162

the rider to take off and clear the fence properly, or has been interfered with in the approach to, or jump over, the fence.

Tension: This may be down to excitement *(see Energy, page 89)* or anxiety (perhaps from a previous bad experience of jumping).

Pain or discomfort: All too frequently, horses are expected to jump with sharp teeth, badly-fitting tack, too-severe bits, on hard ground or with neck or back injuries.

The first step in trying to correct any jumping problem is to take a long, hard look at which of the above may apply. Once any potential source of discomfort or tension has been dealt with, most problems need to be patiently worked through with a capable rider, concentrating on going back to basics and involving flatwork, poles and grids.

TIPS TO OVERCOME PROBLEMS

Rushing: The horse comes into his fences too fast, unbalanced and flat or even hollow. To remedy this problem:

- Remember, horses that rush are always tense. First, pinpoint the source of tension and take steps to rectify this as far as possible. Do not be too quick to create yet more tension by resorting to a stronger bit.
- Work on the flat to improve the horse's outline, suppleness and responsiveness. Make flatwork interesting so the horse has plenty to think about.
- The rider must stay quiet, relaxed and avoid over-strong aids.
- Go right back to basics and progress step by step, always quietly insisting on a calm approach. This means plenty of work over, through and around poles on the ground, firstly in walk and then trot.

Try to avoid over-strong aids when a horse rushes his fences.

A horse that backs off a fence needs positive, confident riding.

- Progress to small grids, again insisting on a calm attitude. Always circle away, settle and re-balance before approaching again.
- When moving on to single fences, trot (and later canter) into a small upright with two poles laid in a 'V' shape behind it.
- Avoid asking for more pace in competition until the problem is overcome.

Run-outs and refusals: The horse backs off the fence from some distance away, puts on the brakes at the last minute, or runs past the obstacle altogether.

- Look for the reason behind the evasion. Lack of confidence or understanding is frequently the cause with youngsters. Older horses may be being badly presented at the fence. Any horse that uncharacteristically begins to refuse to jump is likely to have a genuine excuse such as pain or poor riding.
- Ride effectively to give the horse confidence, and make every presentation active, straight and positive. Sit up and keep the rein contact constant all the way to the fence. A tap down the shoulder with the stick can help a hesitant horse make up his mind to 'go'.
- Work on the flat to improve the ingredients for jumping: impulsion, balance, straightness, rhythm and responsiveness to the leg. With a good approach, the horse should find it easier to take off and jump than to run out or stop!
- Take training back as many stages as you need to regain the horse's confidence, recapping on basic exercises using poles and grids.
- Use placing poles in front of fences to help with judging take-off, or a ground-pole 1ft (30cm) in front to help the horse stand off more if he is consistently getting in too close.
- Do not rush or over-face the horse, or jump too often.

- If the refusals/run-outs occur at 'spooky' fences, do more preparation work with mini-versions of strange-looking obstacles.
- Run-outs, or drifting to the side, can be helped by working over an upright with two poles resting on the top forming a 'V' that funnels the horse in to the centre of the fence.

Carelessness: A careless horse is one which frequently knocks poles, either because he is untidy with his legs or flattening. To overcome this carelessness:

- Work on the flat. Concentrate on a balanced, active, accurate approach. Do not rush.
- Use a variety of basic exercises to encourage rhythm, balance and concentration, e.g. poles and grids.
- Use placing poles, gradually moving them in a little so the horse must take off closer to the fence.
- A grid of bounces (no more than five in a row) or small parallels will help improve neatness and concentration.
- If a particular fore-leg trails, raise the top poles along the grid on that side a little.

Not all horses have the ability, build or mental aptitude to put enough effort into clearing their fences. If this is your horse, then be realistic about your expectations!

Jumping is a huge subject in itself. Although there is not sufficient space here for details on how to tackle specific problems or how to refine your youngster's jumping skills, much excellent advice is available. Arranging a course of sessions with a respected professional trainer with good facilities will help you get the best from your horse and provide the opportunity to work through any difficulties.

KICKING

A genuine kick packs a powerful punch and usually hits its target spot-on. It is in quite a different league to the vague threat offered by a horse that raises a hind-leg when tickled by overenthusiastic grooming, paws with a fore-leg when feeding or kicks out when startled.

Although kicking is an act of aggression from a horse, in nature it tends to be used more in self-defence, usually preceded by a series of warning threats. Aggression is not characteristic of horses as a species, so the reason for any such behaviour always needs to be investigated and dealt with as a priority before remedial action can be taken *(see Aggression, page 25)*.

KICKING AT PEOPLE

Ask yourself why the horse may be kicking. Check there are no reasonable excuses, e.g. rough grooming or handling, irritation from flies or a skin condition. Determined kickers are usually hypersensitive about their personal space. Lack of confidence, or past bullying (equine or human) may have been the original spur for the horse to go on the offensive. Once the horse realises how easily he can keep any 'undesirables' at a distance this way, it soon becomes a habit. Standing to the side when grooming etc. does not get to the root of the problem, which is about re-establishing trust and respect.

Re-establishing control: To try and regain trust and respect, work through the process of habituating the horse to being felt all over his body. With older horses and confirmed kickers, it is best to use a stick with a light cloth (e.g. handkerchief) to stroke the body, so you can keep at a safe distance. Include the legs. Do not be put off, but keep this up until it is accepted, giving vocal praise and reassurance. Progress to rubbing the body all over with the flat of your hand. The horse must understand the rules: you *must* be allowed to enter his space and will not hurt him. However, he must *not* enter *your* space unless asked. Authority must be reasserted but in a reassuring, non-threatening way.

- Successfully habituating the horse to having his personal space entered and his body touched can be achieved through the use of the sacking out procedure (q.v.). The join-up process (q.v.) will also further help build a better horse-human relationship.
- If the horse threatens by swinging his quarters towards you, use the same procedure as for barging (q.v.) – i.e. flick a long stick towards the quarters to send them away, at the same time as directing the head round towards you for a friendly rub and praise.
- Lessons must be frequent and intensive until all signs of threatening behaviour stop.
- Groom thin-skinned horses tactfully, using the hand to remove dried mud from sensitive areas rather than a stiff brush.

KICKING THE DOOR

Banging at the stable door is a sign of frustration rather than aggression. The horse is often eager to get stuck into the bucket of feed he can see or hear being dished up. The confirmed door-banger may simply be shouting "Let me out!"

Re-establishing control: As always, get at the cause of this attention-seeking behaviour, rather than merely denying him the chance to relieve his stress in this way. What will defuse the situation?

- With horses that bang the door continually, the answer is as simple as giving them more freedom to relax in an unconfined space, i.e. at pasture or loose in an enclosed area.

- Kicking at meal-times is a displacement activity *(see Decision Making and Conflict, page 79)*. It is aggravated in yards where different owners feed their horses at different times, and also by an owner who always follows the same pre-feeding routine, allowing her horse to build up to a frenzy of anticipation! If these apply, reconsider your arrangements: your horse may be better suited to a smaller yard where one person is in charge, and varying your routine will help the horse think more flexibly.

- The satisfaction of the noise can make matters worse. After taking the above considerations into account, lessening the noise can help reduce the behaviour. Fit padded sacking or rubber matting to the door to protect it and deaden the sound. In fine weather, a bar can be attached at chest height across the doorway and the door opened.

LATERAL WORK

A horse moves 'laterally' whenever he is asked to take a sideways step. Examples of lateral moves include: moving around to open a gate; lining up alongside the mounting block; and moving onto the verge to avoid traffic. Lateral work describes a set of schooling exercises in which the horse is asked to move both forwards and sideways, the fore-legs and hind-legs moving on different tracks.

Lateral work helps the horse achieve a better outline through development of all the elements required – rhythm, balance, straightness, impulsion and suppleness. It also improves obedience and strengthens the quarters so the horse can move more of his weight backwards, lightening his forehand. Use a combination of the movements regularly in your schooling sessions to exercise every muscle and joint in the horse's body.

Although basic lateral exercises such as turning on the forehand and leg yielding can be performed before the horse has achieved 'collected' paces, the more advanced movements need more collection.

Before introducing any lateral work, the horse must be understanding and accepting of the rein contact and forward leg aids. He should be working on the straight and through turns and large circles calmly and rhythmically, with reasonable suppleness.

Whatever the exercise, during lateral work the horse must:
• Continue to accept the bit.
• Stay in a correct outline.
• Keep going forwards in rhythm and balance.
• Stay relaxed, showing no resistance or tension.
• Not be hurried.

The rider must sit softly and straight, trying not to grip with the legs or stiffen the arms. Each hand and leg will be working independently, so good co-ordination and concentration is required!

TEACHING THE YOUNG HORSE TO MOVE AWAY FROM THE LEG

The horse finds sideways movement easy and natural, so early lateral exercises simply involve teaching him to connect the signal from the leg with that movement.

• As a preliminary step, ask the youngster to move over in the stable, and later under saddle, by nudging him just behind the girth and using the voice command OVER.
• In the arena, move on to the inside track. Now ask the horse to move forwards and sideways back to the outside track using the inside leg.
• Aim for slight bend to the inside, regulated by the outside rein.
• Do not overdo the aid. Strong aids should never be needed in any lateral work.
• Be content with a just a few steps at first and build up from there.

Turn on the forehand.

LATERAL EXERCISES

Riders should be able to do all of these movements well on a trained horse before trying to teach them to a youngster. With young horses, make aids clear and set the horse up carefully for each exercise. Do not hurry – a few steps at a time is enough to earn a reward at first. Aim to get each movement right in walk before progressing to trot.

Turn on the forehand: The horse pivots 180 degrees around his forehand, the fore-legs marching on the spot as the quarters rotate around them. This can be performed in walk, either in, or away from, the direction of the bend. This manoeuvre introduces the idea of moving away from the leg and helps to keep the hips and hocks supple.

- The move should be performed from a square halt on the inside track, parallel to the wall or hedge.
- Ask for one step at a time. Avoid too much bend in the neck and keep up impulsion to prevent any backward steps.
- Do not over-practise the manoeuvre, as it restricts forwards movement, encouraging weight to be taken forwards rather than backwards.
- Ask the horse to go forwards immediately after the turn has been completed.

Leg yield: The leg yield requires the horse to move diagonally forwards and sideways. The horse should be straight except for a slight bend at the poll in the opposite direction to the way he is moving (allowing the rider to just see the inside nostril). The movement is on two tracks – the inside legs pass and cross the outside legs.

Leg yield.

- This move should be carried out in walk and trot, with no collection needed.
- Introduce by leg yielding from the inside track or centre line in a diagonal direction to the outside track or by increasing the size of a 10-metre circle to 20 metres.
- Use the inside leg to move the horse over and keep up impulsion. Maintain straightness and avoid too much bend in the neck.
- Some trainers prefer not to leg yield because it asks the horse to bend the 'wrong' way and can cause confusion when teaching the half-pass later.

Shoulder-in: This involves the rider bringing the horse's shoulders on to the inside track. The horse moves sideways on three (or four) tracks, bending uniformly around the rider's inside leg, away from the direction he is going. The inside fore crosses over the outside fore, but the hind-legs hardly cross at all. The shoulder-in is an excellent exercise for improving suppleness, increasing collection and teaching control of the shoulders. In turn, this improves turns, circles and straightness, the basis of all collected and advanced lateral work.

- The shoulder-in should first be introduced in walk. As soon as the horse understands the move, he should progress to practising it in trot.
- Some collection is needed. Prepare by establishing a balanced, active shortened trot. Doing a 10-metre circle in the corner first helps novices get the correct bend and increases inside hind-leg activity.
- Keep the angle at about 30 degrees so inside fore and outside hind can follow the same track.
- Practise down the long side, centre line or off a circle. Always bring the shoulders to the inside (as if beginning a circle).
- Adjust contact on inside/outside rein to avoid excessive bend in the neck.
- Keep up impulsion and control the swing of the quarters.

- After completing the move, ride forwards around the curve (more advanced horses can be straightened).

Travers (haunches-in): During travers, the forehand continues on the outer track (or centre line) while the hindquarters are moved on to the inner track. The horse is bent around the inside leg and towards the direction of travel.

Shoulder-in.

- Travers is beneficial in preparing for the half-pass and working on control of the quarters.
- The bend should be maintained at about 30 degrees, so that the horse has to keep working on three tracks.
- Introduce this manoeuvre in walk before progressing to trot and canter.

Renvers (haunches-out): In renvers, the quarters remain on the track while the forehand moves on an inside track. The horse is bent around the outside leg. Renvers is a very useful straightening exercise which also develops suppleness. It is usually carried out down the long side of the arena.

Half-pass: When performing the half-pass, the horse should move forwards and sideways (as in leg yield) but looking and bending uniformly towards the direction he is going. The aim of the half-pass is to stay almost parallel to the side of the arena, although novices will work with forehand slightly ahead of quarters. The half-pass is excellent for creating suppleness in the hips, stifles and hocks, as it requires the outside hind to cross over the inside hind. The half-pass can be ridden in walk, trot and canter. Preparation should begin with a half-circle or shoulder-in to create activity and correct bend.

Turn on the haunches (demi-pirouette & pirouette): This is a two-track movement where the fore-legs cross over to make a circle or half-circle around the hind-legs. The inside hind acts as a pivot with the outside hind moving around it. The manoeuvre requires a high degree of collection, through repeated half-halts.

- Initially this move should be performed from walk, although a more advanced horse can begin from canter.

- The shoulder must be free to move.
- Introduce by asking for haunches-in on a small circle, gradually decreasing the size of the circle.
- Keep up impulsion and the rhythm of the walk.

LAZINESS
See Energy, page 89; Responsiveness, page 211.

LEADING
Discipline in leading is crucial as it is the foundation of so much we do with our horses. To fit in with the life he is going to lead in domestication, one of the earliest and most significant lessons the foal must learn is to follow his human 'leader' politely, allowing them total control over his movement and having complete respect for the human's personal space.

This is a huge lesson in acceptance and discipline and sets the tone for everything that comes later. A youngster that has been properly taught to yield to pressure from the lead-rope is unlikely to ever be a difficult leader, or refuse to load or pull back when tied up. He will be conditioned to the rule that he moves when you move and stands when you stand (i.e. does not take matters into his own hands), keeping a respectful distance at all times (i.e. never coming so near as to tread on your toes) (*see Halter-breaking, page 125*).

Taking care when leading reinforces this relationship. Sloppy leading habits will quickly tempt any horse to have a go at reasserting himself. The following are points to remember when leading:
- Expect total respect.
- Always walk level with the horse's head. Here you retain control, are well clear of his feet and are reinforcing the message of submission. Walking by the shoulder allows him to play 'leader'.

- Do not get too close or hold the rope too near the head. There is no need to actively restrain a properly halter-broken horse.

Leading is a lesson in acceptance and discipline.

L

DEALING WITH A HORSE THAT IS DIFFICULT TO LEAD
All too often, halter-breaking is done badly, not thoroughly
enough, left too late, or ignored altogether. The result is horses
who have learnt to use their size and weight against their
handlers, habitually barging their way around, putting
themselves and everyone within range at risk. Overcoming this
behaviour is not easily done, but tactics include:

- Assertive body language (q.v.). This can be used to
  intimidate a pushy horse and remind him to back off your
  personal space. All horses should go backwards a few steps
  in-hand with no protests whatsoever.
- Don't forget your voice. Reinforce your actions with the
  vocal commands for steadying down that he is familiar with
  (generally WHOA).
- Lead strong or difficult horses using a chain lead rather than
  a bridle, which risks injuring the mouth in a confrontation. Be
  sure to stay to the side and slightly in front of the horse's eye.
  Hold the chain between the finger and thumb. This allows the
  rider to administer a short tug, immediately followed by
  release of the chain, should the horse start to pull. Do not jerk
  on the chain or give a constant pull. A chain lead is more
  than a brake. Schooling with the nose-chain can teach the
  horse to accept precise and subtle signals. With young or very
  sensitive horses, use a narrow lead-rope instead.
- Confirmed bargers may need determined handling at first.
  Wear gloves and strong boots/shoes. Use a head-collar with a
  long lead-rope and chain lead (see above). If the horse begins
  to forge ahead, step sideways at a 45-degree angle to him
  and, using the extra leverage this creates, bring his head
  sharply towards you to unbalance him. When he brings his
  head to you, slacken the rope, fuss and rub him in reward.
- An adult horse may need to be effectively re-broken to the
  halter. This will require the extra control of a pressure halter
  (q.v.).

LEANING ON THE BIT (or HAND)
**When too much weight is carried on the forehand, the
horse often helps support himself by leaning on the bit.
This has the effect of pulling the rider forward and is very
unbalancing. Improvement lies in using schooling exercises
to keep the horse supple and encourage him to round his
back and use his hindquarters more, so lightening the
forehand.**
See On the Forehand, page 99; Aids, page 30.

LENGTHENING
See Gaits, page 101.

LOADING
See Travelling, page 262.

LONG-REINING
Long-reining is a vital stage in the process of preparing a young horse for a rider. Two heavy lunge lines (about 30ft or 9m in length) are used, attached to the cavesson (or bit ring for experienced handlers) on each side. The handler stands to the side or behind the horse, directing him and controlling the pace.

USES AND ADVANTAGES
Long-reining:
- Introduces the concept of signals being given by pressure on the bit and on his sides, not only by voice and body language.
- Prepares the young horse for the 'feel' of leg and hand aids.
- Helps teach the meaning of these aids.
- Starts encouraging the horse to 'listen backward' for his instructions, as he will when he carries a rider.
- Encourages balance and self-carriage.
- Increases confidence.
- Reinforces the dominance of the human, who is controlling the horse's movement.
- Desensitises the horse to things draped around and flapping against his sides, quarters and legs.

 Knowing a little about steering and brakes will make the process of backing and riding away all the less stressful or confusing, as he will already understand and accept these

Long-reining encourages balance and self-carriage.

aids. It has many advantages over the more widely-used technique of lungeing, which cannot imitate the feel of the rider in the same way, tends to get the horse thinking round in circles rather than forwards and puts more strain on the limbs.

HOW TO LONG-REIN

Before attempting to long-rein, the youngster must have been introduced to the saddle and protective boots *(see Equipment, page 92)* and be properly halter-broken. Respect and confidence in the handler should also now be the keynote of the relationship. Any confident horse-person can long-rein, although it makes sense to practise on an experienced horse first. Fifteen minutes per session is plenty.

- Work in an enclosed, familiar area.
- To avoid damaging the mouth, use a head-collar or cavesson rather than attaching the reins directly to the bit if you are not sure of your skill. Adjust the stirrups to hang just below the saddle flap. Connect the irons under the belly using a length of twine or strap.
- Stand alongside the horse. Attach the off-side rein (having an assistant hold the horse is useful at first), pass through the stirrup and bring it over the saddle, but not over the quarters. Attach the near-side rein, pass through the stirrup and hold it in the other hand. It is crucial not to alarm the horse by suddenly flapping the reins at him.
- Stay by the shoulder with the reins looped up in your hands. Ask the horse to walk on. Gradually take up a light contact. Now slowly increase your distance away from the horse, staying to the side where you can be seen.
- Ask for HALT, using gentle pressure on the reins. The assistant can help show what is required by moving in front of the horse. Once he stops, release the pressure immediately and give praise. Practise this on both sides. This is enough for the first time.
- Arrange a further session soon. After recapping, gradually move further back and let the outside rein down over the quarters. Stay slightly to one side but, little by little, edge further away until the reins are at their full length. Continue working on walk and halt, now on a large circle as if lungeing.
- When the horse is ready, ask for trot with your voice, body and a flick of the outside rein behind the quarters. Stay slightly behind him. If he offers canter, allow it. Practise transitions up and down, using the walls of the arena or pen to help guide him.

- As the horse settles and starts to listen more to the rein aids, you can drop further back in walk or halt, so he cannot see you. Work towards varying your position between standing to the side and behind.
- Work equally in both directions. Turn by increasing the feel on the outside rein and stepping slightly ahead of his shoulder to slow him. Now move behind the quarters, letting the old inside rein go a little as the horse turns and it becomes the new inside rein. Turn towards the outside fence or wall to help guide the horse round, practising in walk first.
- Keep the rein contact soft throughout. You should not need to pull. The elbows must be bent and reins handled as sensitively as when riding.
- Take care not to move too far forwards unless you intend to use your body position to slow the horse down.
- Work through any resistance patiently and quietly using voice, body and the rein aids. If necessary, stop, reassure the horse and go back to the previous stage.
- With more experienced horses, carefully allowing the reins to fall down the legs at the end of each session will help the horse learn not to fuss or panic in this situation.
  Once the procedure is familiar, long-reining can be used over poles on the ground and out and about around the yard and quiet, familiar lanes.

LOOPS

Loops can be incorporated into schooling sessions in a variety of ways to help improve the horse's suppleness, balance and rhythm. Each loop involves two changes of direction, and so requires the horse to 'bend' twice.

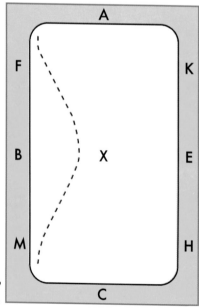

Loops are used to improve suppleness.

It is also made up of smooth curves, not two straight lines connected by a 90-degree turn!

Loops are usually done down the long side of the school and are made either 5 metres or 10 metres (16-32 feet) 'deep'. Good loops require:

- Looking and planning ahead. This will help show the horse where you intend to go.
- Accuracy and consistency. Get to know how many strides your horse takes around each part of the movement. This should be even, out and back.
- Good cornering. Good corners lead to good loops. Riding a balanced corner with the correct bend keeps up activity and prevents the horse falling in by using the inside leg.
- The rider to sit upright and evenly on both seat-bones, with their legs beneath them to keep the horse balanced around the loop. Tipping to one side, dropping a shoulder or taking one leg off the horse's side will all affect the horse's bend and direction.
- Supporting with the outside aids to prevent drifting.
- Resisting the temptation to leg-yield the horse should he move straight.
- Changing the bend before asking for the change in direction. Give him time!
- Laying out poles or cones to help the horse/rider find the correct line at first.

LOOSE REIN/LOOSENESS
Term used to describe the horse moving freely with no restriction on his natural expression. The less tension and stiffness in the muscles, the more loose the horse will be.

Working for spells in a longer, lower outline and allowing time at the beginning and end of sessions for the horse to

At the beginning and end of schooling sessions, give your horse the opportunity to stretch down.

stretch down his neck on a long-rein will encourage greater looseness. Begin teaching the horse to relax in this way as soon as he is going forwards well on a straight line with a light contact. Gradually allow him a 'long' rein then a 'loose' rein (where the rider has no contact) keeping him straight using the legs. He will soon come to recognise a longer rein as a signal to wind down at the end of a session.

LOOSE SCHOOLING
Working a horse of any age loose in a school has many benefits if done well. For the horse, it provides a stimulating new way of exercising, free of a rider. For the trainer it is an interesting alternative training opportunity and a chance to see the horse moving naturally without tack or a rider.

Learning hinges on the process staying calm and controlled. You have only your voice and body stance to control the horse, who should already recognise the vocal commands for HALT, WALK and TROT.

- Choose only a safe enclosed area with good footing, that should be at least 30 metres square or in diameter. With youngsters, it should be a space they are familiar with and should have boundaries high enough to respect.
- Fit a head-collar and boots.
- Carry a lunge whip. Some people prefer to use two; a lunge whip as a 'forward' aid, and a schooling whip in the other hand as a slowing aid. This takes some co-ordination and practice.
- Lead the horse into the arena and release him. Let him have a 'fling' if he wishes, then use your voice to steady him.
- Encourage him to walk, then trot by using a driving stance (i.e. slightly behind the girth) and the whip towards him. To slow and halt, move slightly in front of his shoulder and bring the whip behind you. Walk up and praise the horse when he stops, then repeat in the other direction.
- Loose schooling is an ideal opportunity to introduce canter to the youngster. Get an active trot and use the vocal command to ask him to move up a gear.
- Adjust the length of sessions according to the horse's age and experience:

Yearlings: 10 minutes of walk and some trot per day.
Two-year-olds: 20 minutes of walk and trot, or two spells of 10 minutes.

Three-year-olds: two periods of 15 minutes, including some canter if offered.

Over-threes: up to a maximum of two 30-minute periods.

N.B. Loose schooling may send contradictory signals to a horse that has been joined-up (q.v.), who will associate being sent away with the handler being displeased.

See also Voice, page 274; Introducing Jumping, page 156.

LUNGEING

Lungeing is a useful way of working any horse without a rider, for exercise or education. It has long been a staple ingredient in the training of young horses, helping to:

- **Teach the horse to go forwards on his own.**
- **Develop suppleness, balance and rhythm.**
- **Introduce the idea of transitions.**
- **Give a chance to work off some steam.**
- **Allow the handler to see how the horse moves from the ground.**

Most importantly, it teaches the young horse to respond to the voice commands *(see Voice, page 274).*

Even so, lungeing sessions are best kept relatively short and to-the-point. Too long and the horse could become over-stressed and switch off. Endless circling is extremely boring and puts great strain on the limbs and joints.

- Do not lunge a horse under the age of three.
- Always lunge on level ground in an enclosed space at least 25m (85ft) in diameter.
- Begin by using a snugly-fitting head-collar with the line clipped beneath, or a cavesson (first accustom the horse to being led from the front of his nose).
- The handler must wear gloves and a hard hat and already have considerable experience of lungeing.
- Before starting, the horse should be familiar with the voice commands, the lunge whip and line and all the tack he is to wear (including boots on all legs and roller or saddle with the stirrups removed).
- The idea of lungeing can be first introduced in a large loose-box.
- Commands must be consistent. Remember, tone of voice is more important than the actual words used, although it makes sense to teach your horse the standard phrases.
- Work equally on both sides.

INTRODUCING LUNGEING

Lungeing can be introduced with the help of an assistant on the inside of the circle about a metre from the horse, ready to back up the trainer's commands.

As this has the effect of splitting the horse's attention, others prefer to work single-handedly:

- Fit the lungeing gear. Walk beside the horse around the edge of the area, recapping on the commands WALK ON, TROT, WHOA.
- Hold the rein in the left hand and whip in the right, behind the body, tip to the ground when not in use.
- Gradually move away from the horse about 2 metres (6ft), staying level with his shoulder. Bring the whip carefully forwards, still pointing it down but towards the quarters.
- Bring the horse slowly on to a large circle, still walking with him. Aim for a steady light contact, with the wrist supple and elbow bent so there is a straight line down the rein. Try to get the horse slightly bent to the inside through give-and-take 'feels' on the rein.
- Gradually allow the rein out as the horse gets the idea so his circle becomes larger and yours smaller. If he leans on the rein, squeeze it gently to encourage him to carry himself. If there is any resistance, or the horse rushes off, return to the shorter rein for a while.
- The whip and your body position also give signals to the horse. Pointing the whip slightly up and at the quarters drives the horse forwards. Aiming the whip at the shoulders will send him further out on the circle. Using the whip down and ahead, will slow him down. Always use the whip gently and *never* hit the horse. To move the horse on, make sure you are standing square to the quarters and slightly behind the girth. Moving in a line with the shoulders will slow him.
- Concentrate, be observant and act quickly to correct the horse if he looks like he is speeding up, slowing down or thinking of turning in (in which case, drive him on).
- To change direction, halt the horse on the outside of the circle. Walk calmly up, gathering the rein into loops and with the whip behind you. Praise the horse before starting off the other way.

N.B. Joined-up horses are trained to come in off a circle to their trainer. For this reason long-reining is more suitable than lungeing for these horses.

WORKING ON THE LUNGE

Once the horse has got the idea, lungeing can be used by an experienced trainer to encourage working into a contact. This will require a cavesson and elasticated side-reins, which must be fitted loosely, high up on the girth/or roller (too low will restrict the stride). Initially, the elasticated side-reins must be fitted on the cavesson.

Work on frequent transitions as these encourage the horse to lighten his forehand. Very gradually the side-reins can be shortened a little until the nose is vertical when there is a light contact on the reins. Even slightly-restrictive side-reins will make the horse tense up and shorten his stride, deadening the mouth and teaching him to go over-bent (q.v.). To avoid any problems developing when teaching the lunge:

- Lunge youngsters in walk and trot only, focusing on trot work.
- Make sessions no more than 20 minutes long, working on both reins.
- If you hit resistance, avoid confrontation. Enlist the help of a more experienced lunger, loosen (or abandon) the side-reins or consider using a chambon *(see Schooling Aids, page 225)*. Alternatively, work in a way the horse finds more stimulating and comfortable (e.g. long-reins or ridden work, if backed).
- Aim to get the horse going freely and actively forwards in a steady, even rhythm, using his hocks so he steps right underneath himself with the hind-feet. Keeping the lunge whip pointed at the quarters and shortening the rein slightly sends the horse forwards more actively.

A horse fitted with a cavesson and side-reins ready for lungeing.

Work on frequent transitions, and aim to get the horse moving forwards freely and actively.

- When lungeing is established, it can be done directly from the bit. Pass the line through the inside bit ring under the chin and clip to the outside bit ring (or alternatively, up over the poll and back to the outside bit ring). You will need to swap the sides when changing direction.
- Sessions should last a total of no more than 15-20 minutes for three-year-olds and 20 minutes for four-year-olds.

MEMORY

A prey animal cannot afford the luxury of rehearsals. The horse's excellent memory evolved as a survival essential. From the very start, a young foal had to learn, and learn quickly, those situations which posed a threat. An animal that could not recall from season to season the location of water and shelter, or which plants were poisonous, was not going to stay alive for long either.

Memory records past experiences and the outcomes of previous choices to use as reference points on which to base further decisions in the future. The mechanics of how and where memory is stored in the brain are not yet known, but seems to involve three stages:

Registration: Data is perceived, understood and allocated a slot in the short-term memory.

Storage: If the data is sufficiently important to the horse or well established by immediate reinforcement and repetition, it is transferred for storage in the long-term memory. If not, it gets replaced with other more pressing information.

A foal must start learning – and remembering – from the very start.

Recall: Data is deliberately retrieved from the subconscious and transferred to the conscious mind. How easily this happens depends on how well it was originally encoded and the circumstances of the moment, i.e. what distractions there are and how focused the horse is on the recall request. Horses have an exceptionally long, clear memory for data that has been effectively stored. They are able to recognise familiar people or places years after last encountering them. A well-learned lesson will stick for a long period of time with little, or even no, topping-up. Once learned, a response will alter only if further effective learning extinguishes the original reaction and replaces it with a stronger, better-stored or more important alternative.

MEMORY AND TRAINING

His excellent memory is fundamental to the horse's trainability. Knowing the way his memory works emphasises the need for effective reinforcement (q.v.) of every new lesson.

The potential down-side is equally obvious. Once registered, any experience is likely to stay with the horse for a lifetime – good or bad. Handling and training young horses is therefore a huge responsibility. Any unpleasantness or distress will be logged and the horse will understandably be reluctant to repeat it. Take time to get things right first time.

One mistake does not necessarily spell complete disaster, however. Most learning must be immediately fixed by repetition before it becomes permanent. For the same reason, no horse should be expected to have learned a lesson he was taught and got right once, weeks ago.

The exception is traumatic memories, often with survival significance. A road accident, for example, is likely to leave the horse permanently nervous in traffic. Patient, consistent retraining can mask these unpleasant memories and rebuild confidence, but the old reaction often resurfaces under stress.

MEN – DISLIKE OF
Some horses appear to have an aversion to men, which can be extremely inconvenient when it is time for a visit from a male farrier or vet.

As with all behaviour, there is always logic behind this apparent irrationality. Most frequently the anxiety is a hangover from a previous uncomfortable experience associated with a male, which might be anything from genuine abuse to an innocent vet administering a vaccination. By nature, men are often more assertive in their bearing. These subconscious body cues are easily picked up by horses and may be a cause of stress and alarm for hypersensitive or nervous types.

The only answer is constant exposure to men in all situations in the horse's daily life, emphasising pleasant experiences. Go out of your way to see the horse is handled and ridden by males who are sensitive to the situation and aware of their body language. Ask every man who comes to the yard to say "Hello" and fuss the horse.

Work on habituating the horse to experiences he may dislike (*e.g. see Feet and the Farrier, page 96*). Choose a patient and sympathetic farrier and vet. Most will be happy to spend a few minutes with the nervous horse at each visit to the yard rather than always being linked with something unpleasant in the horse's mind which results in unco-operative behaviour.

MOTIVATION
A motivated pupil – horse or human – learns fast and well, because he *wants* to learn. For the poorly motivated pupil, learning is hard going. The teacher is the 'enemy', forever making unappealing and confusing demands.

Good motivation creates a positive atmosphere for learning that creates a forward-thinking, secure and confident horse. A negative attitude is a huge handicap and soon creates a downward spiral. De-motivation is often the result of misunderstandings between horse and rider, or the horse being unable or unwilling to do what the rider asks.

There is no natural, inherent motivation for horses to do ridden work in the same way that there is for them to eat, drink and reproduce. We have to create it by making learning enjoyable and effortless.

Good motivation is created by:

Communication: Signals must be clear and consistent, giving a sense of security. The trainer must be alert to feedback from the horse.

Variety: Interesting lessons are fun and stimulating, encouraging initiative, flexibility and responsiveness. Boredom leads to resistance. Over-repetition also rapidly desensitises the horse.

Timing: Take things step by step, only progressing once the previous stage has been clearly understood. Let the horse dictate the pace.

Going with horse's own inclinations: An understanding of the way a horse's mind works and the individual's temperament helps a trainer set up lessons so that getting it right becomes easy and natural.

Reward: Make the horse feel good when he suceeds. Praise fosters a sense of achievement, co-operation and teamwork as well as providing instant reinforcement for a particular lesson done well. Whatever the horse's level, rewards should always be given when deserved.

Whenever you hit a problem in training, do not push on or create a confrontation. Try to work out what is behind the horse's objection and find a way of restoring or increasing his motivation using the guidelines above. Remember that, if discipline is needed, it must always be fair, clear and consistent, as with all our communication with the horse.

MOUNTING

From the very first backing, the young horse must learn to stand absolutely still while the rider mounts and until he is given the signal to move off. If this basic lesson is ignored, the horse is forever likely to be a fidget that potentially puts the rider at risk.

Although during early backing lessons the rider will be legged up, do not delay introducing proper mounting. If the experience is comfortable and it is clear from the start what is expected, problems are unlikely. For your horse to adapt to trouble-free mounting:

Use a mounting block to reduce the drag on the horse's back.

- Always check the girth before mounting.
- Work in an enclosed area.
- Use a mounting block to reduce drag on the horse's back (accustom the horse to the block beforehand). Have someone hold the stirrup on the other side.
- The rider must be very careful not to dig a toe into the horse's side, and to sit down lightly into the saddle. Remember to give praise.
- During the early days, have an assistant standing a little to the side in front of the horse blocking any forwards movement or ready to lead the horse on a little if he steps backwards.
- Slight sideways movement can be discouraged by shortening the off-side rein a little. If necessary, another helper can stand that side with a schooling whip to point at the quarters to keep the horse straight.
- Use a vocal command the horse knows as a stop or steady signal, e.g. WHOA or STAND.

THE FIDGETY HORSE

A horses that wanders, or even rushes off before the rider is in the saddle, is obviously a safety risk. He is also showing a lack of respect for the rider that is unlikely to improve during his ridden work. Fidgets have usually been made that way either by never having been properly taught to stand still, or from anxiety about the whole business. This is frequently the result of pain, either from a current physical problem or the memory of an earlier one.

- Have the horse's back and teeth thoroughly checked by specialists. Begin retraining only when there are no physical problems.
- Use the method above consistently and repeatedly. Stay calm and patient.
- If the horse reacts dramatically, school him in-hand in a pressure halter (q.v.). Once he understands and respects the halter's action, use it to reinforce the stand still message as an assistant mounts.

MOUTHING
See Bitting, page 49.

MOVING HOME
Moving house is said to be one of the most stressful situations a human can face. Multiply that stress a hundredfold for the horse, who has no anticipation of the event, and whose happiness and peace of mind revolves around the security of his familiar surroundings, routine, and companions.

We have a way of moving horses around like second-hand cars with little regard for the potential trauma it involves. With a little thought, this can be kept to a minimum:
- Plan ahead to avoid short-term moves where possible. For example, do you need to send your horse away to a livery yard when you go on holiday, or could a knowledgeable friend or professional 'animal sitter' care for them at home?
- Avoid frequent changes of yard. When looking for a new yard, research suitable options thoroughly to increase the chances of getting it right first time.

Moving home is very stressful, and you must give the horse time to settle.

- Be aware of the implications of pair-bonding *(see Herd Behaviour, page 130)*.
- When selling, ease the changeover by close liaison with the horse's new owners. Be sure they know the horse's usual routine, and are introduced to and become familiar with the horse. Allow the new owners to buy or borrow tack, rugs etc. which are familiar to the horse.
- Before the final exchange, make sure the horse has been recently shod, wormed etc.
- When taking on a new horse, bear all the above in mind. Do not expect too much of him straight away – settling down will take time.

MUSCLE DEVELOPMENT
See Suppleness, page 250; Schooling Exercises, page 230.

NAPPING
A horse naps when it refuses to go forwards or tries to spin round or run backwards. Once napping becomes a habit it can be a hard one to break. A large element of 'trying it on' often masks the original cause, as the nappy horse realises that by misbehaving in this way he can dictate when and where he goes. This is the very reason why encouraging a positive, forward-thinking outlook has to be the mainstay of everything we do with the young horse.

CAUSES OF NAPPING
Few horses are stubborn and unco-operative for the sake of it. There are many reasons why a horse may begin to nap. Finding a meaningful solution depends on pinpointing the cause:

Pain: Discomfort from badly-fitting tack, neglected teeth, a back or neck injury or sore feet (possibly from concussion on hard ground) must be discounted before concentrating on obedience.

Poor riding: A bad rider can create a reluctant horse, e.g. through rough 'nagging' hands, by restricting forward movement through too tight a rein, by giving contradictory aids, by using too strong a bit or being excessively nervous themselves.

Napping may be a symptom of insecurity.

Boredom/tiredness: Fatigue or sheer boredom can be enough for some horses to say "Enough's enough". Keep work interesting and at a suitable level for the horse's fitness or stage of training.

Nervousness/lack of confidence: Despite its bullying impression, napping is often a symptom of insecurity in horses. An anxious horse is drawn back so strongly to the safety of home and the herd that he ignores his rider. Napping often develops from shying (q.v.) that has not been dealt with by teaching the horse to face his fears.

DEALING WITH THE NAPPY HORSE

Tackling napping involves four key areas:

Re-establishing respect: The horse must be clear in his mind that you are his 'boss' and leader. His safety zone lies with you, not in his stable or with his companions. Join-up (q.v.) can help in this process. This relationship must be reinforced in every area of handling and riding.

Improving obedience: Work, with the help of a professional trainer if necessary, on improving the horse's understanding of the aids, responsiveness and obedience. Developing suppleness help create a more comfortable horse. School work will also increases your own effectiveness and sensitivity as a rider and the horse's confidence in you.

Boosting confidence & facing fears: Identify any specific anxieties that seem to trigger the napping or shying. Gradual, progressive exposure will help him realise there is nothing to fear *(see Habituation, page 113)*. Sacking out (q.v.) is a useful way to teach spooky and nervous horses to accept whatever comes their way.

Confidence can be boosted generally in many other ways, e.g. long-reining and taking the horse out to as many different places as possible (again, building up from the slightly unfamiliar to the very unfamiliar as his trust in you grows). Riding out with a reliable escort can have its uses, particularly with the confirmed napper. Here the nappy horse is progressively asked to walk further ahead until it is going by itself. However, particularly with youngsters, it is often better to do careful preparatory work, then teach them right from the start that they must face the world with only *you* as the comfort zone. Reliance on another horse is not permitted.

Effective riding: A nervous, rough or novice rider will never be able to cure a nappy horse. If you are in any doubt about your ability to see re-education through, come what may, ask an experienced, confident but quiet rider to help.

The rider must be sensitive to the slightest hesitation by the horse and be ready to send him on positively using strong, clear aids. Keep behind the movement and use a light, even contact to encourage him forwards. Avoid the temptation to simply hit the horse if he stops dead. Turn in tight circles to off-balance the horse before sending him on again. Praise any forwards step.

If he plants his feet completely, sit it out as long as it takes, trying the circles every so often. He must learn that you will not give up.

A change from a negative to positive attitude will take persistence and will not appear overnight.

NEAR
A term used to describe the horse's left-hand side.

NEGATIVE REINFORCEMENT (PUNISHMENT)
See Reinforcement, page 207.

NERVOUSNESS
See Shying, page 236; Head-shy, page 128; Traffic, page 255.

NEUROSIS
See Decision Making and Conflict, page 79; Stable Vices, page 241.

OBEDIENCE
See Discipline, page 82.

OFF
A term used to describe the right-hand side of the horse.

'ON THE BIT'
A horse cannot be said to be 'on the bit' simply because he is going along with his nose tucked in. He must be working in a correct, rounded outline, pushing himself actively forwards using his hindquarters into the rider's contact.
Over-bent, page 194; Outline, page 192.

ORPHAN FOALS
Anyone who has ever reared and trained a foal orphaned at birth will agree that it is a process that takes commitment, patience and determination!

When a foal is left motherless, by far and away the best option is to contact experienced hands (such as the National Foaling Bank in the UK) who can attempt to set up a fostering arrangement with a mare that has lost her own foal. Persuading the potential foster mare to accept an alternative foal is a difficult procedure in itself, with no guarantee of success. However, if bonding does take place, the foal can at least go on to experience a more normal childhood.

The orphan foal needs equine, as well as human company.

Many foals have been successfully hand-reared using artificial mare's milk until they are old enough for weaning. Physically they generally thrive. Psychologically, the effects can be far-reaching if those caring for the foal have little understanding of equine psychology. A bottle-reared foal will imprint (q.v.) exclusively on his human handler. Often this is allowed to go too far, with the foal being treated as a family pet and given insufficient contact with other horses.

In nature, it is the mare who dishes out discipline and, together with other senior herd members, teaches the foal equine social etiquette. Deprived of this relationship, the orphan foal often regards himself as the same being as his human handler. He behaves towards people as one young horse would to another, typically becoming over-familiar, nipping and barging. More crucial than ever for these foals are two essentials for any well-balanced youngster:

- Firm, consistent discipline.
- The company of other horses (preferably of mixed age, including other youngsters).

OUTLINE
The shape of the horse when it is being ridden, looked at from the side, is described as its outline. Outline involves every part of the body, from the position of the head to the way the hindquarters are working.

A correct outline is about more than looking pretty. It means the horse can use his body efficiently and be much more controllable and manoeuvrable. Ideally, outline should stay consistent through transitions and changes of direction – in fact whatever the horse does.

In the early stages of training, aim for a novice outline. This involves the horse:

- Carrying himself (rather than leaning on the bit or getting too much on the forehand).
- Being relaxed and supple with no tension or resistance (a lifted, swinging tail and contented expression are good indications).
- Rounding his back to lift the rider's weight and stepping underneath himself actively with his hind-legs.
- Carrying his head steadily, so the poll is the highest point and his nose is on, or slightly in front of a vertical line to the ground.

If the horse is regularly worked in this way, his muscles will

If a horse is worked in an outline, the muscles will develop correctly.

develop correctly so that he can sustain this outline for longer. In the same way, a horse constantly ridden in an incorrect outline will build the wrong muscles and make carrying the rider increasingly difficult and uncomfortable. Most important is strengthening and keeping supple the top-line muscles along the neck, back and quarters.

It is impossible to start trying to work a horse in an outline if he is tense, reluctant or not accepting the rider's hand or leg aids for any reason.

Greater collection comes gradually. As the horse becomes more advanced he carries an increasing amount of weight on his hindquarters. His centre of gravity moves back, lightening the forehand. The quarters drop and the head carriage becomes more elevated but he retains the flexion at the poll and a relaxed, natural impression. The whole frame is shortened and more condensed. This is an 'advanced' outline.

ACHIEVING AN OUTLINE

- A consistently good outline requires balance, impulsion, straightness, suppleness and rhythm (q.v.) *(see also Schooling Exercises, page 230; Lateral Work, page 167)*.
- First and foremost, the horse must be moving away from the leg and not be reliant on the reins for steering. Focus on pushing the horse forwards into a soft, yielding contact. Work on the exercises for shortening/lengthening the stride *(see Gaits, page 101)* to create impulsion from your leg, first in walk and then trot. Think in terms of asking him to condense his body into a shorter, springier frame like a concertina. Keep rein contact soft and elastic, not fixed. The horse should stay relaxed, gently mouthing the bit.
- Trying to pull the horse's nose in will only cause hollowing (q.v.). Get impulsion first before worrying about outline.
- Avoid an obsession with the position of the horse's head – think in terms of the whole body.
- Encourage the horse to work long and deep using plenty of flexing, turns and circles on a light contact.

193

- Keep it slow. Give the horse time to relax, think about your aids and balance himself. Prepare properly for each turn and transition.
- Check self-carriage by giving away the reins a little to see if the horse can hold his outline.
- Keep sessions short for young horses – working correctly is tiring.
- Encourage stretching after working in an outline by giving a long or loose rein.

OVER-BENT

A ridden horse is said to be over-bent if he is bringing the front of his face behind a vertical line to the ground so that the poll is no longer the highest point.

Horses may over-bend due to several reasons:
- Fear of accepting the bit (possibly due to a mouth, teeth or bitting problem).
- Rider having too strong or fixed a rein contact.
- Rider not creating enough forward impulsion (not the same as speed!).

An over-bent horse finds it easy to evade the action of the bit. Focus schooling on increasing impulsion (q.v.) and encouraging the horse to work through from behind, relaxing and stretching into a longer, lower outline. Use lots of flexion and half-halts to vary the pressure on the bit. Keep the rein contact light, soft and elastic. Yielding the inside rein slightly while maintaining a steady feel on the outside can help teach the horse to seek the contact.

An over-bent horse can evade the action of the bit.

O-P

OVER-FACING
Nothing destroys a horse's jumping confidence faster than being over-faced, i.e. asked to jump a fence that is too high or difficult for his ability or level of training. Over-facing inevitably leads to the horse starting to refuse or run out at fences. Patient schooling is needed to restore confidence, going back one or several stages to work over much smaller, simpler fences.

PACES
See Gaits, page 101.

PAIN
Sadly for the horse throughout the history of his domestication, he has suffered pain and discomfort silently, with the fortitude of a prey animal who must never give away his whereabouts, even when wounded. The ear-splitting urgency of a hurt dog's whimpering grabs his owner's attention in no uncertain terms. The horse also tells of his pain, but in other, quieter ways that require us to be far more observant.

Too often, the horse's willingness to please means his subtle hints are ignored and so he soldiers on, tolerating a pain threshold that then becomes almost 'normal'. He gets used to carrying himself in a certain way to compensate for a poorly-fitting saddle for example, creating an undercurrent of psychological stress and building up incorrect musculature that puts additional strain on his body. At last, when it all finally gets too much, he is forced to react more dramatically – yet is often either further abused or labelled as difficult.

No horse in discomfort can be expected to work at his best. Nothing creates tension more rapidly than pain. Yet most problem horses have been forced into their extreme behaviour by physical discomfort.

SIGNS OF PAIN/DISCOMFORT
Horses are not hypochondriacs – they cannot 'imagine' pain or fake the symptoms. Neither can they alter their own workload or lifestyle to cope with it, or call the vet, the farrier or the horse dentist themselves. All owners should be aware

of the signs of pain and be prepared to dig deep to find and eradicate the cause. This goes further than simply being able to identify lameness or the symptoms of a particular ailment.

General physical and behavioural symptoms of pain include:

- Tightness around the muzzle and nostrils.
- Eyes dull or fixed.
- Ears flopped to the side or slightly back, sometimes tense.
- Tucked-up appearance, possibly with dull coat.
- Irritability.
- Aggression.
- Evasions in ridden work, including reluctance to go forwards, bucking, rushing etc.
- Unsteady head carriage or avoidance of bit.
- Reluctance to be tacked up, mounted or even approached.

Like humans, some horses have a higher pain threshold than others – here again, knowing your own horse tells you how to handle the situation. Also bear in mind that horses do not always react by moving *away* from pain. While a reflex action will make a horse withdraw from a short, sharp stimulus, a constant, nagging ache is more likely to be leant *into (see Pressure, page 201)*.

COMMON CAUSES OF PAIN
- Poorly-fitting saddle.
- Poorly-fitting or unsuitable bridle/bit.
- Unbalanced or rough riding.

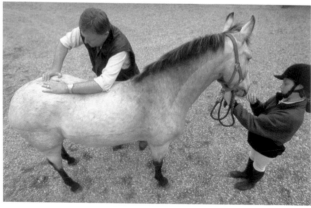

Check for lameness or back problems which could be causing discomfort.

- Neglected teeth.
- Injury to the spine or soft tissues of the neck, back or quarters.
- Chronic lameness or discomfort due to another physical condition (that may not yet have been diagnosed).

Every possibility should be checked thoroughly by a respected professional before any retraining of problem behaviour is attempted.

PARELLI NATURAL HORSEMANSHIP

Parelli Natural Horsemanship is a training method developed during the 1990s by Pat Parelli, a Colorado-based rodeo champion. PNH is a technique which has now achieved worldwide recognition. It is based on understanding and using equine psychology to establish the human handler as the boss, or 'alpha' horse in the herd, doing away with any need for fear or intimidation in our relationship with the horse. This is achieved by the use of body language and repetition of a set programme of games which mimic the way a hierarchy is set up within a natural group.

The student works with their horse through four different levels ('savvys') of knowledge, from basic communication skills to advanced ridden work. The only equipment needed is a head-collar or pressure halter (for more precise instructions), a soft, light, 5-metre (12-foot) rope, and a sturdy stick with short length of rope attached (called the carrot stick) and a hard hat.

Level one establishes a basic understanding of equine body language and sets up a balanced relationship between horse and handler based on respect and trust. It involves learning seven games, all from the ground. Each must be thoroughly understood before moving on to the next.

The first three games teach the horse the alphabet he will need for future lessons: to accept being touched all over, to move wherever asked, to move away from pressure. The others put these together to ask for particular manoeuvres, e.g. to back away then walk towards you, move in a circle around you, to walk sideways at a right angle to a fence and to squeeze through a gap between you and a fixed object.

Once the principles of the system are thoroughly understood they can be used to guide the horse through, in a straightforward, enjoyable way, any activity you may wish to do with him, e.g. loading, introducing equipment or backing.

As trust and skill increases, the programme progresses to riding the horse from a halter with two reins, then a single rein and finally to riding with no reins at all and working the horse at liberty from the ground.

PICKING UP FEET
See Feet and the Farrier, page 96.

PLACING POLE
A pole laid on the ground at a set distance from a fence (usually one non-jumping stride or a bounce distance) to help the horse judge his take-off accurately.

PLAY
Play takes up more of the young foal's time than any other activity besides eating and sleeping. Like all growing mammals, young horses not only love to play, but *need* to.

Young-horse play serves three vital roles:
• It increases physical confidence, co-ordination and balance, and encourages sharp reactions and acute senses.
• It familiarises the young horse to interaction with others. In this way, the young horse becomes at ease in social situations, learning how to use and interpret body language in order to obey the protocols of herd living.
• It provides the chance to practise and perfect survival skills. Foals play baby games which would be recognised by the wild horse – nipping and barging, mock-fighting, spooks, wild turns and hasty exits. Early on, play takes place near the safety of the mare, but, as confidence grows, the foal makes his acquaintance with other youngsters and serious rough-and-tumble starts (the colts, as ever, generally in the thick of it!) that sometimes needs to be put in order by an adult.

Older horses will also play when the feel-good factor is high.

All young horses, not only foals, need the opportunity to play. Preferably this should be with their peer group or a mixed-age group of youngsters where each feels secure and no one individual will always be the under-dog.

Older horses play too, in domestication, generally when the feel-good factor is high. A group stampeding around the field, a stabled horse exploding with bucks when released out to pasture – the sensation of freedom and sheer pleasure seems to reactivate their sense of play. Under saddle this 'joie de vivre' is not always so welcome!

Messing up the bedding or chewing the rug may be the stabled horse's way of fulfilling the urge to play, although constant frustration and boredom creates the neurosis of stable vices (q.v.). With a little thought and effort, it should be possible to arrange management routines so that every horse is able to spend time winding down at liberty in the field or other safe area.

Watching individuals at play gives clues about their character and attitude to life, whether they are bold or shy, worried or curious.

POLE-WORK
Poles on the ground can be used in 1001 different ways in training horses, both to develop work on the flat or jumping.

Pole-work:
- Develops suppleness and agility.
- Improves mental and physical co-ordination, teaching the horse to 'connect' different parts of his body.
- Builds muscle in the right places.
- Encourages concentration and accuracy.
- Encourages the horse to look where he is going and think for himself where he is putting his feet.
- Develops rhythm and balance.
- Boosts confidence.
- Adds variety to schooling sessions.
- Develops impulsion and collection, as the horse lowers his head, rounds his back and engages the hocks.

Exercises over poles are particularly useful for steadying horses that rush, and sharpening up lazy or careless horses.

INTRODUCING POLES
Pole-work may be introduced at any age. The young foal is

ready as soon as he is halter-broken to be walked in-hand over and around poles on the ground. Begin with single poles laid around the arena, progressing to a line of three spaced about 9 feet (2.5m) apart (adjust to the individual's stride).

- Take your time, reassuring the youngster and allowing him to stop and sniff the poles if he wishes.
- He may well knock the poles or stumble over them – even so, it is better not to fit boots as he needs to learn how this feels.
- If he is very suspicious, lay two poles end to end but leave a large gap between. Circle round and through the gap, gradually narrowing it until the horse is walking over the pole.

Include poles in this way in long-reining (and/or lungeing) sessions once these procedures are familiar *(see Long-reining, page 174; Lungeing, page 179)*. When ridden work has begun and the horse has a basic understanding of the aids, poles add a new dimension to home-work sessions.

Begin with single poles and then a line, as above, in walk and rising trot. Move on to some of the exercises below – choose according to the horse's stage of training. Aim for a regular, unhurried rhythm and rounded shape. At any sign of rushing, circle the horse away and work on a circle until he relaxes. If necessary, approach the first pole of a line in walk or go back to single poles.

WAYS TO USE POLES ON THE GROUND

- Set out a line of three or more parallel poles 9 feet (2.7m) apart (for walk/trot/canter) or 4'6" (2 to 1.5m) apart (for trot only). Adjust to suit the individual horse's stride. The hooves should fall mid-way between the poles in trot. Lines can be laid down the long sides of the arena, down the centre-line or across the diagonal.

Aim for a regular, unhurried rhythm when working with poles.

1.) Ride straight down the centre of the whole line (approach off a circle).

2.) Ride down the line but circle away at random points, left or right.

3.) Ask for halt at various places in the line (from walk only). This is useful for tense, excited horses.

4.) Lengthen the stride by taking them at an angle.

5.) Work on a figure of eight, changing the rein between poles.

6.) Work on a serpentine in and out of the poles.

7.) Work on circles of varying sizes, taking in two, three or four poles at a time.

- Lay three poles out in a fan shape (a distance of about 3ft at the inside and 4'6" at the outside will suit walk at the inner end and trot at the outer).

- Work sideways along a single pole, or between two parallel poles.

- Set out several squares of 12ft poles, leaving a narrow gap at each corner.

   1.) Walk in one corner and out another, turning to come back in over a pole, out over the one opposite and so on at random.

   2.) Circle within each square before moving out of the gap and on to another similar square.

   3.) Practise turn on the haunches within each square (size can be reduced for this).

- Set out poles parallel to create an L-shaped tunnel.

   1.) Moves sideways along the L, the forehand on one side of the pole and the quarters on the other, teach the horse to move sideways away from the leg.

   2.) Turn on the haunches or turn on the forehand at the corners.

   3.) Rein back quietly and slowly between the poles.

See also Grids, page 108.

POSITIVE REINFORCEMENT
See Reinforcement, page 207.

PRESSURE
It is a misconception that horses always move away from pressure. In fact, they generally move *into* any prolonged pressure, especially when tense, as anyone will know who has tried to shift a horse that has planted its own foot on theirs! Another example is the horse who sets his jaw against a hard-handed rider with an unyielding contact on the rein, or an unwilling loader who pulls back against the handler trying to drag him up that ramp.

Quick reactions and sensitive handling are needed when using a pressure halter.

The inter-pressure reaction is probably a survival technique: the horse that went *with* the lion's bite had a better chance of escaping with a lesser injury than the one that pulled away from the pain. The inter-pressure response can be used effectively by making all signals involving pressure light and intermittent, giving-and-taking. This applies to all situations, both in riding and handling.

Given this natural reaction, it takes time and patience to teach a horse circumstances when we wish him to move *away* from pressure, such as in halter-breaking. This can only be done by using avoidance conditioning, i.e. making going into the pressure uncomfortable *(see Halter-breaking, page 125).*

USING A PRESSURE HALTER

A pressure halter is a rope halter made up in such a way that when it is fitted, any constant pull on the lead-rope brings pressure to bear on the horse's poll. Because the horse finds this uncomfortable, he moves forward to relieve that pressure.

It can be used, with care, to teach a young horse to yield to pressure in halter-breaking. With a more mature animal that has been inadequately halter-broken and still leans into any pressure on the lead-rope, it is an invaluable aid.

A human will never win a battle of strength with a horse. Consequently, to deal with any horse that pulls back in any situation and retrain him to the halter, humans need to be given an aid to regain the upper hand. Dominance is not the real issue. It is a case of getting into a position where you are *able* to present the horse with a choice of actions, and clearly point to the better choice to make.

It is vital that a pressure halter is correctly used. The handler must be confident, quick-reacting and quick-thinking.

Insensitive handling or abuse of the halter will hurt and confuse the horse. If you are in any doubt about your ability, contact a professional trainer experienced in their use (such as one trained in Monty Roberts's/Richard Maxwell's methods.

- Constant pressure must be kept up on the lead-rope whenever the horse is resisting – whatever he does!
- That pressure must be relaxed the *instant* the horse takes a forwards step towards the handler.
- Any forwards step must be immediately rewarded with praise and a friendly rub or gentle pat.
- Begin schooling the horse to the halter quietly in the yard. Only move on to tackle any particular problem situation once you are certain he is respecting and responding to the slightest pressure, and have checked out other potential reasons for the horse's resistance.

PULLING

As described above, when a horse feels pressure, his natural response is to lean into it. Even when schooled to aids that teach him to back off pressure, this instinctive reaction often resurfaces whenever the horse is tense or stressed. This might be in a schooling situation, causing a horse to lean on to the bit when he is stiff or when the rider's hand is hard and fixed. Or it may be riding out, where the anxious rider pulls to stop a keen horse, only to find him 'taking hold'.

A pulling horse must have something to pull against. Causes of pulling include:
- A rider with fixed or stiff hands.
- Too strong a contact.
- Too severe a bit.

Riders need to work on maintaining a soft, elastic contact. Instead of relying on the rein aids to slow a horse that has begun to pick up speed, use the seat and body weight to steady and re-balance. Keep an onward-bound horse thinking by being creative about your schooling.

See also Bolting, page 55; Energy, page 89; On the Forehand, page 99; Schooling Exercises, page 230.

PUNISHMENT
See Reinforcement, page 207.

REARING

A rearing horse means business. Although rearing is natural behaviour in stallions (being a normal part of mating and fighting display), in mares and geldings the rear is a determined act of defiance. A horse that rears has either been pushed to the limits of its tolerance to resort to such an extreme action, or has come to learn how to intimidate its human handler or rider in this way.

Few horses suddenly start performing a full-blown circus act. The rearing horse usually gives plenty of warning through jibbing (q.v.) and napping (q.v.). If such behaviour is dealt with effectively, the horse should never learn to rear.

CAUSES OF REARING

As with all problems, check out every reasonable excuse before attempting remedial training. Extreme reluctance to go forwards can be provoked by:

• A heavy-handed rider.
• Too severe a bit.
• Discomfort from a badly-fitting bit, bridle or saddle.
• Overuse of schooling aids such as draw reins.
• Pain from injury.
• Fright.

What seems like plain disobedience can often be aggravated by over-confinement or an unsuitable diet too high in energy.

DEALING WITH A REAR

Knowing the horse in question will tell you whether he is just overfull of high spirits and 'trying it on', or if he is genuinely frightened and so needs further work on boosting his confidence, or whether he is single-mindedly trying to remove his rider.

Those that fall into the first two categories need:

• Plenty of varied and interesting work in the school that focuses on getting them going forwards and responding to the rider's leg.
• Strong, positive riding with a light, steady contact.
• Confidence-boosting measures *(see Napping, page 188).*

Where the horse is genuinely frightened, it makes sense to avoid the offending object/place until work has been done to make the horse less nervous.

The horse which has been confirmed as a rearer is a different matter. Once the possible causes have been investigated, he needs to be tackled by a very capable rider who can balance without the help of the reins and is also knowledgeable about horse psychology. Ask a professional for help if necessary, as this is a potentially dangerous situation. Attempting to hit the horse over the head with anything, as in many traditional 'cures', is usually ineffective, dangerous and cruel. Instead, try the following techniques:

- At the first signs (i.e. jibbing and half-rears) drive the horse forwards and unbalance him by pulling the head and neck to one side while using a strong inside leg.
- If possible, turn in a small circle.
- If the horse goes right up, the rider must act fast to go *with* him, holding on to the mane or around the neck if possible and leaning slightly to the side. At all costs, avoid hanging on by the reins which risks pulling the horse (and rider) over backwards.

A capable rider with a secure seat can persuade the horse that rearing is not such a smart idea in the following way:

- When riding a rearing horse, the rider carries with him a whip or short, soft rope.
- As the horse goes up, he leans his body forward but also reaches down to the side and flicks the whip or rope under the horse's belly.
- As the horse comes down, the rider drives him forwards strongly.

Few horses will expose such a vulnerable area to attack in this way repeatedly. Moreover, as it is coming from below, the smack is not associated with the rider in the way that numerous swipes from a whip or jabs with the spurs would be.

From this point the horse must be taken back to basics with his schooling to build a more positive, forward-thinking attitude.

REFLEXES
Reflexes are the simplest behavioural patterns: high-speed, automatic, subconscious responses to a stimulus. The reaction is immediate, short-lived and very specific, e.g. a cough to remove an irritation, the blink of an eyelid in bright light, or the flick of a muscle to dislodge a fly. A complex network of reflexes combine to synchronise muscles, controlling body movement and keeping the

horse on his feet.

The brain is not usually involved in a reflex action, but can have some influence. For example, it can command the horse not to react to every tiny movement in the corner of his eye. In training, habituation (q.v.) aims to damp down instinctive reflex actions in this way, using repeated exposure to increase the horse's tolerance threshold.

REFUSALS & RUN-OUTS
See Jumping, page 156.

REIN-BACK
A schooling exercise where the horse steps backwards in a straight line, moving his legs in diagonal pairs. He must keep a relaxed, rounded outline and take calm, even steps.

The idea of moving backwards is best introduced in-hand. Psychologically the horse is reluctant to move backwards, as he equates it with 'giving in'. It is also a difficult movement for the young, stiff horse to co-ordinate. A light touch with a schooling whip on the lower fore-leg helps indicate what you are asking.

Take time and care introducing rein-back as each horse may need slightly different aids to understand what is being asked. The rider sits lightly and gives the forward leg aids into a soft but resisting contact. Ask for just a few steps, one at a time. Having an assistant to gently push the horse back can help.

Rein-back is a useful exercise for helping bring the horse's quarters underneath him.

Take time and care introducing rein-back.

REINFORCEMENT

Reinforcement is any means used to encourage the horse to do the same thing next time he is asked the same request (positive reinforcement). Or, in the case of an unwanted action, to discourage him from doing the same thing (negative reinforcement). Knowing when, how much and what kind of reinforcement to use is essential to train a horse effectively *(see Conditioning, page 71).*

POSITIVE REINFORCEMENT

Any meaningful reward strengthens the link between a cue and a reaction, increasing the horse's motivation to repeat the response another time. Praise and rewards, and even bribery, are effective forms of positive reinforcement.

Praise and rewards: Horses are social beings. They have a natural inclination to want approval, which can be used by the handler to great effect. Show your appreciation of every correct reaction, not only your disapproval of mistakes or wrong responses.

For the horse to link the reward to his action (so encouraging him to repeat the action on the same cue or aid) it must be given during, or immediately afterwards (within three seconds).

Cessation of the stimulus, is a kind of reward in itself . A horse will not repeat his response to a signal if that signal goes on and on being given however he reacts to it! Back this up with more active praise or reward. Tidbits are appreciated momentarily but can lead to nipping and are little use to reward a horse on the move. Just as appreciated and much more effective in motivating horses and improving horse-rider communication, is passing on good vibes with liberal verbal

A reward must be given within three seconds of the action for a horse to make a connection.

praise, scratching the horse on the neck etc., i.e. natural signs of friendliness and approval.

Points to remember when using positive reinforcement:

- An action can be a reward in itself, e.g. ending a good flatwork session with some jumping, if that is what the horse enjoys most.
- Be patient, especially with young horses. Ignore mistakes and focus on consistently rewarding correct responses.
- Once a response is thoroughly learned, save the rewards for more challenging lessons so they retain their value.
- Make every learning experience as far as possible a positive, enjoyable one.

Bribery: The promise of a future reward can be a useful motivator. Bribes are most effective when they utilise a strong natural urge, e.g. asking a young horse to follow an older horse over a fence, or enticing the reluctant loader with a bucket of food. The effectiveness of the bribe depends on the individual and the circumstances.

See also Motivation, page 184.

NEGATIVE REINFORCEMENT

An action will be discouraged or avoided if it becomes linked with an unpleasant sensation or consequence.

Avoidance conditioning: With good timing, negative reinforcement can be used constructively, training the horse to respond to a lighter and lighter cue, e.g. the horse learns to yield to the slightest contact on a pressure halter by moving his head in the direction of the pull to avoid discomfort.

We use negative reinforcement in this way all the time. It is easy and often instant, but overused or misapplied, it stops working or has the opposite effect. Using it repeatedly without release will only cause the horse to ignore the signal, e.g. if the rider's legs keep banging against horse's sides even when the horse responds, the horse will begin to ignore the signal.

Punishment: Punishment, given after an undesirable action in order to discourage its repetition, is not well suited to horses for numerous reasons:

- Instant punishment *can* stop an action for the short term, but if that action is an old habit, it will recur.
- A horse has limited understanding of being punished for something he has *not* done, e.g. not taking off over a jump. Though an action may be performed to *avoid* punishment, it is generally repeated grudgingly with minimum effort,

rather than willingly.

- To be effective, any punishment must be lightning-fast (during, or within three seconds of, the misdemeanour). More often than not, this is physically impossible. If punishment can be administered within this time, the rider/handler must be certain the horse is at fault (i.e. it was not rider error, lack of understanding, physical inability, discomfort etc.). He must also ensure there is no confusion about why the horse is being punished (e.g. the horse refuses a jump, is turned away, then hit: here the turn rewards his refusal, but the smack then punishes him for the turn).

Any punishment creates tension and fear, which blocks learning. Furthermore, horses seem to become habituated to ineffectual punishment very quickly, e.g. shouting at a horse for banging its stable door at feed-time. In fact, having succeeded in getting your attention, this bad behaviour is actually being rewarded by your response, so is sometimes best ignored.

Punishment is therefore often counterproductive and has limited effectiveness as a way of conditioning a response. Negative reinforcement can also sometimes be ineffective because the horse has other more important things on his mind, e.g. a bolting horse will take no notice of the rider's rein aids, and a horse that does not load that often, does not seem to care how many times he is hit on the quarters.

If the horse is kept as calm and relaxed as possible about a learning experience, he is unlikely to need a very loud or strong negative reinforcement to discourage him from certain bad habits. Learning is far more effective and thorough when based on positive reinforcement. Praise and reward are motivations, whereas punishment demotivates. It is open to misuse, creates tension and misunderstanding, and blocks communication.

Discipline: Horses are not saints. Deliberate disobedience and testing of the boundaries of their relationship with humans will happen, even with the most docile of personalities.

Discipline is a constructive and necessary part of the horse-human relationship, but should be based on mutual respect as it is in the herd. Horses respond to being firmly and fairly treated. Discipline must be fair, quick, consistent, in tune with the crime and meaningful to the horse.

The good trainer gives the horse freedom to make mistakes, at the same time making the right response come naturally and easily. There is no need for force or fear. Breakdowns in communication are responsible for most inappropriate behaviour. Unable to escape a frightening or confusing situation, the horse fights it. It is up to us to learn to tell defiance from confusion or anxiety and act accordingly. *See also Discipline and Respect, page 82.*

REINFORCEMENT CHECKLIST
- Remove any negative reinforcement, i.e. discomfort, as soon as the horse responds. Reward each step towards a goal.
- Act quickly if the horse is to make a connection.
- Force is not necessary. Remember, the horse is a sensitive creature.
- Re-evaluate your use of positive/negative reinforcement if no progress is being made, or if increasingly strong reinforcement becomes necessary. Try to examine the problem from the horse's viewpoint.
- Use negative reinforcement only when absolutely necessary, or the horse will learn to ignore it.
- Make all learning experiences as positive and enjoyable as possible.

RELAXATION
See Tension, page 254; Play, page 198; Stress, page 241.

REPETITION
Although horses can learn from an experience that has happened only once, (particularly if there is a strong survival element), most lessons need cementing into the memory through repetition. Repetition acts as a powerful reinforcement as it strengthens the connection between a cue and an action.

Consistency is important if you want a horse to repeat an action. Psychology dictates that unless circumstances change, the pupil is most likely to do the same thing as he did before *(see Habit Strength, page 115)*. If you wish the horse to do something different, something has to change!

Too much repetition, of course, can have the opposite effect and becomes a type of negative reinforcement.
See also Reinforcement, page 207.

RESISTANCE
See Evasions, page 94.

RESPECT
See Discipline and Respect, page 82.

RESPONSIVENESS
As in the human race, there are horses whose one aim in life is to get away with making as little effort as possible! Breeding has much to do with attitude to energy-expenditure *(see Energy, page 89)*, **but other factors such as boredom, tiredness and even discomfort can play a part. This is evidenced by the number of switched-off riding school horses which undergo a complete personality change when finding themselves in a more stimulating environment, such as out for a hack, a cross-country round or sold to a private home.**

Personality aside, your target should be to teach every horse to react to the lightest of aids. A responsive horse will be far happier and less open to abuse than one whose riders feel they have to constantly thump or whip to get any kind of response.

CREATING A RESPONSIVE YOUNGSTER
Most youngsters take time to get used to the idea of having their movement directed by a rider. Few are naturally forward-going in their early days under saddle. Even so, from the start, aim for a quick response to the lightest possible signal. Bear the following pointers in mind, when trying to train your youngster:
- Do not confuse lack of understanding with reluctance. Make aids clear and short. Release and repeat if necessary until the horse responds. Do not rush lessons.
- There is no need to 'shout' with your aids! Use a light aid at first, only 'turning up the volume' gradually if there is no

Aim for a quick response to the lightest possible aid.

reaction.

- Nagging aids soon desensitise horses. A flick with the schooling whip when necessary, behind the girth, gives all the amplification you need. Back up with voice aids at first.
- Take care not to block GO aids with too tight a rein contact, or to jab the horse in the mouth if he jumps forwards suddenly.
- Praise quick responses.

IMPROVING RESPONSIVENESS

General points include:

- Keep sessions short and sweet.
- Establish obedience in an enclosed space before asking for it outside the arena.
- Make sure the horse fully understands what he is being asked (i.e. the exercise suits his level of education and the rider is being clear and effective).
- Over-strong aids in the past may have 'deadened' the horse. Avoid compounding this with ever-heavier signals. Use lots of positive reinforcement.
- Make a clear difference between when your horse has got it right (by ceasing the aid and praising him) and when he has got it wrong (by giving a stronger aid).
- After giving each aid, allow the horse a moment to respond before increasing the strength of the signal. Use a planned sequence of increasing the severity and releasing or yielding between each stage. For example, in downward transitions, first squeeze the rein; fix the elbows and squeeze; then use a short tug plus a voice aid; followed by a short tug with the horse directed towards fence/wall. Or, to increase impulsion, the following can be used: first squeeze briefly with the lower leg; then nudge firmly; followed by a sharper nudge plus a voice command; and finally, a sharp nudge plus flick of a whip behind-leg.
- Competent riders can use blunt spurs for clarity when the horse does not respond immediately to the original aid given without the spur.
- Remember over-bitting or harsh hands will make the horse reluctant to go forwards. Resistance may be exaggerated by a drop-type noseband or straight-bar bit.
- Boredom often causes laziness and evasion. Make work varied and *fun!* Include pole-work, jumping and games. Get out of the school!
- Take care not to overtire the horse. Rest between exercises by walking on a loose rein. Increase work gradually as

*Make learning fun –
take the opportunity
to get out of the
school as often as
possible.*

fitness improves.
* Improving the horse's all-round obedience will have a positive knock-on effect on his responsiveness under saddle.

SCHOOLING THE LAZY/UNRESPONSIVE HORSE
* Be positive! Vague, half-hearted aids will not inspire enthusiasm. All aids need to be accurate, clear and consistent.
* Keep an effective position. Avoid tipping forwards in an effort to urge the horse on – the lower leg must stay relaxed, beneath you. Hold the hands correctly for maximum sensitivity.
* Begin as you mean to go on. Make working-in brisk and businesslike.
* An early canter can motivate an idle character (try taking up a slightly forward position to really energise him). Now maintain this activity. Ask for some canter whenever you need an energy injection.
* Keep up an active rhythm throughout but avoid hurrying your horse. Know his natural rhythm – big horses often have a naturally slow tempo.
* Plan each move properly, so the horse is as balanced as possible. Give him a reasonable chance of complying with your request.
* Create energy, then control it. Focus on getting the horse going forwards from the leg, then reacting to the hand. Once he responds smartly to start, stop and steering, niceties like outline will come more easily.

IMPROVING RESPONSIVENESS IN SPECIFIC AREAS
Mobilising the quarters: Ride lots of transitions in quick

succession (this also gets the horse's attention). Be accurate and assertive, backing up slow responses with another aid or instant flick of the whip. Stop as soon as the horse reacts. Use exercises such as lengthened strides *(see Going Forward, page 100; Impulsion, page 143; Lateral Work, page 167)*. By improving longitudinal suppleness, energy created behind can be controlled by the hands rather than drifting out the front door.

Improving responsiveness to the hand: Work on a circle. Practise squeezing the rein in halt until the horse 'gives' and brings in his head, then immediately soften the contact. Move on to achieving the same in walk (try on a 10-metre circle at first), then trot.

Work on improving the front-to-back connection, getting a balance between hand and leg. Use circles and bends to encourage softness, pushing from the inside leg to the outside hand. Keep legs on and contact light and elastic. Test the contact by loosening the inside rein to see if the outline is maintained *(see also Outline, page 192; Impulsion, page 143)*. Allow stretching every so often, but keep up forwards momentum.

RESTRAINT

In an ideal world, your horse would stand quietly, accepting whatever you need to do to it, however uncomfortable or unpleasant. Real life, of course, is different!

The horse is a prey animal whose instincts drive him to avoid any threats to his survival. A systematic programme of training based on sound equine psychology will certainly go a long way towards building up trust and obedience. This will pay off when the horse is asked to face a stressful situation or is asked to tolerate sensitive or painful areas being touched.

However, the strength of the instincts that drive him to flee from, or fight against, any threat or pain is enormous. Sick or injured horses are often particularly anxious and unpredictable. To enable first aid and other procedures to be carried out safely and properly, physical restraint is sometimes necessary for the sake of all involved.

The degree and type of restraint you may need to use depends on:
• The horse's level of education.
• His physical maturity.
• His character.

• What needs to be done.

The handler should wear sensible footwear, gloves and a hard hat and get knowledgeable help if necessary. Choose an enclosed area with safe footing. Always hold the horse on the same side as the person giving treatment or working with it. Begin with the minimum restraint, only increasing it if the horse does not respond.

METHODS OF RESTRAINT

Controlling the head: Control of the body and limbs is almost impossible without gaining control of the head.

• A bridle gives more control than a head-collar, but there is a risk of damaging the mouth if the horse resists violently.
• Consider the use of a chain lead or pressure halter for horses schooled to respond to one.
• Avoid hanging on to the head. Use short pulls if necessary.
• Talk quietly to the horse to calm and distract him. Giving a hay-net can sometimes help.

Holding up a fore-leg: This can be sufficient for well-handled horses. It has the advantage of keeping the horse still and preventing cow kicking *(see Feet and the Farrier, page 96 for tips on picking up feet).*

• Position the horse four-square with his weight evenly spread.
• Have a helper hold up the fore-leg on the same side as the procedure (or the opposite one if a fore-leg is being treated).
• Where a hind-leg is being dealt with, hold up the fore-leg on the same side.

A twitch stimulates production of the body's natural sedatives.

- Do not allow the horse to lean on the assistant holding the leg.
- Grip and squeeze a handful of loose skin on the side of the neck, near the base. This is good for head-shy horses, but will only work for short procedures, e.g. bandaging.

Twitch: This is thought to work by stimulating production of the body's natural sedatives, endorphins. A proper humane twitch is preferable to an improvised broom-handle with loop of string.

- Use a twitch on the top lip *only*. Never use on the lower lip or on the ear (this is illegal in the UK).
- Stand to one side, never in front of the horse.
- Gather as much of the upper lip as possible into the loop. Twist slowly until the pressure is firm and the loop cannot slip off. Knot the lead-rope of the head-collar to the twitch handle to stop it swinging about if the handler loses grip. Scratch the neck and talk calmly to reassure the horse.
- The twitch can be loosened or tightened slightly if the horse gets restless.
- Clamp-type twitches can be applied then fastened to the head-collar to leave one hand free.
- Relax pressure on the twitch at regular intervals.

Holding a horse down: This is used to prevent injury when the horse is lying flat-out but periodically struggling without success to get up.

- Put a head-collar and lead-rope on the horse.
- Using your full weight, kneel on the extended neck and put a hand on the head.

Restraining foals: Foals and weanlings are easily panicked and must be restrained carefully and calmly.

- Handle foals close to the mare. Cup one hand around the neck and the other around the rump so the body is cradled.
- Weanlings can be backed up against a wall with the tail held firmly near the base to prevent flipping backwards or sitting down. Work the hand gradually up the neck, cup the ear and squeeze it firmly but gently to help restrain the head.
- For weanlings, a figure-of-eight bandage can be useful alongside a head-collar and lead-rope. Pass a soft rope, webbing line or bandage around the quarters. Knot at the withers and run down the shoulders and over the chest. Pressure can be exerted on different parts of the web to control movement.

Using sedatives: It is obviously not desirable to resort to sedating a horse regularly. However, if there is a procedure that throws him into total panic, it may be safer and less traumatic for all concerned to administer a sedative (either orally, or if a vet is present, by injection). With a calm horse, you then have the opportunity to use the occasion as a constructive learning experience rather than another confrontation.

REWARDS
See Reinforcement, page 207.

RHYTHM
Rhythm refers to the regularity of the strides or the steps within each stride. Each should have a clear beat, cover an equal distance and be of equal duration.

A horse can only keep up a consistent outline if he is moving in rhythm, and to do this he must also be balanced. Finding balance difficult, young horses often have an erratic rhythm, but schooling helps teach the horse to move as in balance and rhythmically with a rider as he does naturally, so he can then use his body just as efficiently.

WAYS TO IMPROVE RHYTHM
- Concentrate on maintaining the same speed. Using music with a strong beat (or a metronome) while you school can help create and maintain a tempo and adds an element of fun.
- With young horses it is easiest to work on rhythm in rising trot first. Remember to change diagonal frequently.
- Note the number of strides used between certain points around the school and aim to always use the same amount. Pole-work is also useful.
- Do not go too fast or hurry the horse along. Staying balanced and keeping steps regular is easier when the rhythm is slow.
- Increased suppleness front-to-back helps with rhythm, freeing the back so it can 'swing'. Work long and low, without letting the horse collapse onto its forehand, to help keep the back supple and strengthen the quarters.
- As the trot becomes more balanced and rhythmical, the canter steps will improve. Walk (q.v.) is generally the last pace to develop and the most difficult. Take care not to force the horse to shorten his steps.

RIG
A rig (cryptorchid) is a male horse that has retained a

testicle in its body after castration. Although apparently a gelding, a rig will show some stallion-like behaviour, often becoming aggressive and trying to mount mares. He may be able to mate successfully.

Suspected rigs need to be examined by a vet, and surgery is needed to remove the remaining testicle.

ROBERTS, MONTY

A former US rodeo rider, Monty Roberts made a name for himself in the UK after being asked to demonstrate his Join-up method of 'starting' young horses to HM The Queen. His techniques were developed from years of observation of wild horses in Nevada and as an alternative to rough and domineering techniques of horse-breaking commonly used on ranches in the American West at that time.

A relationship of trust and respect between horse and man is set up using communication via body language the horse understands (termed *Equus* by Roberts). Once the deal has been struck, the horse is ready to accept the man as his herd leader and look to him for security and direction.

Public attention has focused on Roberts' demonstrations showing how join-up enables even an unbroken young horse to be tacked up and ridden in a matter of minutes. However, join-up is only one part of a much broader approach that seeks to create this partnership with the horse from its earliest days, consolidate it long-term using many other conventional, tried-and-tested methods and also includes effective remedial work.

Students of Monty Roberts, who have taken up and developed his methods in the UK, include Richard Maxwell, Kelly Marks, and Michael Pearce.
See also Join-up, page 153.

ROLLING

Most horses love to roll. Rolling is an action which serves a useful purpose too. Horses leading a natural life will roll both to help relieve themselves of itching parasites, and to impregnate their coats with the scent of their herd's territory. Dusty or muddy spots are usually preferred (snow, sand and fresh bedding are also favourites).
When about to roll, the horse will sniff and paw at the ground before bending at the hocks and knees and going down fore-

Rolling relieves itchiness, and it also impregnates the coat with the scent of the herd's territory.

hand first. A supple horse will roll right onto his spine to get a satisfying scratch along the withers, neck and poll before rolling over to do the other side. Older, stiffer horses usually do one side, get up, then go down again to do the other. Getting up is done fore-hand first with a push from the hindquarters and is usually followed by a good shake.

The speed and relish with which a sweaty horse gets down to roll in the mud after a ride shows how much he appreciates the chance to relax, scratch himself and restore circulation in this way.

Watch regularly to check when and how your horse rolls. A horse that rarely rolls may be tense, insecure or have a physical problem. Struggling to get up afterwards is another warning sign.

ROUTINE
We are all creatures of habit. When life is predictable we all feel safer and more secure. No sudden shocks or nasty surprises mean no need to be constantly on the alert for threats of danger. If this is true for humans (the hunters), imagine how much more it means to the horse (the hunted).

Living alongside humans throws up constant challenges to the horse's natural behaviour. The domesticated horse is dependent on people to fulfil every one of his most basic needs and drives, including food and water, company and freedom.

If these needs are met adequately and regularly, he can relax, as experience tells him there is no cause to worry. On the other hand, if he does not know from one day to the next when (or even if) his meal will arrive, whether he will be turned out or not, or who his companions will be (friend or foe?) he is in a constant state of anxiety.

A yard with a sensible, established routine that avoids continual alterations in the way things are done will have much more settled, contented horses than the one where timings, staff and horses are forever changing.

Some horses are so hypersensitive or lacking in confidence they are affected by even the slightest changes to accepted routines, such as in the way they are ridden, the place they are fed or who grooms them. Planning and sticking to a better routine always has a calming effect. When there is a specific event or activity that causes excitement or stress, making that activity part of the regular routine will help the horse to accept it as unremarkable and not worth making a fuss over.

Habit strength (q.v.) can have its drawbacks, however. Too rigidly-fixed a routine can make some horses over-dependent on things always happening the same way. Your horse should receive constant reassurance, but not lose his adaptability. This can be achieved by:

- Exposing all youngsters to as many different variations on every experience as possible, teaching them flexibility *(see Discrimination, page 83)* and increasing their confidence to take life as it comes.
- Encouraging all horses to take decisions, and to think flexibly and independently, e.g. to stand still without

Horses thrive on routine.

If a rug is comfortable and fits well, you should avoid the problem of rug-tearing.

needing to be tied up, or kept in a yard where he can choose to come in or out of the stable at will.

RUGS
See Equipment, page 92.

RUG-TEARING
We humans choose our clothes carefully and if they are not comfortable we take them off and swap them for something else. A horse does not have the same option, although many try, and some succeed!

The horse that bites at and tears his rugs is making a statement as clearly as he knows how. Finding the cause of his frustration and relieving his discomfort is entirely up to his carer. Horses tear clothing because of:

Irritation: Choose rugs with care for sensitive-skinned animals, opting for cotton or synthetic linings rather than wool.
Discomfort: The rug does not fit, or is making the horse too hot.
Boredom: "Well, it's something to pass the time..."
Frustration: Rug-tearing can be a displacement activity, expressing annoyance at a different, unrelated issue.
See also Stable Vices, page 241.

RUSHING
See Jumping, page 156; Bolting, page 55.

SACKING OUT

This is an excellent way of desensitising very tense, excitable or flighty horses of any age. The horse is taught to accept any strange or unexpected sight, sound or touch. Consequently, he is able to realise there is no need to be in a constant state of anxiety.

The following steps can be taken to accustom your horse to sacking out. Correctly implemented, sacking out should result in a horse which is quieter and more relaxed in every way:

- Take a large sheet of plastic (at least 6ft x 4ft, approx 2 x 1 metres). Fold it up until it fits in the palm of your hand.
- Begin in a familiar enclosed space such as the stable. Fit a head-collar and tie up or hold the rope loosely.
- Wipe the plastic all over every part of the horse's body, starting with the neck and sides but moving gradually to include the head, ears, legs and belly. Once complete, begin again, this time 'scrunching' the plastic as you go.
- Whatever the horse's objections, continue until he is totally relaxed about this. Give plenty of praise for the right response.
- Once this is accepted, unfold the plastic *once*. Repeat.
- Progress by unfolding the sheet *once* only when the horse is completely accepting of the previous stage.
- Continue until you are able to wipe, scrunch and even flap the entire sheet, unfolded, over and around the horse's whole body, including his head.
- Work on being able to do this outside the stable.
  Remember that sessions should be frequent, but not too long (15 minutes is plenty at first). The whole process could take between two sessions and 20 sessions (a matter of hours or weeks). When starting a new session, recap the previous stage.

SADDLE-FITTING

Any piece of equipment fastened on the horse's back will restrict his natural movement to a degree. A well-fitted saddle should keep this to an absolute minimum, allowing the horse to move as freely as possible. Conversely, a badly-fitting saddle can cause considerable psychological and physical damage. A horse forced to move and carry a

rider in a saddle that not only restricts his movement but, in some cases, actually causes pain, must be in a constant state of stress and trauma.

For years saddle trees (frames) were created in dozens of different styles to suit the rider's taste, yet only three basic shapes (narrow, medium or wide), to fit every single horse. Fortunately, studies of the way horses move have now led to advances in design and much greater emphasis is now placed on the comfort of the horse. Advanced techniques have helped horses that have proved difficult to fit with saddles, by locating pressure 'hot-spots' and developing equipment that can adapt and flex with a horse's motion.

SIGNS OF POSSIBLE SADDLE PROBLEMS
Any of the following may be a symptom of a problem in the soft tissue in the back or bones of the spine, either caused, or aggravated, by a badly-fitting saddle:
• The horse is 'cold-backed', reluctant to be saddled up or have the girth tightened.
• The horse lifts its back, tenses or fidgets when mounted.
• Bucking.
• Rushing.
• Hollowness.
• Napping.
• Sensitivity to being touched around the saddle area.
• Lack of level bearing or stiffness to one side.
• Reluctance to accept the bit and go in correct outline.

GENERAL POINTS ON SADDLE-FITTING
• Each horse must be fitted individually for his own saddle. Saddles should not be shared by horses. Just because a saddle comes with a horse, do not assume it fits him!

A saddle must be fitted to the individual, taking into account their particular conformation and movement.

- Horses change shape according to their age, condition and fitness level. Reassess the saddle fit regularly.
- Saddles change shape as the stuffing settles and moulds to the horse's body. Reassess the saddle condition regularly.
- Saddle fit should be assessed by a professional, who is knowledgeable on horse anatomy and movement, and aware of up-to-date thinking. It should be checked both with and without a rider, standing still and on the move. Never buy a saddle without fitting it to the horse.
- The saddle should sit level on the back, with the lowest part of the seat mid-way between the pommel and cantle. There must be no twisting or rocking when the rider is rising (posting) to the trot.
- Daylight should be visible down the whole gullet, even with the rider leaning forward or back. Several fingers should fit between the withers and pommel at all times. Any movement side-to-side at the withers suggests too wide a fit. Pinching at the sides of the withers indicates too narrow a fit.
- No part of the saddle should impede movement, even with the shoulders at full stretch. At the back, the saddle should not reach beyond the last rib or over the weak loin area.
- The panels are the shock-absorbers of the saddle and should spread the rider's weight over as wide an area as possible. Stuffing should give good protection but not be over-tight.

SAFETY
People who work with horses hardly need reminding that they are big, strong animals that will never be totally predictable. Even so, every day at almost every yard, experienced riders and handlers can be seen taking safety risks. Nine times out of ten, even 99 out of 100, we get away with it. However, accidents do happen, sometimes serious ones. Most are avoidable.

Being aware of safety issues is more important than ever with young horses, whose behaviour can be erratic or challenging. Always:
- Wear the correct gear for the job: including a helmet, gloves and strong, safe footwear.
- Use the correct gear on the horse, properly fitted.
- Consider and work with the horse's natural inclinations, not against them.

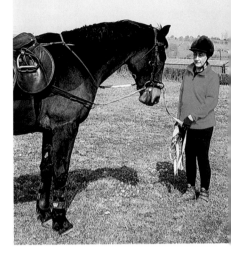

Always wear the correct gear when working with horses.

- Expect respect and discipline from the start with youngsters. When taking on an older horse whose manners are not up to scratch, work through the problem logically, using fair and consistent discipline that is meaningful to the horse.
- Never get into a physical battle of strength with a horse. You cannot win.
- Do not provoke confrontation by asking too much of the horse. Look for the reason behind mistakes and misunderstandings.
- Seek help and advice from an experienced professional about serious behavioural problems.

SCHOOL MASTER
An experienced, well-mannered and reliable horse ideal for a novice rider or to use alongside a young or nervous horse for reassurance and giving confidence.

SCHOOLING AIDS
Schooling aids are items of equipment used by trainers to help indicate more clearly to the horse how he is expected to go.

The use of schooling aids has always been controversial. Riders who look upon 'gadgets' as a short-cut to avoid the input of time and patience required for calm, effective schooling, or to compensate for ineffective riding, are both misusing the gear and missing the point.

Schooling aids have their place, but are not a magic wand that will transform a stiff, resistant or very novice horse into a dressage star. However, used appropriately, with care and respect, an aid is able to help a rider or trainer at any level to:

- Communicate clearly and speedily to the horse how he is expected to work.
- Improve control.
- Increase obedience.
- Develop suppleness and work the muscles needed for a correct outline.
- Remind the horse how to perform a particular manoeuvre.
- Overcome schooling or communication problems.

USING SCHOOLING AIDS

Consider the use of a schooling aid carefully. It is not a fashion item. In the wrong hands all of these gadgets are capable of doing more harm than good. Just as with any equipment an athlete would make use of in the gym, they should always be used with care and with respect. Ask yourself:

Does the horse really need it? Perhaps the rider needs to give clearer aids, work in a different way or check for possible causes of a horse's resistance or tension (such as physical discomfort). Ask the advice of an experienced trainer before opting for a gadget.

Is the horse going forwards with enough impulsion? This is crucial. Schooling aids work by 'catching' the energy created by the quarters, so encouraging the horse to round his back. This frees up his forehand and enables him to lengthen his strides. If there is not sufficient energy coming from behind to start with, all that will happen is that restriction of the horse's movement will shorten his stride further. The effect will be the opposite to the one intended.

Is the equipment fitted so as to encourage, rather than hold or force, the correct outline? No training aid should come into effect unless the horse raises his nose *beyond* a vertical line to the ground. All aids should be fitted so they do not come into play when the horse is carrying his head parallel to this line, or a good hand's width past this point. Fastening any tighter than this will only teach the horse to over-bend (q.v.), shorten his stride and create tension, or even create panic.

General points to bear in mind include:

- Choose with the help of someone who has successfully used the aid before. But remember every aid depends on the ability of the person using it.
- Any new equipment should be introduced gradually and loosely until the horse gets used to its action.

- Familiarise yourself with the way the gear fits. Take great care when putting it on and taking it off.
- Work the horse in well before fitting the aid and remove to allow stretching afterwards.
- Working in this way is tiring, particularly for the young, novice or stiff horse. Build up slowly from 5 minutes to a maximum of 30 minutes, working equally on both reins. Do not use the aid for your whole schooling session.
- Look on the aid as a short-term means to an end. It is a way to produce an effect that can then be recreated using the seat and legs only. If there is no improvement, it is not working. Keeping it on all the time is pointless!

TYPES OF SCHOOLING AID

There is now a huge range of 'gadgets' available, some designed for use when lungeing, others only for riding and others for combined use. Take advice from an expert on your ability and the level of difficulty for the horse, before choosing and using any aid.

Draw reins and running reins: Running reins attach under the saddle flaps and feed through the bit rings back to the rider's hands. Draw reins loop from the girth, through the bit ring to the rider. Both apply pressure to the bars of the mouth, making the horse bring in his head, stretch his top-line and come into a short, round shape. Draw reins also have a lowering effect.

- The rider should be competent at using two sets of reins, to avoid relying solely on the training rein.
- Fit draw reins from the inside to the outside of the bit ring.
- Feed through a loose neck-strap for safety.
- Elasticated reins allow for more flexibility.
- Ride forwards from the leg, up to the rein. Avoid the temptation to pull the horse's head in, making him over-bend and run on. Allow and return to using the direct rein as soon as the horse understands what is required and complies.

Market Harborough: A type of rein and martingale in one. It runs from the girth to a neck-strap, where it splits into two. Each strap runs through a bit ring and clips on to the normal rein about half-way along. Acts like a running martingale when the horse is going correctly, but exerts strong pressure on the bit if the head is brought up or out.

- The Market Harborough is very useful in discouraging hard pullers or to regain control when working through a problem.

A Harbridge encourages the horse to lower his head.

- Avoid fitting it too tightly and causing resistance.
- The rein is operated by the horse rather than the rider, and so is less easily misused by novice hands.

Harbridge: This fastens to the girth and splits at the chest into two elasticated straps that clip to the bit rings.

- It is a useful basic item to encourage the horse to lower his head and prevent him raising it too far.
- It can be used when riding or lungeing.

De Gogue: The De Gogue fixes to the girth and splits at the chest into two straps that pass over the head-piece, down each cheek, through the bit ring and back to a clip at chest level. It puts pressure on the poll and bit to encourage the horse's head down and in, raise the shoulders, round the back and engage the quarters.

- It should be fitted so that a triangle shape is formed equally on both sides.
- It can be used for riding or lungeing.

The Chambon is used for lungeing only.

Flexi-reins help to produce a constant contact.

- It works independently of the rein.
- The De Gogue requires knowledge and experience for correct use.

Chambon: This passes from the girth, splitting at the chest up to a special head-piece with pulleys either side, then down the sides of the face to the bit rings. It develops suppleness in the back by encouraging the horse to lower and stretch his neck out and down, and creates a free, swinging stride.

It is useful for those horses that tend to tense their necks and come behind the bit.

- Use the Chambon with a loose neck-strap to avoid the leg becoming caught.
- It should be used for lungeing only.
- Avoid fitting the Chambon too tightly.

Side-reins: *see Lungeing, page 179.*

Pessoa Training System: A set of ropes pass from the girth through the bit rings, back through D-rings on the sides of a roller, around the horse's quarters to the top of the roller. These ropes encourage more active use of the quarters as well as developing balance and correct outline. The PTS exercises and develops correct muscles along the back and neck.

- The fitting of this aid is adjustable according to the horse's level of training.
- The PTS should be used for lungeing only.

Equilonge: A rope passes from the girth to feed through a pulley attached to the bit ring, up the side of the face, over the poll, through the pulley the other side and back to the girth. Pressure is exerted on both poll and bit if the head carriage goes too high.

- Use the Equilonge for riding or lungeing.

- Fit carefully to avoid too much 'swing' or unsafe, loose straps.
- The Equilonge is adjustable according to the horse's level.

Flexi-Rein: Short elastic inserts that fit between the end of the rein and the bit, designed to produce a constant contact and absorb jarring or tension from the rider's hand aids.
- These are very simple to use.
- Flexi-reins are ideal for novice riders, young horses or horses unwilling to accept the bit.

Schoolmasta: Leather reins are connected by a strap to a specially-designed numnah with a pulley. The effect of this aid is one of lightening the forehand and therefore discouraging pulling, leaning on the bit (as the horse only pulls against himself) and snatching at the bit (as it gives a consistent but not fixed contact).
- Can be used with, but independent of, ordinary reins.
- The aid is suitable for riding and lungeing.
- It should be adjusted loosely at first, gradually being brought in until the correct head carriage is achieved.
- Suitable for novice or experienced riders.

Abbot-Davies Balancing Rein:
Attached to the girth, splitting at the breast into two, each rein passes through a pulley either side of a strap connecting the bit rings. The reins then clip on to the ordinary reins about half-way along. The balancing rein helps to maintain correct balance and head position without restricting the horse, and develops correct muscles.
- The rein produces the same kind of effect as draw reins but is more suitable for the less experienced user.
- It should be used for short periods only at first, when the horse should be ridden forwards well.

SCHOOLING EXERCISES

Riding around the outside of the arena doing the odd circle or loop might exercise a horse, but will not go far towards improving his way of going. Perhaps the rider is not sure what else to do with their horse. Or so preoccupied with trying to get their horse going 'on the bit' they are not actually making use of techniques that will help the horse to do just that.

By structuring your sessions around schooling figures you can make the most of time spent in the school, knowing that every move correctly ridden is bringing you closer to your objective of a supple, balanced, active and obedient horse.

INGREDIENTS OF A SCHOOLING SESSION

The exact questions you ask of your horse and your
expectations of him will depend on his level of training.
However, the basic ingredients of the recipe remain the same:
straight lines, curves and transitions.

Straight lines: It is impossible to work on straightness on the
outer track. Move off the outer track on to the quarter, centre,
three-quarter lines and diagonals. Practise keeping the fore-
feet stepping on the same track as the hind-feet while doing:

- Half-halts.
- Transitions.
- A few lengthened strides.
- A few steps of shoulder-in or leg yield.
- Turning accurately onto the line.
- Giving and re-taking the reins.
- Making a shallow loop off the line.

See also Straightness, page 248.

Curves: Any movement involving a turn, bend or curve is
encouraging suppleness and balance. Include in your session:

- Large (65-feet/20-metre) and small (32 to 40-feet/10 to 15-
  metre) circles (the more stiff or novice the horse, the larger
  the circle should be).
- Corners and turns.
- Figure of eight loops (this can also be incorporated within a
  large circle, or to practise changing canter leads).
- Serpentines (q.v.).
- Loops (q.v.).
- Spiralling in and out from a large circle.
- Transitions on the circle.
- Lateral work (q.v.).
- Giving and re-taking the rein (particularly the inside one, to
  check the horse is not leaning on it).
- Flexing to the outside for a few steps.

  Riding movements involving curves require the rider to
concentrate on accuracy, creating uniform bend through the
horse's body, giving clear aids and preparing the horse well
for each change
of bend.

*See also Curves and Circles, page 76; Steering, page 247;
Suppleness, page 24.*

NOW BE CREATIVE!

These curves and straight lines can be combined to create a
limitless number of different movements to make up your

schooling session. There is no need to get 'hung up' on sticking to traditional school figures. As long as what you ask your horse is sensible, he has space and time to do it and is well prepared for each change of pace or direction, simply focus on keeping things flowing smoothly.

Remember that it is only by constantly asking your horse to bend his body one way, straighten it and bend it again the other way that he will become more supple. Likewise, it is only by preparing for each movement properly

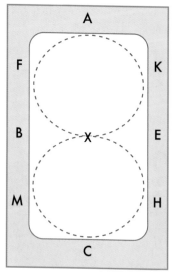

A figure of eight can be used to practise canter leads.

and asking clearly that your horse will learn to respond to aids obediently.

- Keep moving! Try to achieve more than simply going large around the school.
- Avoid too many 20-metre circles. Even if the horse is very novice or stiff, incorporate other movements with shallow curves.
- Working in a properly-marked arena will help you ride positively and accurately.
- Keep off the outside track as much as possible. Make all transitions during movements.
- Remember to work equally on both reins.
- Schooling figures work the horse hard. Allow regular relaxation on a loose rein, particularly if your horse is young or not used to much exertion.
- If you school by yourself, try to develop 'feel' for the quality of the way your horse is going. Award yourself a 'mark' for each movement, as if you were a dressage judge. If you felt a figure was not as good as it could have been, come around and try again.
- Allow yourself plenty of time for what you hope to achieve. Stay calm and cool – there is always another day. Training your horse is a serious business, but you will both enjoy

S

schooling sessions more if you look on them as 'playing about in the arena' trying this and trying that, rather than as a life-or-death situation!
- Try to end on a good note. If you are having problems, go back a stage to an easier exercise and do that again well before finishing.

SEAT
See Aids, page 30.

SERPENTINE
A schooling movement consisting of a series of half-circles joined by a series of straight lines, creating an S-shape. The serpentine movement is excellent for suppleness and balance, making sure the horse is worked equally on both sides and teaching the rider to co-ordinate the aids.

Any number of loops can be ridden but the more loops, the more supple the horse must be. Three, four and five loops are enough to begin with.
- Make sure each half-circle is a full and accurate one.
- Keep all the loops an even size.
- Ride a few straight strides across the centre line. Use this time to prepare for the next change of bend and to change the diagonal.
- Focus on sitting centrally and giving clear aids.
- Make changes of bend and direction smooth by preparing the horse using half-halts and a slight squeeze on the inside rein.
- Aim for a consistent, relaxed rhythm throughout.
- An accurate serpentine should start at A (or C) and finish at C (or A).

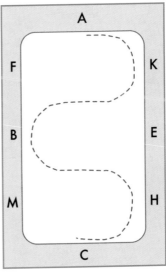

Keep all loops of a serpentine equal in length.

- For variation, try a serpentine of shallow loops in walk down the centre line. More advanced horses can work on a serpentine in canter, either coming back to trot to change legs over the centre line, or doing a loop in counter-canter.

SEXUAL BEHAVIOUR

Few horses, apart from those living in the wild, have the chance to indulge in completely natural patterns of sexual behaviour. In fact, most owners pay little attention to their horse's sex life, even though in their natural state, reproduction is their very 'raison d'être'.

MARES

Mares are only 'interested' in sex, i.e. fertile and receptive to a stallion's advances, when in-season (in oestrus). This is a short period of around five days every three weeks from spring through until autumn. Seasons are dictated by the hormones, which are activated by the longer daylight hours.

Behaviour influenced by the drive to mate also varies during the reproductive cycle, according to the time of year and the individual. Natural behaviour during the week building up to the oestrus period typically involves 'flirting' with males, raising the tail and squirting small amounts of urine. All of this behaviour is designed to attract a stallion's notice, but the mare may often become aggressive when he approaches. After a few days her attitude then becomes more docile towards the stallion, although she may become temporarily aggressive towards other mares (i.e. the competition!).

In the domestic situation few mares come into regular contact with stallions. Even so, their behaviour during the breeding season can be inconsistent, as it is still influenced by their hormones. Typical behaviour by a mare in oestrus includes:

- Irritability (towards humans and other horses).
- Resentment of being crowded in by others, outside or in the stable.
- Flirting with geldings (who may show interest even though they have no sexual ability. This can lead to jealousies and skirmishes in the field).
- Ultra-sensitivity to being saddled or any other forms of pressure on the back.

For mares in work, the unreliable pre-oestrus period of testiness does seem to be prolonged, which can cause difficulties with other horses. It may also manifest itself as a

A mare in oestrus will flirt with geldings by lifting her tail and swinging her quarters towards them.

reluctance to work or lack of usual sparkle. All this is natural behaviour and with well-managed and well-disciplined horses does not pose undue problems. Most trouble occurs when fluctuating hormones aggravate general bad manners.

Avoid making too many demands on a mare known to be particularly 'touchy' when in-season. If you face serious difficulties at these times, or her seasons seem erratic, too frequent or infrequent, consult your vet.

STALLIONS

The majority of entire males sadly (and unnecessarily) spend most of their time in solitary confinement, cooped up in a stable to avoid 'antisocial' antics and given limited exercise. To many, life revolves around being brought out to serve a

With good management, a stallion should be allowed to live a relatively natural life. This is the Arab stallion Chatanz owned by Lesley Dunn.

235

mare, usually with the briefest of introductions. Such abnormal conditions often produce abnormally aggressive behaviour, most of which would be avoided by firm but sympathetic handling and a more natural lifestyle.

COURTSHIP
At the stud, breeding is generally carefully controlled. The mare and stallion are brought together after the briefest of introductions, only when the mare has been proved ready (usually by the use of a 'teaser' stallion). This is a marked contrast to the natural courtship process, which is prolonged and intense and based on a set of very precise behavioural cues. The stallion must interpret these correctly to get the 'green light'.

Survival dictates that no time is wasted, so mating itself is a brief affair taking less than a minute. By serving the same mare several times over a 4-5 day period, the wild stallion maximises the chance of conception.

SHYING
Nervousness is part of being a horse. Such a tasty, meat-packed meal was unlikely to make it far up the evolutionary tree if it just sat back and let things happen. As a result, everything about the horse, from his sensory early warning system to his bodily build, lightning reactions and superb balance, is designed to allow him to react instinctively and decisively on the slightest suspicion of danger.

A few thousand years of living alongside humans has done little to dampen these life-saving reflexes. A horse's eyes are still geared to act on the tiniest movement in their lateral field of vision. A horse's every instinct still tells him to run first, think later.

It is not surprising, then, that horses are easily startled by sudden loud or strange noises, or 'spooked' by unexpected sights or movements such as a plastic bag blowing across the ground or a bird flying out of a hedgerow. Shying is a natural reflex action – a quick 'jump', either to alert the body for action, or turning forehand to investigate more closely.

There is an element of individuality about 'spookiness'. Breeding and personality makes some horses more aware of their surroundings and more reactive than others. However, in most horses a shy is just that – a side-step, or momentary

Shying is an essential part of a horse's survival equipment.

startle, easily controlled by an effective rider. Careful habituation (q.v.) has taught the horse to accept strange occurrences and experiences and realise they rarely pose a threat to survival.

A relationship of trust with the rider or handler is the background to this more laid-back attitude. Where shying becomes a significant problem, the horse is usually full of tension or anxiety, making him feel constantly under threat and insecure. The solution lies in boosting the horse's self-confidence to face whatever comes his way, teaching him to relax and to look to his human handler/rider for any reassurance he needs.

It is as well to work at a significant shying problem, as horses like this can be a real danger, particularly on the roads. A shying habit easily develops into napping or even rearing.

DEALING WITH THE NERVOUS OR PANICKY HORSE
- Make sure the horse's lifestyle is as stress-free and natural as possible.
- Habituate youngsters thoroughly and systematically to all new experiences.
- Expose the horse to as many experiences as possible, in a non-threatening way.
- Do not create tension by the way the horse is fed, kept, ridden or handled.
- Work on the basics of obedience and responsiveness in the school before venturing out.
- Use the sacking out procedure (q.v.).
- When riding out, make use of a sensible companion if you wish, though make your objective boosting your own horse's independence.

- Ride calmly and effectively. Stay relaxed in the saddle, but be alert and prepared for potential 'frighteners' out on rides.
- Sit up and use plenty of outside leg to keep the horse's quarters from swinging out. Teach the horse shoulder-in in the school. When passing a 'spooky' object out hacking, shoulder-in past it to allow the horse to 'look' without losing control of his body.
- Set up situations where the horse can face any specific fears in a controlled, safe situation, gradually building up his exposure (e.g. to traffic).

SLEEP
Adult horses sleep for short periods at a time, totalling about seven hours in every 24. Most sleeping spells are spent standing up, using the 'hitching' mechanism in the elbows and stifles called the stay apparatus, designed by evolution to facilitate a quick getaway. At least one sleep each day, however, is usually deeper and more restful. This involves lying down either flat on the side or balanced on the breastbone with the feet tucked under the body.

Lying flat-out is a vulnerable position for a prey animal. In a group of horses, it is rare to see all of them lying down at the same time. At least one is usually on 'look-out' duty. This behaviour is observed in stable yards as well as in the field. Under the mare's protective gaze, young foals frequently lie flat-out asleep, but as they grow they spend less and less time resting.

Research suggests that horses dream, and that getting enough satisfying 'deep' sleep is essential to mental and physical health. To feel able to relax enough to sleep in this way, however, a horse must feel totally safe and secure. If your horse never lies down, ask yourself why.

'SOUR' HORSE
A sour horse may be actively evading or resisting his rider, or simply be 'going through the motions'. Whichever it is, he is clearly unhappy and not getting any pleasure from his work.

Boredom and stress are the most common causes of sourness. Inject enthusiasm back into his life by lightening up! Add variety and interest to his work. Stick to activities you know the horse enjoys and are well within his capabilities. Take a look at the broader aspects of his lifestyle to keep it relaxed and stress-free.

SPREAD FENCE

A fence that uses more than one pair of jump stands, creating depth as well as height. Spreads are generally inviting as the fence shape corresponds to the arc of the horse's outline as he jumps. Types include:

Ascending spread (or oxer): The front pole is lower than the back pole on this fence. It is ideal for novices.

Triple bar (or 'staircase' fence): This is three poles deep, with the second and third poles progressively higher. It requires more impulsion to make the spread. The horse must not take off too far away.

Pyramid (or hog's back): This fence is three poles deep with the highest pole in the centre. Again, it requires impressive impulsion and a reasonably close take-off. It is useful for practising at home as it can be jumped from both directions.

Parallel: On the parallel fence, the front and back poles are at the same height. The parallel is the most demanding shape to jump as horse must jump up, as for an upright (q.v.), and out to make the spread.

STABLING

Horses did not evolve to live in caves or cages. Safety and security for a horse means freedom, an open horizon and familiar companions. They might appreciate the shelter in very bad weather, but given the option most horses would be just as happy under a thick hedge or tree in the field.

We stable horses purely for our own convenience. As a completely unnatural way of living for them, stabling potentially exposes them to numerous stresses:
Physical problems which can occur as a result of stabling include:

- Stiffness and poor circulation, as a result of restriction of movement for long periods.
- Respiratory disease, due to poor ventilation.
- Foot conditions and/or skin diseases, resulting from a dirty environment.
- Dietary-related problems due to poor feeding management; in particular, insufficient forage or a diet which is too high-energy.

Make stables as horse-friendly as possible.

Mental problems which may result include:
- Stress from over-confinement.
- Claustrophobia.
- Stress from the inability to escape unwanted intrusion of personal space.
- Depression from lack of sight and/or tactile contact with other equines.
- Lack of confidence, due to the inability to satisfy their natural curiosity.
- Stress from the inability to graze.

At the extreme, these frustrations can lead to neuroses such as stable vices. Despite these drawbacks, many horses have had to come to terms with to spending long periods of time in stables. Thoughtful management can minimise the stress of stabling *(see Stable Vices, page 241)*.

THE HORSE-FRIENDLY STABLE

It is the horse that has to live in his stable, not the owner. Stable design should make the horse's needs a priority:
- Where possible, give the horse the choice of being in or out, e.g. by fencing off a safe corral so he can walk in and out of the stable at will.
- Arrange stabling so horses can see and, ideally, touch each other (i.e. with 'talk' grilles).
- Provide at least one, and preferably more than one interesting outlook.
- Make stables as big as possible: consider 12ft x 12ft (4 square metres) an absolute minimum.
- Ensure ventilation is good. Never shut the top door. Instead, provide extra rugs in cold weather.
- Provide sufficient bedding to encourage the horse to stale and lie down.

STABLE 'VICES' AND STRESS

Horses showing abnormal, obsessive behaviours (technically known as 'stereotypes') can be seen in every stable yard. Traditionally these actions have been described as 'vices', although this could hardly be more unfair. Far from being malicious, horses with these habits are often the most sensitive and vulnerable of all.

Stereotypical behaviours include:

Weaving: Where the horse swings his head or rocks his whole forehand from side to side.

Crib-biting: Where the horse rests the front teeth of the top jaw on to a fixed object, e.g. stable door.

Wind-sucking: This is the same as crib-biting, but the horse then gulps in air.

Box-walking: The horse paces obsessively around the stable.

Rug-tearing: Where the horse bites at or rips off clothing.

Dung-eating: The horse eats his own droppings.

WHAT IS HAPPENING?

Nature designed horses to move around steadily all day, constantly chewing and digesting a steady trickle of low-energy fibrous food, safely surrounded by others of their own kind. We keep them in solitary confinement in a space in which they can barely turn round, occasionally producing small bundles of forage plus a few additional bucketfuls of high-octane fuel a day. For the stabled horse there is no way out.

An open barn is ideal housing for settled companions.

Stable 'vices' are far more than simply an expression of boredom, as was once believed. Unknown in the wild, these displaced activities *(see Decision Making and Conflict, page 80)* are a direct consequence of artificial management methods that prevent a horse from being able to fulfil his natural repertoire of behaviour and inbuilt urges. Such repetitive actions appear to provide a way for the horse to cope with a situation he finds intolerably frustrating, stressful and depressing.

It is not long before this stress affects the horse's physical as well as mental health. Stress triggers the continual release of endorphins, the body's natural emergency pain-killers, keeping the horse's body in a continual state of 'red alert'. In addition, the repetition of an action produces the hormone cortisol, which affects the immune system, temperature, digestion, drinking and sexual habits. It seems that stable vices are addictive. Repetition of the same behaviour results in the equine system quickly becoming addicted to the chemicals that behaviour releases internally.

The fact that not all horses show abnormal, stereotypical behaviour does not mean that some stabled horses must live totally happy, stress-free lives. More likely an explanation is that they are simply better able to cope with stress. Genes, breeding and personality certainly play a part in giving some animals higher tolerance thresholds than others.

PREVENTION & MANAGEMENT
Stereotypical habits are difficult or impossible to cure. Prevention is clearly the better option! Keeping the pressure off your horse by providing as natural a lifestyle as possible is the only way either to prevent the development of abnormal behaviour, or to minimise it once it is established. Where horses must be stabled, give thought to occupying and enriching their lives, particularly for more nervy and 'anxious' personalities.

Some prevention and management tips are:

Feeding: Many stereotyped actions reflect the horse's unfulfilled urge to chew and to occupy his digestive system.
- Give stabled horses access to ad-lib forage.
- Use small-holed hay-nets to increase eating time.
- Stable 'toys' such as the Horseball, that make the horse work for his concentrate ration, are good boredom-busters.
- Keep to a set routine where all the horses in a yard are fed at the same time to reduce anxiety.
- Overfeeding concentrates can trigger 'hyper' behaviour.

Stick to a low-energy fibre-based diet unless the horse is working very hard.

Activity: Mentally the horse is programmed to be free and on the move, in an open area where he can exercise his escape option if need be. A stabled horse has no opportunity for relaxation or play, and no ability to move away from an invasion of his personal space.

- Turn out *all* horses as much as possible. Horses can stand the cold, providing they are well rugged up and shelter is available.
- Split exercise into several short spells a day.

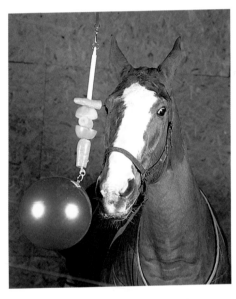

Boredom-busting toys help to relieve the tedium of stabled life.

- Consider two hours per day a minimum exercise period for a fully stabled horse (this could be ridden exercise, loose schooling or turn-out).
- Stables should be as large as possible, with a high ceiling and at least one, preferably two, interesting outlooks.

Social interaction: As a herd animal, the horse feels acutely vulnerable and under pressure when isolated. Company also provides entertainment and mental stimulation and develops social skills.

- Provide grazing companions (preferably equine, although any livestock is better than none). As far as possible, keep groups settled.
- Arrange stabling so horses can see, and preferably touch each other in safety (e.g. through dividing grilles).

• Be sensitive to relationships between horses stabled next-
door to each other.

Weaving grilles, cribbing straps and other mechanical devices
may relieve human frustration at stable vices but do
absolutely nothing to reduce the animal's distress. In fact,
they simply prevent the horse from accessing his only way of
dealing with his stress.

A stabled horse performing a stable vice is no different to a
zoo animal pacing up and down or biting at its own fur. The
answer is not to make the cage smaller or muzzle the animal.
It lies in trying to see life through the horse's eyes and taking
steps – drastic if necessary – to reduce or eliminate the stress
he is under.

TYPES OF STABLE VICE BEHAVIOURS

Eating	Movement	Irritation	Social Interac
Chewing	Pacing	Box-Kicking	Head-stretchin
Licking lips	Weaving	Rubbing	Box-kicking
Licking enviroment	Pawing	Self-mutilation	
Crib-biting	Tail-Swishing	Head-tossing	
Wind-sucking	Kicking door	Head-circling	
Wood-chewing		Head-shaking	
		Head-nodding	

OTHER SOURCES OF STRESS

A relaxed horse is not only happier but healthier and easier to
handle. Providing a lifestyle as close to nature as possible will
help reduce stress, but will not necessarily eliminate it from a
horse's life. Unsympathetic management methods are only
one of several sources of stress that domesticated horses are
exposed to on a daily basis. Others include:

Bad or inconsistent riding or handling: Any horse handled
or ridden roughly or inconsistently is constantly confused and
fearful. Frustration with the situation may show as depression
or evasion (frequently dealt with by physical force that merely
piles on more pressure).

Consistent, confident handling will increase his confidence
in you. Continually work on improving your riding and horse
management skills.

Incomplete habituation: Unless the horse has been carefully
habituated to potentially alarming new experiences, he will
react to them with perfectly natural 'fight' or 'flight'

A weaving grille does nothing to alleviate the horse's distress.

behaviour, i.e. running away, resisting, or napping back to the 'herd' *(see Habituation, page 113).* Allow your horse time to introduce new experiences carefully so that his normal fears can be overcome. Take things one step at a time and do not make unfair demands. Be aware of how frightening unfamiliar environments, such as shows, can be.

Weaning: Abnormal behaviours such as stable vices often become a habit after beginning at times of trauma, such as weaning that is too early, too abrupt or leaves the foal in unnecessary isolation *(see Weaning, page 278).*

STALLIONS
Everything about a male entire horse programmes him to be the best, the strongest, the brightest, and the bravest etc. This can make him a very special and satisfying horse to know and to work with, but also a very challenging one.

The qualities of a stallion, alongside the potential for stud fees, persuade many people to keep their colt entire. Yet bringing up a colt to become a well-adjusted member of society takes an above-average level of experience, confidence and sensitivity. If you want an entire, firstly ask yourself if you are up to the job – for his sake as well as your own.

THE MALE 'PSYCHE'
Successful training of a stallion revolves around appreciating the natural drives that make him different. Entires are:

- Physically strong.
- Usually intelligent and quick on the uptake.
- Generally confident, assertive characters.
- Hypersensitive to all issues involving leadership. Respect will only be accorded to their handler if the stallion feels it has been earned. Stallions will frequently refuse to be bullied into submission, and will constantly test the worthiness of their leader (handler).

More than ever, aim at creating a respectful partnership, as opposed to one based on physical mastery. If a stallion does decides to question your authority, his size and muscle-power make any challenge a potentially frightening proposition. You must be prepared to face that and not back down.

However, correct training never relies on brute force. Real problems should never develop if ground rules are solidly established and learning carried out systematically along the same principles as with any young horse. Keep consistency, firmness and fairness as your key-words and you will not go far wrong.

HANDLING THE ENTIRE

A well-mannered stallion should lead as normal a lifestyle as possible. In turn, this can help him stay relaxed and on-track. Ridden work rarely presents any problems if handling from the ground has been effective.

- Be self-disciplined: set the rules clearly and keep to them at all times.
- Stick to a set routine.
- Insist on respect for personal space.
- Halter-break early and thoroughly, reinforcing the lesson in all situations the horse will face.
- Deal with challenges calmly and reasonably, but firmly.
- Make sure all handlers know what they are doing.
- Manage the horse as naturally as possible, ensuring he gets freedom, company and a suitable diet.
- Integrate with other horses as far as possible.
- Make his lifestyle stimulating and varied. The stallion must learn there is more to life than covering mares.
- Keep sides of his life totally separate so that he knows what is expected of him in different situations, e.g. covering or being ridden.
- Assert your authority with effective use of body language, not physical force.

Halter-break an entire early, and reinforce the lesson in all situations.

- Expect and make some allowances for stallions doing what comes naturally, but never excuse bad habits or allow the horse to 'take advantage'. Be observant and act before a small disobedience becomes a serious problem.

PROBLEMS FREQUENTLY ENCOUNTERED WITH ENTIRES

Biting: Entires are naturally 'mouthy'. Teach them early on that this is unacceptable with humans *(see Biting, page 41).*

Rearing: This is a normal part of horse courtship and fighting rituals. The stallion must learn when this behaviour is not appropriate *(see Rearing, page 205).*

Aggression/territorial behaviour: This is natural to a certain extent, particularly when hormones are running high. Nevertheless, be certain to look for causes of over-aggression.

STARTING

This term is now generally used rather than 'breaking in' to describe the early education of a young horse.

STEERING

Start, stop and steering are the young horse's ABC – the foundations from which everything else he learns are built.

Most young horses are stiff and unbalanced. Steering using the reins alone only results in the neck and head being pulled around, with the rest of the body generally carrying on in a straight line!

When teaching the youngster to turn, start as you mean to go on, by using the legs to encourage the whole body to bend.

- Prepare for a turn by half-halting and asking for slight flexion to the inside a couple of strides beforehand.
- Always use the outside leg to ask for a turn. Stretch the inside leg down and apply the outside leg to push the horse around the bend.
- Turn your body slightly to indicate the direction you wish him to move and to help his shoulders around the turn.
- Use an open rein, i.e. move the hand slightly away from the body.
- Coming out of the turn, use the inside leg so that the horse comes to distinguish the way the legs are used: both for going straight, outside only for turning.
- Be patient – this will take a while to sink in. Work in walk at first before moving on to a slow, steady trot. Do not worry about outline for now.
- For exercises to improve steering, bends and turns, *see Curves and Circles, page 76.*

CORRECT CORNERS

Try to ride correct, deep corners from the start, going right in rather than encouraging sloppy short-cuts at the ends of the arena. The following exercise helps teach the horse to listen to the outside rein as well as the inside leg to really use himself around a corner.

Ride a large diamond. Imagine there is a cone at each corner you must edge around. Halt at the corner and ask for a step or turn on the forehand to push the quarters over, then praise him and ride forwards.

- Open the inside rein a little.
- Give short inward nudges with the inside leg then relax.
- Keep the outside leg and hand contact to stop him swinging his shoulders or quarters too far out.

Work deep into the corners of the arena to improve steering.

- Do not rush. Give the horse time to understand what you are asking.

  If the horse tries to cut a corner when going large, halt and use the same exercise.

STRAIGHTNESS

Straightness does not come naturally to horses. In the wild a horse has no particular reason to travel in a straight line. Straightness is worth achieving for a riding horse, however. A horse that continually moves crookedly will be stiff and unbalanced. As the muscles will develop unevenly, this may lead to discomfort and even unsoundness.

Achieving straightness with a rider on board is far more difficult than we would think. The horse's natural balance reflexes make him constantly adjust himself slightly to one side or another to support the rider's body weight more efficiently *(see Aids, page 30)*. In addition, every horse is naturally one-sided *(see Handedness, page 127)* and, as he is wider at the quarters than the shoulders, will tend towards moving crookedly!

Schooling can help achieve true straightness, where the hind-legs follow directly in the tracks of the fore-legs on either a straight line or circle.

IMPROVING STRAIGHTNESS

To be straight, a horse must first be supple (q.v.). Any schooling exercise that improves suppleness will help with straightness.

- Check the rider is sitting evenly. Any leaning or collapse to one side will off-balance the horse.
- Look up and straight ahead! Keep an even contact on both reins.
- Make sure you have enough impulsion and a regular rhythm. If the horse is not going forwards, he is more likely to wander off a straight line.
- Work on circles, bends, loops and serpentines to increase lateral flexibility.
- Lateral work will improve responsiveness to the rider's leg and control of the shoulders and quarters.
- Focus on controlling the shoulders.

  If the quarters fall in, reposition the shoulders back in line with them rather than trying to push the quarters back out. Do not use too much inside rein when doing this. Rather,

To be straight, a horse must be supple.

use the outside hand and leg to straighten the neck, then shoulder-in (q.v.). Falling out through the outside shoulder can be helped by a little counter-bending, i.e. flexing the horse slightly to the outside down the long side of the school.

- Do not always work on the outside track, as horses quickly come to rely on the support of the wall or fence. Use the centre and quarter lines too. Arrange a line of poles end-to-end about 2 metres (6'6") in from the side. Aim to ride centrally down this channel. Gradually remove the poles, maintaining the same straight path. Now try this down the centre line or across the diagonal.

- Good turns make it easier to achieve straight lines with the minimum of readjustment. Prepare well for turns with slight inside flexion and half-halts. Turn the horse's body using the legs, not the reins. Afterwards, remember to readjust your aids to ask for straightness *(see Steering, page 247).*

- Horses quickly learn to anticipate turns. Incorporate a variety of random straight lines in your schooling sessions, such as: down the centre line (not always to change the rein); and down the ¼ or ¾ line changing the rein across the long diagonal; down the ¼ or ¾ line changing the rein across the short diagonal; down a half 10-metre circle and then returning to the track.

- Do lots of transitions, especially WALK-HALT-WALK, focusing on controlling the shoulders.

SUBMISSION
In the training of horses, the term 'submission' has a specific meaning that has nothing to do with domination. The submission a judge is looking for in a dressage test is a horse that is:

- Listening to his rider.
- Obeying the aids willingly without any delay.
- Accepting the rein contact and leg aids with no signs of resistance.

In other words, the horse must not only respond to the aids but be happy to co-operate because he is enjoying his work. The only way to achieve this is through giving clear,

consistent aids and a progressive programme of schooling
using plenty of repetition and reward.

SUPPLENESS

**A supple horse is totally relaxed, showing no sign of
tension or stiffness anywhere in his body. Suppleness is
one of the basic ingredients of schooling. A stiff horse is
not using his body efficiently, so is prone to injury or
unsoundness and finds carrying a rider difficult. He
cannot respond as the rider wishes or be correct in the
way he moves.**

- A stiff rider will exaggerate a horse's stiffness. The rider
  must be supple and absorb the horse's movement without
  collapsing. Any tension or lack of balance will affect the
  horse's ability to move. Work on problem areas.
- Just as with human athletes, horses should be warmed up
  before being expected to participate in any suppleness-
  promoting exercises. Begin by walking forwards actively on
  a long-rein.
- Work slowly at first. Pushing too hard or for too long will
  increase tension. Work progressively, only increasing
  demands when the horse is ready. Developing flexibility
  takes time.
- To see improvement, exercises must be accurately ridden
  with every part of the horse's body under the rider's control.
  To improve lateral flexibility, the horse must bend around
  turns and curves uniformly through the whole body. Ride
  from the inside leg to the outside hand, using the inside
  hand to encourage inside flexion. Change bend and
  direction continuously in smooth, flowing curves.
- Avoid over-compensating for stiffness by using stronger
  hand aids on one side.
- Regular massage sessions can also help loosen and relax the
  muscles.
  The horse needs to be able to bend in two directions:
  laterally (i.e. through the rib-cage, from side to side) and
  longitudinally (i.e. flexing the spine from nose to tail).

LATERAL SUPPLENESS

Carrying a rider involves using muscles quite differently to
those used when moving loose. As a loose horse naturally
moves slightly crookedly *(see Straightness, page 249)* the
muscles to the inside of the body will be tighter than those to

the outside. Until the young horse has progressively learned to work with a rider, he will be stiff, unbalanced and one-sided. A supple horse will be able to go straight, or to bend around a curve equally well on either rein through his whole body.

Schooling exercises are aimed at balancing this unevenness, so the horse can flex easily and equally from side to side. Exercises to improve lateral flexibility include:

- Circles, turns and loops (use cones to help with accuracy).
- Serpentines.
- Figures of eight.
- Changes of rein.
- Lateral work.
- Counter-flexion (i.e. bend to the outside of a circle).
- Spiralling in and out when riding a circle.
- In-hand work.
- Long-reining and lungeing.
- Loose schooling.

LONGITUDINAL SUPPLENESS

The horse will not be able to achieve a correct, balanced outline (q.v.) and work 'on the bit' until he can soften his jaw, arch his neck and round his back, so he can bring his quarters further underneath his body. This requires the ability to flex the muscles along the spine from the poll to the tail and tighten the abdominal muscles, so lifting the back to support the weight of the rider. Front-to-back flexibility is particularly important for jumping.

See also Outline, page 192; Hollow, page 138.

Exercises to increase longitudinal suppleness include:

- Pole and grid-work.
- Rein-back.
- Half-halts.
- In-hand work.
- Long-reining and lungeing with side-reins.
- Loose schooling.

Lungeing with side-reins will help to improve suppleness.

In the stable, feed from the ground to encourage stretching of the muscles along the neck and back. Offer the horse a carrot by holding it at his shoulder or between his fore-legs to make him really stretch to reach it. Holding the carrot under his bottom lip, or fixing his feed-bowl to the door, means he must flex at the poll.

ASSESSING STIFFNESS

Spend time locating your horse's areas of stiffness and target these in your schooling. Signs of stiffness in particular areas include:

- Unwillingness to canter on one leading leg.
- The horse appears to find lateral work more difficult in one direction than the other.
- Tension or hollowness in the back.
- Uneven 'loading' of weight on the limbs.
- Holding the head/neck at an angle to the shoulders.
- Reluctance to bend or turn easily in one direction.
- One or both hind-legs are not tracking up or are over-tracking.

A knowledgeable person on the ground will help detect problem areas. Persistent stiffness usually has a physical cause. Conformation and age can both be contributory factors. If a horse finds flexing to one side or the other, or softening to the bit, particularly difficult, this must be thoroughly checked out. Common causes include:

- Uncomfortable, badly-fitting tack (especially saddles).
- Neglected teeth.
- Other physical injury.
- Unbalanced riding.

Once the problem has been put right, begin working patiently through all the exercises designed to increase suppleness.

TEETH

As the horse's lower jaw is narrower than the upper jaw, the sideways grinding action of eating causes uneven wear on the outer edges of the molar teeth. This results in sharp edges, which if left can lead to severe discomfort and problems with eating, digestion and ridden work.

Sharp edges of the teeth will need to be rasped.

Every horse's mouth and teeth need checking, and any edges filing ('rasping' or 'floating') by a vet or specialist horse dentist every six months or once a year. In the UK, only veterinary surgeons are legally allowed to perform more complex operations such as extraction and orthodontic work.

SIGNS OF MOUTH & TEETH PROBLEMS
- Dropping excessive amounts of food when eating ('quidding').
- Bad breath.
- Loss of condition.
- Head-shyness.
- Reluctance to be bridled.
- Evasion of the bit, unsteady head carriage, snatching at the reins, and yawing.
- Reluctance to go forwards, e.g. napping, bucking.

TEMPERAMENT
See Individuality and Temperament, page 144.

TENSION
Tension is a huge barrier to learning and performing well. Every effort needs to be made to find and eliminate its source and encourage the horse to relax and enjoy his work.

A horse may be tense for any number of reasons. These include:
- Confusion, or not understanding what is expected of him.

- Fear or anxiety.
- Discomfort.
- Rider tension.
- Stressful environment.
- Overexcitement.

Tension will create stiffness throughout the whole body, making the horse unable to stretch his muscles and move freely enough to go correctly. He may even show active resistance, gnawing at the bit, swishing his tail or lashing out. Not only is he mentally in a state of anxiety, and therefore not listening to his rider, but he is also blocking out other stimuli. This means he is not listening to or responding to the rider's aids.

See also Energy, page 89; Suppleness, page 250.

TERRITORY

Horses are not excessively territorial animals. Although a wild stallion will defend his harem against takeover by a rival, the idea of bravely defending his 'territory' against all intruders is wrong. Feral bands generally range over a familiar area that will vary from just a few to several dozen square kilometres, depending on the quality of the pasture. Often these overlap with the home ranges of neighbouring groups and are marked by the distinctive smell of their dung piles. If the grazing is good, there is no need to roam further.

Domesticated horses also tend to stick to their own 'ranges', even staying in fields with gaping fences or an open gate unless a strong urge attracts them further afield (e.g. there is little there to eat or the horse has been left by himself and wants to find a friend).

Aggressive protection of territory, sometimes seen in stabled horses, is usually a sign of anxiety or insecurity.

TIMING

Timing is all about choosing the right moment. This can be anything from choosing the right time to introduce a young horse to a saddle, to choosing the correct time to initiate the sequence of manoeuvres necessary for jumping. Getting the timing right can make all the difference to training a horse.

To get the timing right it is important to:
- Introduce new tasks at optimum times in the horse's life *(see Age, page 22).*

- Time specific lessons for when the horse is in a receptive frame of mind.
- Increase demands progressively and at the individual's own pace.
- Use conditioning effectively, i.e. judging the right moment for a cue or aid so it is most likely to get the right response. This often requires the rider to anticipate what the horse is about to do.
- Reinforce learning experiences effectively (see Reinforcement, page 207).

These skills can take years of practice. Hopefully, an instinctive 'feel' will develop as a result. Training a horse well takes a very able rider, someone who is quick-thinking and adaptable, able to focus and stay calm, and who is in complete control of their body and reactions.

TONGUE OVER THE BIT
See Bitting, page 49.

TRACKING-UP
A horse is said to be tracking-up when his hind-feet fall into, or in front of, the footprints made by his fore-feet. In other words, he is stepping right underneath his body and really using his quarters effectively.

TRAFFIC & ROAD-SENSE
Taking avoiding action from any sudden noise from behind or unexpected movement out of the corner of their eye is a totally reflexive action for a horse. Yet every day we see horses barely batting an eyelid as huge lorries rumble by within inches, cycles creep up silently then whirr by, or trailers clatter and rumble past them.

That these animals' instinctive fears have been so completely overcome is down purely and simply to good habituation. They have been trained to realise that these things pose no threat.

Habituation (q.v.) is the key to training a horse to be reliable in traffic. A horse used to sights and sounds from an early age has no reason to expect trouble from them. This is a long process, but a totally necessary one, for both the horse and rider's sake. Horses and roads are not a good mix, but one there is no avoiding. Few horses have much of a future if they are unreliable on the road. Accidents will always happen, but it is up to every owner of a young horse to put in the time and effort to make him traffic-proof. It could be a life-saver.

FIRST INTRODUCTIONS TO TRAFFIC

Do not leave exposing your youngster to traffic until you want to long-rein or ride him on the road. This is a long-term process that cannot be rushed. Any fright can be a real setback, but a really bad experience may scar a horse for a lifetime.

Make sure your horse makes his first experience with traffic a positive one.

- Ideally, make sure that an introduction to traffic is part of the early imprinting (q.v.) process.
- Accustom the young foal to following the mare past and around parked vehicles of all types: parked, stationary (but with the engine running), with the door open and then as the door is open and shut. Continue once he is halter-broken, also introducing vehicles moving slowly past.
- Turn out the horse with an older companion in a field (with good fencing, obviously) alongside a reasonably busy road.
- Expose the youngster to the usual comings and goings of vehicles at the yard (including, if possible, farm vehicles, e.g. tractors).
- Have a car, lorry and/or tractor parked in the field for a while. Youngsters need to be given time to investigate and accept strange objects. Remember that on the road, these things whizz past in seconds.
- Accustom him to walking through puddles and having his legs splashed *(see also Water, page 277)*.
- Hang up old feed bags and other light objects from the roof of his stable *(see Head-shy, page 128)* and use sacking out (q.v.) to accustom him to accepting odd and unexpected movements and sensations.
- After bitting, start venturing further afield but stick to quiet lanes. Arrange for helpers to drive by slowly in different vehicles. If necessary, take a quiet, experienced horse for reassurance, but avoid over-reliance on having company. Always use a bridle when leading horses on the road and make sure you are both easily visible. Lead on the left-hand side of the road (UK), putting yourself between the horse and traffic. A light schooling whip in the right hand can be flicked at the quarters to help keep the horse straight if needed.
- Once the young horse is happy with the above and is

familiar with being long-reined in the arena, he can be long-reined on quiet, familiar roads.

RIDING ON THE ROAD

Only attempt to ride on the road once the youngster is calm and unworried by traffic and understands and responds to the aids.

- As before, keep to quiet lanes the horse already knows at first.
- Make trips short at first.
- If the lane is not wide enough for vehicles to pass well clear of the horse, find a gateway where you can stop and turn him slightly so he has a clearer view of what is approaching.
- Use clear hand signals to indicate to drivers to slow down or stop (but do not wave the whip about!).
- Be aware of traffic around you if you come across something that may spook your horse. Wait for it to pass rather than risk a shy at a bad moment.
- Stay alert but relaxed.
- Be aware of the horse's body tension and prepared for anything, but avoid being over-cautious. Ride positively. Do not shorten the reins in anticipation of trouble or the horse will think there is something to be afraid of.
- Counter any thoughts of sideways movement with strong aids from the right leg and hand. Trying to pull the horse over with the left rein will only make him swing his quarters into the road. Keep a light contact.
- If a loud or large vehicle is approaching, shoulder-in slightly to allow the horse a better view. With his eye on the vehicle, his quarters stay by the verge.

With careful training, a horse will be unperturbed in traffic.

- Avoid busier roads until the horse is very experienced – and then use only when essential.
- Never ride on the road in poor visibility conditions. Also be aware of the dangers of low sun.

SHOULD YOU RIDE ALONE OR ALONGSIDE?

Young horses need to learn to go out quietly and confidently by themselves. Those that have been long-reined outside the arena usually accept riding out on the roads by themselves readily. If this is your youngster, then build on this positive start by 'going it alone' from the beginning. This teaches him to look to his rider for support and reassurance in a strange situation.

Introducing the horse to the roads, walking on the inside of a mature, reliable companion, also offers reassurance. Be aware, though, that you must progressively wean the youngster off his companion before he becomes too reliant on being nannied in this way. Otherwise you may find yourself with a horse that continually spooks when ridden on his own, or worse, naps. Gradually encourage him to take the lead until he is going single-file in front of the other horse, then progressively further away.

THE TRAFFIC-SHY HORSE

Many horses are unflappable from the start, whatever comes their way. Others are always a little jumpy, particularly of vehicles passing too fast or noisily. Some are genuinely terrified, often as a result of a traumatic experience. Even these will improve, with time, patience and persistence.

- Be aware of what particularly bothers your horse, e.g. tractors or motorbikes. Concentrate on habituating him to this.
- Do not put yourself at risk by trying to 'school' a horse on the road.
- It is too risky to insist a horse unreliable in traffic faces it alone. In these circumstances, always put him to the verge-side of a steady companion, his nose level with the other horse's girth. Aim to gradually move him forwards to walking alongside. Pick only quiet routes where you can ride in this way.
- Stay calm, relaxed and positive.
- Get out of the way into a gateway or lay-by if possible if a potentially scary vehicle is approaching.

TRANSITIONS

A transition is a change of pace (e.g. walk to trot) or change within a pace (e.g. working trot to medium trot). It can be progressive (from one pace to the next, e.g. trot to canter) or direct (missing out the intermediate gait, e.g. walk to canter).

To achieve your objectives, your schooling must be underpinned by good transitions. However perfectly your horse may go within each pace, it is meaningless if every time you 'change gear' all that balance and impulsion is lost in a poor transition.

GETTING GOOD TRANSITIONS

To stay balanced through a transition, the horse must be going forwards. Even in downward transitions, it is therefore the energy-creating aids that the rider must think of and use first (i.e. the legs, knees, seat and back). The rein is used last, and only if necessary.

Giving the aids accurately and smoothly is crucial if you want an accurate, smooth transition. It is not easy!

Upward transitions: First check your position. Then:

- Prepare the horse with one or more half-halts to catch his attention, channel impulsion and re-balance him.
- Apply pressure with both legs to ask him to go on forwards. Do not give a prolonged squeeze but a short, inward nudge with the calves.
- Keep a soft, but not over-strong contact.
- Allow him a second to react. If there is no response, give a more definite aid or quick flick of the whip to clarify and reinforce your signal. Use your voice aid if necessary.
- Stop the leg aid as soon as he responds.

Downward transitions: First achieve forward momentum, a rounded outline and soft contact before asking. Tension in the pace before will worsen during the transition down. Then:

- Think slow. Focus on the tempo of the slower pace into which you are moving.
- Check your position: sit and look up, with shoulders back.

Upward transition: Walk to trot.

Tighten the back but not the seat muscles, as you need to be relaxed to absorb the movement, but not collapsed. Think of bringing the pelvis forward towards the hands.

- Make a series of half-halts with the outside-rein slightly stronger. Focus on riding forwards into a non-allowing hand. Squeeze and release, squeeze and release, making each squeeze firmer if there is not enough response. Use the rein as little as necessary. The aid should be restraining only, *not* restricting. Do not pull back or the horse will only tense and lean against the rein.

- Keep up the forward impulsion from the quarters or the horse will tip onto his forehand, hollow and the following pace will begin badly. Ride half-halts to concentrate the impulsion before the transition down. Support with your legs. Do not take them off just when they are most needed.

- Give with your hands once the horse responds correctly so forward movement is not restricted.

INTRODUCING TRANSITIONS TO THE YOUNG HORSE
Until his balance with a rider improves, a youngster finds transitions tricky. Moving up a pace, he is often too quick or too slow to respond. Going down, he may resist and falls easily onto his forehand. As a result, the following pace is unbalanced and tense. Only plenty of practice will improve things.

Upward: walk to trot: Establish a good walk. Squeeze the knees for a few strides with the lower legs on to activate the walk. Release the knees and use the lower legs to positively ride the horse on into trot.

Downward: trot to walk: Shorten the strides by squeezing the knees slightly and half-halting. Keep a steady contact and squeeze the reins a little.

USING TRANSITIONS IN SCHOOLING
Good transitions do not only allow the horse to flow smoothly from one pace to another, but also to improve the quality of the paces and the way he carries himself, by encouraging him to use his hindquarters more effectively to create energy and balance.

Incorporating plenty of transitions in schooling sessions also helps to keep the

Downward transition: trot to walk.

horse's attention and interest, wakes up an idle horse or can steady an excited one. Make sure you do at least one transition every circuit of the arena!

- Once the horse understands the basic signals, work on increasing his responsiveness to ever more subtle aids.
- If your horse misunderstands, gets uptight or runs on instead of changing pace, stay calm. Steady him, re-establish your pace, prepare better and ask again. If you can tell a downwards transition is going wrong, push on out of it and set up for another try.
- Aim for a relaxed transition with the outline maintained throughout. Too abrupt a change will knock the horse out of his rhythm.
- Asking on a circle or curve will help the horse stay balanced.
- Ride every transition accurately, even out on hacks. In a dressage test, the horse should make the transition as his body passes the marker. Work out exactly where you need to half-halt and give the aids to achieve this.
- When progressive transitions are established, introduce direct ones:

Walk to canter: Ask on a 10m circle, from a very active walk. Bring your outside leg behind the girth, then nudge with both legs as the inside fore comes to the ground. Allow with the hands but keep up an even contact.

Canter to walk: Get a steady but bouncy canter on a 20m circle. Decrease the size of the circle slightly to slow the horse a little. Squeeze and release the rein, keeping the legs on. Ask again if necessary. Once in walk, yield the rein and do not hurry the horse on.

Direct transitions can be practised during schooling movements (q.v.) to ride changes of rein.

TRAVELLING & LOADING
To have a broad, confidence-building education, and go on to a secure and useful future, a young horse must learn to accept loading and travelling as a routine and unalarming part of everyday life. A difficult loader or traveller creates endless aggravation and distress for everyone, the horse included. So why are there so many around?

In many ways it should come as no surprise. Travelling is potentially the ultimate stressful experience for a horse.

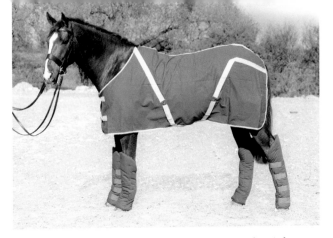

A horse will travel safely if he is equipped in the right gear.

Competition animals exist with this undercurrent of travel stress, even after years of being almost constantly on the road and apparently travelling well.

Stress is both mental and physical. Horses are naturally claustrophobic creatures (q.v.). Survival instincts have also made them obsessive about staying on their feet. In the lorry or trailer they have to constantly readjust their balance 'blind' and in the narrowest of spaces. Poor ventilation, restricted movement, dehydration, all add to the pressure, not to mention possible bullying by an incompatible companion.

The fact that so many horses repeatedly allow themselves to be put into this vulnerable situation, standing calmly inside a dark, low, rumbling and vibrating box, is testament to two things: generosity and thoroughness of training that reduces these stress-factors to a minimum.

As usual, the key lies in a systematic, sympathetic introduction to the idea.

TEACHING THE YOUNGSTER TO LOAD

- If you have the opportunity to imprint (q.v.) the new-born foal, include loading as one of his earliest experiences.
- Park the lorry or trailer in the field which houses the mare and foal, or the youngster. Lower the ramp from the lorry. Allow the youngster to explore it at will. Put feed inside.
- Establish respect of the halter before trying to load. Once he If so, is thoroughly halter-broken, load and unload regularly.
- Allow as much time as it takes. Make the lorry/trailer inviting and safe. Keep the whole business as calm and low-key as possible. Praise and encourage.
- Build up from loading and walking through, to standing while the breast-bar is fixed, standing while the ramp is raised, and finally, going for a short journey.

With sympathetic handling, loading need not be a trauma.

- Make sure the youngster is well used to travel gear before putting it on to actually travel.
- Practise often. Establish happy travelling before planning an important journey.

COMMON CAUSES OF LOADING/TRAVELLING PROBLEMS

Although many a worldly-wise horse or pony has quickly learnt how disruptive refusing to load can be, do not be too quick to label a difficult loader 'stubborn' or 'awkward'. Most problems originally arise through anxiety, due to:

Inadequate or poor training: The horse is confused about what is expected, has been rushed, pressurised or forced.

Fear: The horse is concerned for his own safety. Common worries involve:

- The ramp, e.g. the sound made by the feet on it, the gap between the ramp and floor, or the feel on their rump.
- The floor. What will he be standing on?
- The ceiling. Many trailers seem very low from a horse's eye view.
- The partition. The horse may feel trapped, sensitive to pressure on his sides, or unable to adjust his balance freely.
- The chest bars. These may be too high or too low.

Bad previous experiences: These may be due to:

- Insensitive or forceful handling during loading.
- Inconsiderate driving.
- A previously rough ride where he had difficulty balancing (often due to over-narrow partitioning).
- A stressful experience at a previous destination.
- A traumatic accident.
- Fear of excessive noise or vibrations from inside or outside.

CHECKS BEFORE RETRAINING

Look into and eliminate all possible underlying problems before starting rehabilitation of a difficult loader:

- Is the lorry/trailer as inviting as possible? e.g. light, airy.
- Is the floor solid, safe and with a suitable covering? Rubber matting offers good grip, allows the horse to see what he is standing on and adjust his foot position easily.
- Is the ramp inviting? e.g. solid, easily seen, with good grip, not too steep (often slippery) or flat (this makes the roof appear very low to the horse).
- Are the partitions set wide enough? Partitions that reach right to the floor narrow the horse's options for balance adjustment. Some horses react against the feel on their sides. Do you really need the partition? The more space the better, particularly for reluctant loaders.
- Does the travelling position worry him? Some dislike having to turn and stand crossways in a lorry. Research suggests travelling tail-forwards as the least stressful option, but this is not possible in a normal trailer without adaptation to allow for altered weight distribution.
- Is the vehicle or coupling unduly noisy when moving?
- Does the horse dislike backing out to unload? Try a front unload design.
- Is the driver careful enough? The best of vehicles is only as good as its driver.

DEALING WITH THE PROBLEM LOADER

This is a difficult problem and re-education can take time and stretch patience to its limits! Various methods of persuasion have been used to get horses inside trailers and lorries.

Enticements: (e.g. a bucket of food or a familiar companion). These can help if the horse is merely hesitant. Take care not to narrow the entrance still further or set too many precedents or provisos for next time. Ultimately the horse must learn to load anywhere, anytime, by himself or with others.

Coercion: (e.g. a broom up the rump, or 'reeling' the horse in using lunge-line crossed around the quarters). The drawback here is that the horse is being pushed in against his will. These methods may work once or twice, but do little to solve the problem long-term except to convince the horse how unpleasant the whole business is.

Persuasion: The only worthwhile long-term method. The horse must choose to go forwards into the trailer himself. This can be achieved by following this procedure:

- Respect for the halter must be re-established first. This can be done using a chain lead or a pressure halter (see Halter-breaking, page 125; Leading, page 172). Perfect this lesson away from the problem area before trying to load. TTEAM and Parelli Natural Horsemanship techniques provide helpful alternative approaches (q.v.) towards defusing the situation and rebuilding a sense of partnership.

- Next, get set up for success, but be sure to allow plenty of time.

Position the trailer on soft but level ground, alongside a solid wall. It is best to be out of earshot of companions in the yard. Have knowledgeable help on hand (though only one person should deal with the horse). Avoid creating a sense of 'ganging up' on him. Open the front unload door. Remove any bedding.Create a channel guiding the horse in using straw or hay bales.

- Keep the horse relaxed. Use TTEAM touches (q.v.) and Parelli (q.v.) games beforehand. Fit a pressure halter or chain lead, depending on which the horse is known to respond to. Lead the horse towards the ramp. Do not hold on to his head too tightly. Give him time to stop and sniff the ramp if he wishes. If there is resistance, put pressure on the halter (or nose if using a lead chain). Instantly the horse gives or takes a forwards step, release the pressure and give praise. Be patient and avoid confrontation. Do not give up until you get the desired result!
- Once the horse goes in, reward and make him stand before walking forwards out of the trailer. Repeat several more times that session. Have another session later that day and regularly afterwards, incorporating short and steady journeys.
- Some horses load willingly but immediately go into rapid-reverse. These must be given plenty of space and taught to think 'forwards' through retraining to the halter or using TTEAM or Parelli methods.

With this type of problem, never back the horse out of a trailer. Once in, he must always move forwards to come out, so use a front-unload only.

- Others load but then start to panic as soon as the vehicle starts. Look at possible on-the-move frighteners, in particular whether balance is difficult. If the horse is sensitive to pressure on his sides, remove the partition, pad the sides/walls or take time to accustom the horse to this feeling by practising in a mock trailer at home.

TROT
Trot is a two-time pace in which the horse's legs move in diagonal pairs, creating two distinct hoof-beats separated by a moment of suspension when all the legs are off the ground.

Trot is an ideal pace for schooling. It is full of natural forward energy (which the rider has to learn to absorb if they are not going to be constantly thrown off-balance). It also has a strong rhythm, making it easier for the horse to balance himself (as long as the rider stays balanced on top). With the foot-fall sequence the same on both sides, changes of direction can flow with minimum resistance or loss of balance.

TROT POINTS

To help the horse stay balanced, the rider must sit to the correct diagonal (q.v.). Avoid having to keep looking down to check. Practise developing 'feel' for the way the horse swings when it uses a particular diagonal.

Rather than tensing against the bounce during the moment of suspension, use it to push you up out of the saddle. This will give you more than enough of a rise in rising trot – in fact, focus on controlling this upward energy. Think not so much up and down off the stirrups, but of moving the pelvis forwards and slightly upwards then softly down again.

A good trot needs to go places. Do not over-restrict with the hands. Keep the contact still and even. Focus on creating energy in the quarters to propel the horse forwards from behind, not pull him from the front.

Sitting trot allows for more control and closer contact, though should be used sparingly with a young horse:

- Sit as lightly as possible, encouraging the horse to stay round.
- Keep the trot slow.
- Ask for just a few strides at first, e.g. down the short side of the arena.
- Sit up and relax, keeping the hips open to absorb the movement.
- Aim to keep a constant rhythm and outline, including during changes of bend and direction.

Trot is an excellent pace for schooling.

- Avoid simply 'going large'. Keep moving and changing the rein (see Schooling Exercises, page 230).

IMPROVING THE TROT
- Develop activity and engagement in trot using trotting poles (see Pole-work, page 199).
- Lungeing in trot helps you see the way the horse moves. Include some work over poles.
- Do plenty of transitions to and from trot, progressive and direct (e.g. HALT to TROT, and TROT to HALT). Focus on keeping the forehand light and making the quarters do the work.
- Free the shoulders by asking for some lengthened strides on a large circle (on both reins) before lengthening on a straight line. Return to working trot and ride a 10-metre circle to condense and channel all that impulsion.

TTEAM
The Tellington Touch Equine Awareness Method (TTEAM) is a system of non-invasive manipulations and ground exercises aimed at increasing body awareness and developing a better understanding with the horse. The techniques are now used all over the world by ordinary horse owners and top professional riders.

TTEAM was developed by Canadian trainer Linda Tellington - Jones following her work with Israeli physicist Moshe Feldenkrais. This research discovered that human paralysis sufferers found relief through the opening up of 'non-habitual' neural pathways.

Tellington found that much resistance which was often labelled intentional or unchangeable, actually stemmed from pain or stress-induced bodily tension. This stress prevents the horse being able to think rationally. Instead he panics, instinctively responding with either flight, fight, freeze or faint reactions (see Decision Making and Conflict, page 79; Instincts, page 147).

TTEAM techniques aim to re-route impulses along newly activated, alternative routes. By releasing the paralysing effect, the panic reflex can be overridden and the vicious circle of pain, resistance and punishment broken. The horse is then given the chance to 'think' and choose from a full range of options. It is suggested that not only can behaviour and personality be changed in this way, but the horse's learning capacity is actually increased.

TTEAM TECHNIQUES

TTEAM uses a system of gentle touches plus ground exercises to:

- Improve the horse's bodily awareness: balance, co-ordination and suppleness.
- Increase concentration.
- Develop self-confidence.
- Reduce stress and encourage relaxation.
- Relieve tension.
- Enhance healing.
- Work on specific behaviour problems.
- Boost performance through improved athletic ability, confidence and learning ability.
- Develop the bond between horse and rider/owner.

The wand is a 4ft long schooling stick used as an extension of the handler's arm.

An initial exploration of the horse's body is made by feeling it all over with the back of the hand and then the palm, to note any variations in temperature, sensitive areas, areas of varying texture, tightness or tension that might indicate a problem.

Tellington touches are a series of circular touches using the hands and fingers in different positions and applied with varied pressure, depending on the desired effect. The foundation is a movement called the Clouded Leopard (each type of touch is denoted by an animal-oriented name). Others are designed for every part of the body including the legs, ears, mouth and tail.

Ground exercises work the horse through and around poles arranged in various patterns. The aim is to give the horse time to think about how the parts of his body connect and where they are placed. A spirit of co-operation is developed, alongside increased suppleness, co-ordination and confidence. A basic exercise is the Labyrinth, where the horse is led through a grid of six 12-foot poles laid out as below:

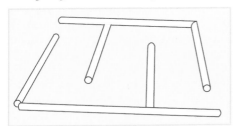

The Labyrinth.

Equipment used in TTEAM work includes:

Lead chains: This is a short lead-rein with light 30-inch chain which passes from the handler through the side-ring on the head-collar, over the noseband, through the opposite side-ring, up the cheek to clip on the top ring. The head-collar must fit well. This allows for lighter, more precise control of the head.

The wand: This is a 4ft-long white schooling stick used as an extension of the handler's arm, to help the horse to relax under a gentle touch and indicate what is required.

Neither piece of equipment is *ever* used to force or punish.

TURNING AWAY

After the intensity of being backed and early lessons in ridden work, the young horse is ready for a holiday in the field. The timing and length of the break depends on the individual, but if the horse has been backed as a three-year-old he is usually turned away late that year for a period of about six weeks.

This rest gives the youngster time to mature a little physically and mentally (big ones in particular), to absorb the new experiences of the previous months and to relax and unwind.

Turning away will be of little help, however, if:

- It involves a total change in routine which the horse finds very unsettling.
- Early lessons have not been completed successfully – the problem will not go away!
- Regular handling is neglected or given up completely.

Education must continue without any break. Catch and handle the youngster daily. If he is simply left to go wild, you will find yourself having to start all over again – with a bigger, stronger and far more opinionated individual than you put out in the same field a few months back! Other ways to keep stimulating his mind without riding him include in-hand and ground work, e.g. TTEAM and Parelli techniques.

Youngsters turned away for the winter must be kept well fed and warm. A better time for a break is autumn. Light work can then be re-started over winter when the horse can spend some time learning about what it is like to be stabled and to be ridden in less-than-ideal conditions. He will then be ready for another short break in the spring on some good grass.

Turning away is important. There is only so much a youngster can learn in one go, and the initial backing and riding away process is plenty for one dose. Youngsters that are pushed on too long or too quickly soon saturate their learning capability. They can lose all enthusiasm, becoming sour and switched off.

TURN ON THE FOREHAND
See Lateral Work, page 167.

TURNS
See Curves and Circles, page 76; Steering, page 247.

TYING UP
Standing quietly when tied up is a part of horse handling we take for granted, forgetting it is something that has to be learned and accepted by the horse like everything else we do with him. Allowing such restriction and total control of his freedom to escape is far from automatic for a youngster.

Being tied up is a lesson he must learn early on as part of his training to the halter. If halter-breaking has been effective there should never be a problem, so if difficulties crop up with a young horse, go back over this procedure until the lesson is completely understood.

Complete halter-breaking in-hand before trying to tie a youngster up *(see Halter-breaking, page 125)*. Teach the vocal command STAND. Tie up at first with quarters towards a solid barrier, e.g. a wall. Tying up the youngster so that he directly faces a solid wall, and allowing him to fight the restriction until he realises it is pointless, is risky and traumatic, as the horse can easily panic, slip or injure his neck.

A more effective approach for first lessons is to use a lunge-line attached to head-collar, passed through a tie ring on the wall and held by the handler. The handler carries on grooming, etc. and is able to 'reel in' the horse if he steps back. A light whip can be used to tap the quarters forwards.

The youngster should already be well halter-broken and trained not to fight against pressure on his head.

Never leave a horse unsupervised when it is tied up.

An alternative technique is to let the line slacken to any resistance, so the youngster has nothing to pull against. However, this does not reinforce the vital lesson of halter-breaking, which is to teach him to go forwards *away from* pressure on the poll. Praise the horse whenever he stands still or takes a step forwards after resisting. Do not use breakable string for teaching tying up. The youngster must not learn it is possible to get himself free. Only leave foals and young horses tied up for a few minutes at a time.

GENERAL POINTS ABOUT TYING UP

- Take care never to alarm any tied-up horse. Restricted horses panic easily.
- Do not tie up with too short, or long a rope.
- Tie only in a safe place: to a fixed object where the horse cannot reach or get hooked up on anything and not near any open door.
- Never leave a horse unattended when tied up.
- Tie with a genuine quick-release knot, i.e. one that will completely release itself in an emergency.
- The use of a breakable string loop as a safety measure is generally recommended. Bear in mind, though, that a horse soon realises how this works! It is preferable to tackle any pulling-back problem by retraining and afterwards, for peace of mind, use a head-collar with quick-release inserts.
- Rather than always reaching for the head-collar, work towards a situation where your horse accepts that he stands still whenever you are working with him, e.g. grooming or tacking up. When it is safe to do so (i.e. in a confined space like the stable) there is then no need to restrict him. If he chooses to stand, so much the better for your relationship.

THE HORSE THAT PULLS BACK

A different proposition to the youngster naturally worried about being restrained, is an older horse who has realised he can get free by pulling on his lead-rope until it breaks. Anyone who has ever dealt one of these characters knows what a hassle – and safety hazard – this can be.

- Work in a safe, confined area. Make lessons frequent until they are successful.
- Try the lunge-line method – attach the lunge-line to the tie ring using a quick-release knot. Pass it through the head-collar ring, around the horse's thighs and back to the head-collar. Any backward movement puts pressure on the

quarters and sends the horse forwards again. Expect a
struggle that might look alarming, but do not interfere
unless strictly necessary. It is important to allow the horse
to teach himself without interference. Praise any forward
step or acceptance of the restraint.

- Go back to basics with halter-breaking (q.v.) using a
pressure halter (q.v.) if necessary.

UPRIGHT

**A fence with height but no width, and set at a vertical
angle to the ground (sometimes called a 'vertical') is
called an upright. Examples include a gate, wall, planks,
or a single set of jump-stands using pole(s) and a filler.**

VARIETY

**Round and round in circles, up and down one stretch of
road, standing staring at the same four walls. Any of these
is enough to switch any horse's brain off at the mains, or
persuade him to try some kind of evasion, simply to liven
life up a little!**

When it comes to native cunning, the wild mustang would
find himself way above most Thoroughbred racehorses in the
IQ stakes. This is all to do with exercising brain cells. We do
so much for our horses that, compared to their wild cousins,
they have very little to challenge them or fill their time,
especially when stabled.

*Include as much
variety in your
horse's work as
possible.*

If you want to have a horse that is a lively, stimulating, all-round 'can do' character who thinks for himself, then you must give him a lively, stimulating environment that gives him something to think about. A one-dimensional existence will lead to a one-dimensional outlook and is the surest way to create a dull or unco-operative animal.

From the earliest days, create as many opportunities to stretch your youngster's mind and body as you can. Give him variety in his everyday life and his training programme. All it takes is a little creativity and commitment.

VICES
Vices are antisocial equine habits, which officially should be declared when selling a horse or pony. They include biting, kicking, rearing or napping and so-called stable vices such as weaving, cribbing or wind-sucking (q.v.).

Fortunately, many horse-people are at last becoming aware of how these behaviours are usually symptoms of stress and are best tackled by methods that take natural horse behaviour into account rather than by force or suppression.

VIDEO
Recording your schooling session, dressage test or jumping round on video is an extremely useful way of being able to pinpoint and analyse problem areas, either by yourself or with the help of your trainer.

VOICE
Despite using a language that is primarily visual, horses have finely-tuned hearing and respond well to vocal signals and commands. Most of us underestimate the importance of simply talking to our horses in building friendly relations. It also makes safety sense to always speak when approaching a horse in the stable or field.

The voice is also an invaluable aid in training, especially with youngsters. Horses can be taught to recognise and react to specific word commands or the voice can be used more generally to soothe, praise, encourage or chastise.

Less important than the actual words used is your tone of voice and inflection. Ever sensitive to mood and tension, the horse will interpret the way a command or phrase is spoken according to whether it conveys anxiety and agitation, or reassurance and calm.

USING THE VOICE

- It is best to teach your horse 'standard' commands, as these are then transferable to other trainers and riders in his future.
- Use voice aids to back up other signals, e.g. OVER when asking the horse to move over in the stable, WHOA whenever he halts, and STAND whenever he is asked to stand still.
- Use the same command and tone of voice whenever giving he aid, to avoid confusion.
- A brisk command, ending in an upward inflection, will have an activating effect. Drawn-out commands with a downward inflection have a steadying effect.
- Vocal commands really come into their own when lungeing and long-reining, minimising the need to use the whip and the rein and helping to keep the horse moving in rhythm. Teach the commands at first alongside the whip/rein, gradually working towards using the vocal aids only. The underlined parts of words below show the part that should be emphasised. For example:

To go forwards:
- To walk say, "WALK <u>ON</u>".
- To move to trot say, "TER-<u>ROTT</u>".
- To move to canter say, "CAN-<u>TER</u>".

To slow down:
- To slow down to trot say, "<u>TER</u>-ROT".
- To slow to walk say, "<u>WA</u>-ALK".
- To stop say, "<u>WHO</u>AAA".

Preceding each command by "AND..." helps prepare the horse for a new instruction.

VOLTE
A small 6-metre circle – a schooling movement for advanced horses.

WALK
Walk is a four-time movement, in which the pattern of foot-falls is right-hind, right-fore, left-hind, left-fore. In order to maintain balance while grazing, walk allows at least two feet to remain on the ground at all times.

A good walk should show rhythmic, regular steps of equal length.

Despite being the slowest and steadiest pace, at which both young horses and novice riders begin their training, walking is the trickiest of all the gaits to master. The quality of the walk depends a great deal on the horse's natural movement. There is a relatively limited amount the rider can do to improve a horse's natural walk, because it has little in-built impulsion. Having no moment of suspension, the walk is more difficult to collect or extend.

In walk the horse should:

- Take rhythmic, regular steps of equal length.
- Swing his shoulders freely forwards.
- Go straight.
- Track-up (look for a momentary 'V' shape as the fore-foot coming back almost touches the hind-foot on the same side coming forward).
- Flex his knees and hocks the same amount with each step.
- Have no tension.

Most schooling work is done in medium walk, with the horse going actively but calmly forwards (for collected, extended and free walk, *see Gaits, page 101*). It is important in these variations to keep the same rhythm, even though the steps are shortened (collected) or lengthened (extended and free walk).

WALK POINTS

- It is all too easy to restrict the walk. Aim to maintain the looseness of the horse's natural walk under saddle. Do not interfere with the walk unless it is really necessary. Use a long-rein only for young horses at first, gradually shortening it once he has learnt to accept the aids in trot and canter.
- Keep a constant but light contact by following the movement of the head, with elbows bent and wrists relaxed.
- Stay relaxed in the saddle, allowing the hips to swing slightly with the horse's back. Tension in the body or legs will shorten and stiffen the horse.

- Use free walk for warming up, cooling down and reward breaks during schooling sessions. Allow the reins to slip through the hands to encourage the horse to stretch his head and neck down low, but keep a slight contact. Quiet leg aids, in time with the strides, will keep the hind-legs swinging right underneath the body. Avoid tensing up or hurrying the horse.

IMPROVING THE WALK
- Use walking time out on hacks to ask for lengthening or shortening of the walk steps between markers (e.g. trees),some leg-yielding or shallow loops.
- Work on hurrying in walk by incorporating regular free walk periods in your schooling, encouraging the horse to relax and stretch. Think a slower walk, using subtle half-halts to steady the horse rather than nagging away at the bit. Use lateral work.
- Horses that break from walk into a jog or trot need to be encouraged to relax (q.v.). Allow a young horse to settle into the pace better by making each spell of walking a reasonable length. Ride a series of 10-metre circles in medium walk, walking between each on a long-rein before picking up the contact again for the next circle, which should be on the opposite rein to the one before. Keep sessions varied so transitions up to trot are not anticipated and the horse never quite knows what is coming next. Focus on keeping up a regular rhythm.
- Encourage a lazy horse to track-up better in walk, by working on his general responsiveness (q.v.) and suppleness (q.v.). This will also help him to stretch more in free walk. Working in trot and canter first will increase impulsion and make him want to stretch when returning to walk. Use this and prompt your horse to walk lots of bends and curves, e.g. serpentines, encouraging more flexion and swing in the back.
- Walking over poles on the ground helps all-round improvement. Adjust the distances correctly so your horse can negotiate the poles comfortably and in a good tempo – around 9 feet (2.5 metres) suits most horses.

WATER
The source of any aversion to water usually lies in a horse's fear for his own safety in some way. The water is seen as an unknown quantity that might pose some kind

of threat. More often than not, inconsiderate handling or inadequate habituation is at the root of the problem.

The horse that hates to be bathed may be terrified of the hose-pipe (after all, it does look and sound like a snake!) or in the past may have been bathed with cold water on a cold day. Who would enjoy that?

The horse who dances around every puddle, or flatly refuses to get his toes wet, let alone take the plunge into a water jump or cross a stream, has probably never been convinced that the footing he cannot see beneath that water is safe. Fear of water has to be overcome. A horse's fear may be a very natural and understandable reaction, but his avoidance antics may take him straight into the path of a car.

Like every other expectation we have, careful introduction is the key to avoiding or overcoming water shyness. From early days:

- Allow the youngster to spend time out in wet weather (but always make shelter available).
- Walk through puddles.
- Trickle water from a sponge up and down his legs.
- On a warm day, progress gradually to wetting the body.
- Introduce a hose-pipe, turned off at first, giving him chance to investigate, sniff and nibble it.
- Halter-broken foals can follow the mare on rides that include shallow streams, ditches and puddles.
- Bathe regularly when weather conditions allow.

Once ridden work starts, continue finding water to negotiate. Nip puddle-avoidance in the bud with firm, calm insistence. Set up a situation where the horse is channelled into going over a puddle in a confined area, e.g. the menage, rather than risking a confrontation on the road. Pick as wide a puddle as possible, so there is less room for the horse to duck around the side. Do not rush or pressurise the horse, and allow him time to sniff if he wishes, but avoid any backward steps. Once he is in front of the puddle, he must go through it.

A youngster that is confident about being bathed and walking through water should not pose any problems when it comes to jumping into or over it later on. Even so, water obstacles need careful introduction. This can be done by working over shallow ditches and mock water trays in the field, and at a purpose-built cross-country practice course with a safely-constructed 'baby' water obstacle. If necessary, a more confident older horse can help give a lead.

WEANING

In the wild, weaning usually takes place naturally at around nine months old before the mare's next foal arrives. A strong bond remains between her and her earlier foal, but as he has been suckling less and less and gradually been drifting away, evolving into his own social group, there is little trauma in the separation.

Leaving the older foal with the mare is not always an option in domestication, although many youngsters would be weaned naturally if nature was allowed to take its course.

Traditional weaning practice with most breeders could not be more different than the natural one: at around six months the foal is abruptly removed from his mother and often isolated in a stable or field. Left confused and afraid, this distressing experience is now believed to be at the root of many adult insecurities and neuroses. Even where the foal is removed and put in with other youngsters (sometimes unfamiliar), the level of stress he goes through is enormous and weaning can be a huge setback, mentally and physically.

Fortunately these methods are now increasingly being replaced by more thoughtful and humane ones, where a gradual separation is planned. Ideally this should involve:

- Establishing the mare and foal in a settled group with other pairs well in advance of weaning.
- Regularly handling the foal, taking opportunities to increase the distance and periods of separation between him and the mare.
- At weaning time, either: separating the foals from the mares with a strong, safe fence but one they can see the mare through; or introducing one or two 'nannies' to the group (i.e. mares without foals), before taking away one mother at a time (starting with the dam of the most independent foal).
- Weaned foals are then best kept in a mixed-age group of three or more. Within a group of this size, socialisation is more natural and discipline more even-handed. In a

Be there for your weaned foal – it is your job to take over where his mother left off.

group of others all their own age, the pushier characters soon learn how to get everything their own way and the shyer individuals become increasingly insecure.
- Be there for your weaned foal. This is an optimum time for you to replace mum's support in the youngster's eyes.

WEAVING
See Stable Vices, page 241.

WEIGHT AIDS
Once a rider has an independent seat (i.e. can give their rein and leg aids without moving their body in the saddle), they can develop the skill of using their body weight to influence the horse:

- By bracing the back muscles slightly to increase the weight on both seat-bones, the horse is encouraged to step further underneath himself.
- Stretching the inside leg down into the stirrup to increase weight on the inside seat-bone will help balance around a turn or circle.
- Weight aids also help accurate lateral work.
    The rider must be able to sit totally still at other times, otherwise the horse will be confused between what is routine loss of balance and what is meant to be a weight aid!
See also Aids, page 30.

WHIP
A whip can be one of two things: a helpful aid to training, or the quickest way to create a resentful, abused horse.

Used well, a long, light schooling whip can be an extension of the arm or of the leg. It can help to clarify or confirm an aid or remind the horse to listen more carefully. A short whip can be used in emergency situations as a forward-driving aid.
    Problems arise when tempers get frayed, or when the incompetent or inexpert handler or rider thinks the whip can be used to punish, threaten or coerce a horse. Whip or no whip, a human can never beat a horse in the strength stakes, so hitting is ultimately pointless. Willing co-operation is essential, and will never be achieved through force.
See also Reinforcement, page 207.

WIND-SUCKING
See Stable Vices, page 241.

WORKING-IN

No serious athlete would dream of turning up at the gym or track and launch straight into his training session without religiously going through his warm-up routine of stretch exercises.

A horse is an athlete in exactly the same way and the schooling session or competition class you are about to do is his work-out. Take warming-up seriously, as a time to:

• Relax the horse mentally.
• Gradually ask him to turn his attention to his rider.
• Focus your own thoughts.
• Gently stretch the horse's muscles, on both sides of the body and from front to back by asking him to flex a little laterally and to work 'long and low'.

Once you have achieved these objectives, you can start taking up more of a contact and asking him to really start using himself. In a pre-competition warm-up you may want a little last-minute practice of moves from a dressage test, for example, or pop over a few small fences. However, always begin with general stretch exercises such as large circles, figures of eight, serpentines and transitions on both reins. It is important that your horse is at his most supple before you begin.

Get to know your horse and what works best for him. Some horses perform better after relatively little working-in, whereas others need a good 20 minutes (or even more, prior to competing).

X-Y-Z

EX-RACEHORSES

Of the 16,000 Thoroughbreds in training in the UK each year, around a third leave the racing game. Of the 5,000 foals registered at Weatherbys, barely 4 per cent actually make it to the race-track. Whether from lack of speed or inability to stand up to training, the 'rejects' create a pool of relatively-inexpensive, quality young horses available to be redirected into other careers. Handled with care, they can be a pleasure to ride and own, and many have gone on to success in various competitive disciplines.

Weigh up the pros and cons before taking on an ex-racehorse.

Taking on an ex-racehorse has both benefits and drawbacks. If you are thinking of this option, weigh these up thoroughly beforehand.

General points: Be sure you want a Thoroughbred at all. Remember they make high demands:

- They need stabling at least overnight in winter, rugging and feeding well.
- They are not generally as sound or robust as a less highly-bred horse.
- They are potentially hypersensitive, reactive and not very forgiving of mistakes or mishandling (although individuals vary, as in any breed or type).
- They require plenty of exercise and/or turn-out.

Consider the type you require. Ex-Flat horses tend to be small and light-boned, whereas ex-National Hunt horses tend to be taller with more substance. Always find out about a particular horse's training and racing history if possible.

Plus factors:

- He will have been bred to be a brave athlete, so should have a head-start as a performance horse – in particular, an eventer.
- He will have been well handled and is probably good to shoe, box, clip etc.
- Routine healthcare, e.g. vaccinations, will have been carried out.
- He is likely to be good on the roads and working in groups.
- He is used to noise, bustle and lots of change.
- He will probably have only been ridden in a snaffle, and not been subjected to any attempts to force him into a 'correct' outline.

Minus factors:

- Have a thorough vetting to ensure soundness for the activities you intend to do. Teeth have often been neglected.
- Many young males will still be entire and require gelding.
- Breaking-in may well have been a no-frills affair, limited to START, LEFT, RIGHT and GALLOP (with little in between) and, hopefully, STOP. The horse is unlikely to have had any work aimed at establishing balance or outline. The wrong muscles may have been developed. Brakes may be a problem.
- You will not be able to simply get on and go. Whatever his age, the horse will have to be taken right back to square one with his training, i.e. completely re-started, and brought on again slowly.
- Bear in mind the sorts of methods used in racing yards which the horse will be used to, e.g. not wearing a normal saddle, having a rider legged up rather than being mounted; a contact being taken up or the rider moving his weight forwards is an indicator to 'GO!'
- Some horses come with problems from rough or impatient handling, or spoilt mouths through being continually held back by a hard-handed rider.
- An independent attitude may take time to develop, as horses in training are rarely taken out by themselves.
- Expect to have to buy at auction, with all its inherent risks. A dealer or bloodstock agent may be a better option.
- Allow time for the horse to be turned away to wind down for a few months before starting re-schooling.

None of the possible drawbacks need pose any real problem to a competent rider or trainer with patience and skill. An ex-racehorse will respond to kind, progressive training in the same way as any other horse. All ex-racers are certainly not unmanageable or likely to bolt as soon as their feet touch grass. Remember that the racehorse on the track is hyper-fit and exploding with energy. On a more 'normal' management regime, he may well be a totally different character.

X-COUNTRY (CROSS-COUNTRY)

Cross-country jumping is 90 per cent about confidence. For this reason, it is best to get the young horse going forwards in a reasonably balanced way in the arena over coloured poles before asking him to tackle any natural obstacles.

At home, if you can, be sure the ground is level; you have a better chance of getting an accurate approach and are able to work through any problems in more ideal conditions without the added excitement and distractions of the big wide world. Poles which knock down are also less likely to bump the horse and put him off jumping early on, when inevitable mistakes are made.

Even so, general preparatory work for cross-country can have been started well before the youngster is backed, by getting him used to being led or long-reined up and down slopes and over ditches in the field.

A horse which is jumping confidently at home should be happy to move-on to cross-country fences.

FIRST NATURAL FENCES

The first natural fences to ask a horse to jump should:
- Be low enough to be jumped from a standstill if necessary (i.e. no more than 2 feet/0.5m).
- Be sited on level ground with safe footing.
- Have a genuine ground-line – logs are ideal.
- Be taken from trot.

Little logs and ditches can certainly be tried out hacking, perhaps behind a schoolmaster horse, but it is difficult to be sure you can get the ideal situation here. Also, there is the risk of unforeseen problems, perhaps from slippery ground or overexcitement. These could turn into a setback. Most people are best arranging schooling sessions at a purpose-built cross-country course where there is a variety of small, well-designed fences with safe approaches and landings.

ASKING FOR MORE

As a four-year-old, the horse can be introduced to walking through shallow water, stepping up on to and down off a low bank and popping over a shallow, narrow ditch.

By this time he can be asked to canter towards a straightforward natural fence as long as he is show-jumping confidently, i.e. he is balanced enough to be able to lengthen and shorten his stride in canter and take on small combinations happily from canter.

If jumping training at home is going well and he has settled into a good techni-que, the five-year-old can be introduced to a greater variety of cross-country obstacles at a schooling course.

SCHOOLING POINTS
- Expect a degree of tension and excitement, but stay calm.
- Work in properly, focusing on rhythm, balance and forward momentum.
- Approach each obstacle steadily but with impulsion.
- Be ready to sit up and drive if the horse hesitates, and to slip the reins and stay balanced if he makes a mistake on landing.
- Only attempt fences you know the horse can get over.
- Jump lots of small fences of different types rather than a few big but straightforward ones.
- Introduce only one new experience at a time, making sure the horse is confident before trying another.
- An experienced horse may provide a useful lead, but do not let your youngster get too reliant on a 'nanny'.
- Introduce combination fences by splitting into separate components and tackling one at a time before gradually putting them together again, e.g. coffin (ditch, fence in and ditch, fence in and ditch and fence out), or drop into water (step down, walk through water, step down into water).
- Practise each obstacle until there is no hesitation.
- Move on to combining groups of fences, focusing on keeping up rhythm and forward impulsion.
- Do not rush to compete until your horse has successfully experienced every possible type of obstacle.

YAWING
See Bitting, page 49.

YIELDING THE REIN
A term used to describe the way the rein is released slightly after giving a hand aid and returned to its original position. This takes the pressure away from the rein and so acts as a reward to the horse for responding to the signal.

ZEST
A term used to describe the amount of enthusiasm you and your horse put into training and your relationship!

INDEX